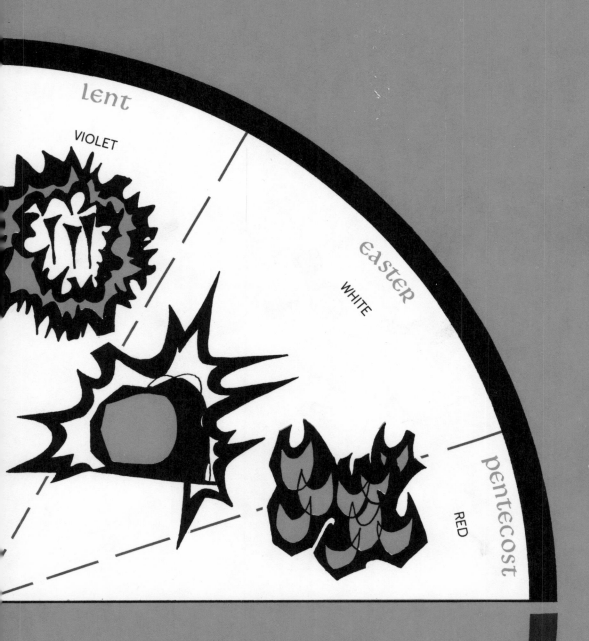

lent

VIOLET

easter

WHITE

pentecost

RED

SAVIOR

and live under him

Written by *GEORGE W. HOYER*

Illustrated by *GERALD F. BROMMER*

CONCORDIA CATECHISM SERIES
Walter M. Wangerin, Editor

CONCORDIA CATECHISM SERIES

PRIMARY LEVEL

God Loves You
God Makes Me His Child in Baptism
God Invites Me to Pray
God Gives Me His Law
God Made You Somebody Special
God Comes to Me in My Worship

ADVANCED LEVEL

When God Chose Man
This Is the Christian Faith
And Live Under Him

Authorized by The Lutheran Church—Missouri Synod for development by the Board of Parish Education, Arthur L. Miller, executive secretary, guided by the catechism committee: Harry G. Coiner, Frederick Nohl, Arnold C. Mueller, Waldemar W. Affeldt, Lewis C. Niemoeller.

Bible quotations are from the Revised Standard Version, copyright 1946 and 1952 by the Division of Christian Education of the National Council of Churches, and are used by permission.

Concordia Publishing House, St. Louis, Missouri
Concordia Publishing House Ltd., London, E. C. 1
© 1967 Concordia Publishing House
Manufactured in the United States of America

cuRtain time!

Studying this catechism is almost like going to the theater—not to sit in the balcony but to act on the stage.

Does the thought of acting in a drama make you a little nervous? This is not unusual. Veteran actors and actresses confess to stage fright just before curtain time. But as soon as the play begins, their artistry and preparation enables them to make a brilliant performance.

This catechism teaches you the script for the drama in which you act. But it does more: It brings you to an encounter with the almighty God, whose Holy Spirit enables you to join the drama of the redeemed life to His glory and your joy.

This is Book 3 of three catechisms. Book 1 relates the history of God's plan of salvation. The lessons take their order from the account of the acts of God recorded in the Holy Scriptures. The lessons of Book 2 follow the outline of Christian doctrine from Martin Luther's Small Catechism. I hope you have been able to study both of these catechisms.

The companion book is your Pupil Guide. Your careful use of it will make the message of the catechism more meaningful to you. Your teacher's copy of the catechism includes many ideas to help you in the classes.

These lessons follow the church year and help you "Do your liturgy" in the Sunday service and every day.

I pray that your study in this catechism will give the Holy Spirit the opportunity to make you a happy participant in the drama of the redeemed life. Jesus redeemed your life so that you can LIVE UNDER HIM in His kingdom.

Walter M. Wangerin, EDITOR

contents

pROGRAM nOTES

The table of contents for this catechism looks like the program for a drama. This *is* a drama.

Drama is conflict. Drama shows struggle. Drama shows wickedness and goodness. This catechism shows the drama of the redeemed life. First we were lost sinners. Then came the most dramatic thing that ever happened on earth: God in Christ rescued mankind from certain death. Jesus Christ as our Savior wrestled with the powers of darkness and Satan. Jesus Christ won the conflict. The Apostles' Creed summarizes that great drama.

A most exciting and important feature of this drama is that *we* are in the cast! Dr. Martin Luther's explanations of the Apostles' Creed make this clear: "I believe that God has made *me* and all creatures. . . . I believe that Jesus Christ . . . redeemed *me*. . . . I believe that the Holy Ghost has called *me* by the Gospel." God did it all, and God does it all. He sent His Son to be our Redeemer and our Lord. The purpose of all God did and does is "that I may be His own, *and live under Him* in His kingdom, and serve Him."

That's the title of this catechism: *And Live Under Him.*

A one-word summary of this title is *worship.* When we praise God, when we call Jesus our Lord, we worship Him. This is not an easy thing to do. In fact by ourselves we can't do it. God knows this. That's why He gives us His Word; His grace comes to us in the Scriptures and the sacraments. Through these means His Spirit gets to us.

"I believe that I cannot by my own reason or strength believe in Jesus Christ, my Lord, or come to Him; but the Holy Ghost has *called me* by the Gospel, *enlightened me* with His gifts, *sanctified* and *kept me* in the true faith."

This isn't a one-man battle. It's a war, and the whole Christian Church is in on it. That's why, if we're to understand what's going on and if we're to do our part with courage, we need to be clear on

all that God has been doing for His people before we came on the battle scene. We've got to become a part of the strategy that is already in operation.

"Even as He calls, gathers, enlightens, and sanctifies the whole Christian Church on earth, and keeps it with Jesus Christ in the one true faith."

All of these words are in the titles of the sections of this catechism.

Here are some explanatory notes for the table of contents—the program of this drama of the redeemed life.

To make sure we realize that *we* are on the stage, that *we* are today's Church, the program begins with

SETTING THE STAGE. Lessons 1 to 13 tell how we are God's people, who are to live under Him. In worship we pledge our allegiance to Him who alone brings us to life.

THE PROLOGUE. Lessons 14 to 16 describe God's purpose in His creation. He created all things to worship Him. God *calls* a worshiping people.

ACT I. Lessons 17 to 21 relate the story of God's people of Israel and how they were to display God's love for men. God *gathers* a worshiping people.

ACT II. Lessons 22 to 26 show the real Light of the world, Jesus Christ. When He came, God showed the world Himself! God *enlightens* a worshiping people.

ACT III.

Lessons 27 to 31 bring us God's present-day plan. The Holy Spirit moves among men to make people holy. God *sanctifies* a worshiping people.

THE EPILOGUE.

Lessons 32 to 62 make up the longest section of this drama. This is the part of **LIVING UNDER HIM** that is still going on. In fact it doesn't end until our Lord returns. Since it's about us and our worshiping lives, it is divided up into the weeks of our church year. God *keeps* us living worshipful lives.

When the director is ready for the play to go on, he calls out, "Places, everyone!" That's what must be said now.

When you hear the words, the sound will be that of the teacher's or pastor's voice, but don't miss who really is speaking to you! It is God who wants us all to find our places among the people of God. Even when the place is at our desk studying a catechism, remember, it's where God wants to see you.

When we're in our place, the way to begin is in worship. Once we've begun, we just go on **LIVING UNDER HIM.**

The lessons of this catechism are a series of Word-of-God directions about the way to live God's kind of life. The action that sums up this life is worship. Then the way to use this book is *to worship.*

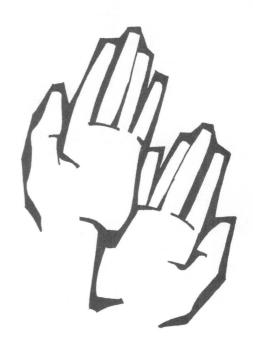

Each lesson has a section called "Worshiping with the Church." Here you will find suggestions for worship activities. Some of them seem very simple: When you wake up each morning the first thing to do is to "Think God!" That may be something you are already doing. Keep it up. Some of your fellow members of the body of Christ haven't caught on to that important idea yet. Let them catch up. We want to help one another worship together.

Notice the suggestions about evening prayer and about "doing the liturgy" each Sunday with the congregation. Perhaps you have been doing that, too. But perhaps you haven't always realized that the whole Church is joining you in that service of God. Take time to study the suggestions for "Worshiping with the Church." And be serious about *doing* them together as members of the Church. In worship we not only need to understand what we are doing and learn to do more, we must also make sure that we're *thinking* the things we do, as we do them.

God works in us. He made us members of the Church, His family, and brought us together in this catechism class. He keeps coming to us with help from His Word so that we *can* do the acts of worship. Now it is up to us to follow through. We must *begin* to worship. Deliberately kneel before your God, and God lifts you up. Deliberately join with the members of the class in worshiping with the Church, and God will make the Church ever more real to you.

Enough talk about the book. Let's get on with working through it. It's up to you. Each lesson is arranged for you to study *before* the class meets. If everyone is all set to talk about the lesson when the class meets, everyone will grow.

Here's Lesson 1.

1

WE ARE the church

"Be yourself!"

It disturbs us when people say that. Have we been trying to be someone else? We check back on how we've *been* acting. We begin to wonder, "Who am I?" "Who are we?"

It's bad enough if we've been acting bigger than we are. But isn't it just as big a mistake to live smaller than we are?

If the President of the United States were to act like the gardener and putter around all day with the White House lawn, we'd say to him, "Be yourself. Be the President." If the queen of England spent all her time dusting Buckingham Palace, people would say, "Be yourself. Be a queen!"

"Who am I?" Does the name written on the front page of this book identify "me"? Bill, Esther, Barbara, Henry . . . student, tackle, forward, class president . . . fool, darling, daughter, son, boy, girl—is my *self* there?

Or am I more? . . . at least a king's son, a king's daughter! Are "we" more than the total of all the "I's"? What is expected of us—if we are of royal family?

WORD and work

I

We ask the One who made us; the King who adopted us. We do just that when we study these passages in the Sacred Scriptures. Who are we?

Galatians 3:26 to *4:7* — False teachers were telling the Galatians that everyone must first keep the Old Testament laws before he could be accepted by God. St. Paul urges them to realize who they *are*.

John 15:13-15 — Jesus loves us with the greatest love possible. Look what He calls us!

1 John 3:1-2 — Jesus Christ is the only-begotten Son of God. What are we?

Ephesians 1:3-6 — God is not surprised to find us in His family. God planned it all.

1 Peter 2:9-10 — We have been brought into God's light in order to shed light on the great things God has done. We have received mercy in order to show mercy.

II

How can a person be sure he's a king's son? If suddenly a boy were told, "You're a prince!" he'd ask, "What happened?" How can we be sure we are children of the King: sons and saints and heirs? In the passages above and in others like *1 Peter 1:3-5, 10-12, 18-23 (18* ✠*); John 3: 5-6* ✠*;* and *Titus 3:5-7* ✠, we see how God made us His children.

Draw comparisons between the ideas in the following paragraphs and the things the Bible passages tell us our God has done to make us His people.

1. A prince is usually born into a royal family. A birth certificate would help him be sure he was the king's son. Sometimes a child has physical characteristics that indicate a family resemblance.

2. Sometimes a man adopts a boy to be his son. Even though he once had a different name and a different home, he now takes his new father's name. He is his son and heir.

3. A newly elected president could read the headlines and be sure that he has been elected. He might say, "I can scarcely believe it." But the words would convince him. The ballots would prove it.

4. Sometimes an act of God makes a man president. The president dies, and overnight the vice-president becomes the president.

Dr. Martin Luther's explanation of the Second Article of the Apostles' Creed brings all of these thoughts together for us. (Knowing it "by heart" keeps it in mind.) Some One died—and we are the sons of God!

The Word got out! Through Scripture and the sacraments God made us His own.

III

Is the class simply made up of the names written on the front pages of all our books? Is that all we are— names? Or are we something *more?*

When a boy is adopted, he not only gets a new father, he gets a new family. When a man is elected to his government's highest office, all his relationships change. The people he lives and works with are different—they look at him in a different way. He sees them through different eyes. His address changes. It could be "The White House" or "No. 10 Downing Street."

We have a new address, new friends, new countrymen, new relatives. We can check that as we read *Ephesians 2:19-22.* We're in God's family.

We are not only *in* the Church— we *are* Church. We are "blood relatives" through Jesus Christ with all the sons and daughters of God and with one another in our class!

How do we begin to feel at home in the family of God? How would one go about feeling at home in the White House? . . . Move in. Introduce yourself. Keep reminding yourself who you are. It's the same in the Church. We keep reminding ourselves who we are. We introduce ourselves to one another—"My name is Christian." We see one another as "family." Since we're "living stones," we act. We hold one another up. We help keep one another in place. Together we are the Church. Be yourself!

worshiping with the church

Everyday

We just *have* to worship! Because God tells us to — but more: God has revealed Himself to us as our Father through His Son, Jesus Christ. His Holy Spirit has given us His new life. Every 24 hours He gives us a new day. We're bound to adore Him, to praise and thank Him — to worship.

As members of the Church we are *one* in Christ. What we do we do together. What we do together helps us all to be ourselves — the Church. As a class we can do nothing more important than to agree to join in the discipline of worship.

It takes a lifetime — an eternity — to worship God fully. We must begin somewhere.

A place to begin is in the morning as we begin the day. A good beginning is to think about the God who made us "sons of God" and to remember that we're "in the family." This is the Catechism's suggestion: "In the morning when you get up, make the sign of the holy cross and say: In the name of the Father and of the Son and of the Holy Ghost. Amen. Then kneeling or standing, repeat the Creed and the Lord's Prayer. . . . Then go joyfully to your work. . . ." We could use any sign as a kind of reminder — but would anything remind us of our loving God better than the sign of the cross? Could we all agree to begin our day in the adoring response to the eternal God who revealed Himself to us and made us the Church? Let's be ourselves — the Church!

2

WE ARE IN THE WORLD

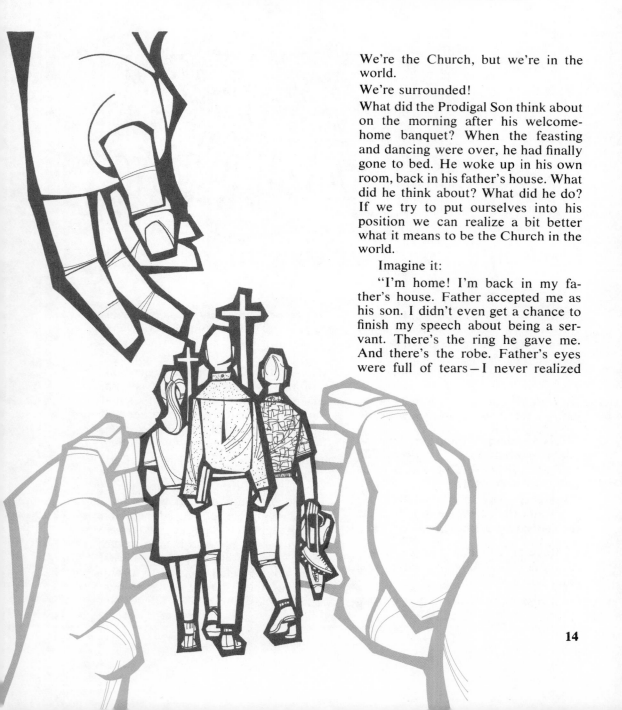

We're the Church, but we're in the world.

We're surrounded!

What did the Prodigal Son think about on the morning after his welcome-home banquet? When the feasting and dancing were over, he had finally gone to bed. He woke up in his own room, back in his father's house. What did he think about? What did he do? If we try to put ourselves into his position we can realize a bit better what it means to be the Church in the world.

Imagine it:

"I'm home! I'm back in my father's house. Father accepted me as his son. I didn't even get a chance to finish my speech about being a servant. There's the ring he gave me. And there's the robe. Father's eyes were full of tears—I never realized how much I hurt him and how much he loves me. The fatted calf—was it good! I'm my father's son again!

"But my older brother wouldn't celebrate. We asked him what was wrong. He was really sore. I don't blame him actually; I know how he feels. But he's so different from Father. There he goes now—slamming the door as he leaves for the fields. He's not *that* much of an eager beaver. He's trying to show me up. Well, here we go again—working with *that* brother, on *Father's* farm, under *Father's* orders.

"Come to think of it, that's what irked me before I ran out. I hate to take orders. I wanted to be on my own. I still do. Farm work will be as boring as ever. The old routine. What I'd really like to do today is stay in bed. How about that?—Father didn't really *say* I'd have to get started first thing in the morning. After all, it's my first day home.

Maybe I could touch him for an advance and go to town and get a few more clothes—things I need. You can't get by with just one robe.

"Wonder if the old gang is still around? The things I have to tell them! Their eyes will pop! That robe's not bad for now . . . this ring too . . . ought to be able to get one of the girls to think twice about me when she sees that. It might even be worth getting up for."

In too many ways we are like the prodigal! In his first words we can spot the forgiven person's joy at being in the Father's family again. Can we spot the temptations, too? . . . from right in the middle of the family of God? . . . from inside the Christian himself? . . . from the world around him?

This is a serious business. A forgiven son could be a prodigal again the very next morning, if the devil had his way.

WORD AND WORK

I

Let's start there. This is a devilish world. God warns us about it in passages like these: *1 Peter 5:8-9* ✠*; Ephesians 6:11-12* ✠*; 1 John 2: 12-17; 1 John 3:8.*

Never underestimate the power of the devil. It isn't necessary to have been bitten by a lion in the jungle before we will obey the sign on the lion's cage at the zoo: "Keep out." We can't keep out of this world. We are *in* the world. So is the devil; but we don't have to pet him. The Bible uses the word world to include everything opposed to God's kind of life. Look around. See the devil in the world and the world's temptations very close to us.

II

Let's take a second look. The devil doesn't stay in the world. The devil goes to church. Our problem is to be able to recognize him. We can spot the devil in these examples: *Acts 5:1-11; James 2:1-10.*

It's the devil who tries to convince us that we can be in God's family and still not act like God's child. The devil tries to persuade us

that the Father who has taken us home again doesn't expect us to work.

III

There's a third problem. Sometimes *we* feel like the devil, think, speak, and act like the devil. The evil power tempts us. More than that, it still controls a part of us—even of us Christians. The Bible calls the old sinful part of us our "flesh." It doesn't mean our body, as though our bodies were not part of "us." The Third Petition of Luther's Small Catechism groups our enemies as "the devil, the world, and our flesh." We should think about *ourselves* when

we read passages like these: *James 1:13-15* ✠ *; James 4:1-17 (7 and 17* ✠*); Romans 7:15-25 (Romans 7: 18-19 and 24-25* ✠*).*

IV

Three problems: the devil is in the world, the devil is working in the Church, and the devil still tempts inside each one of us. But we ought to go back to the starting point again. We are the Church. We are sons and daughters of God! The Spirit of God dwells in us. By Him we can live as the Church in the world. His Son gave up His life for us as a sacrifice. His death and resurrection defeated the devil, redeemed the world, and made us able to live our lives as sacrifices. That kind of living is our reasonable service. In the passages below God not only tells us what to do, but helps us do it! *(John 15:13-17; John 17: 14-18; Romans 12:1-2)*

Perhaps when he woke up the Prodigal Son *remembered* he was the father's forgiven son, a member of the Church-on-the-farm, the Church-in-the-world. If he did, what would he have said? What would he have done?

worshiping with the church

Every Night

As long as we are in the world we're in danger of forgetting who we are. Whenever we talk with the heavenly Father we're reminded. We are His children—His Church. For that reason the way we end the day is as vital for us as the day's beginning. The refrain through all the creation story is, "The evening and the morning were the first day . . ." and so on. That suggests *tomorrow begins tonight.* A time of adoring worship evening and morning are a discipline we accept for ourselves if we are to *live under Him.* We do it together. Then our worship helps us to draw closer to one another and to be ourselves—the Church.

Let's use the Catechism's Evening Prayer. It begins in adoration by using the Invocation. Using the sign of the cross connects us with all God's baptized people. It will be helpful to add our own prayers. Review the day; admit shortcomings. With the Prodigal Son say, "Father, I have sinned. . . ." Leave the past day in God's hands. Look to the new day. With sleep He will give us strength for tomorrow's life of service.

3

the church's service

After teen-agers from a Jewish synagogue had attended a service according to the order of the Holy Communion, one of the group asked, "Why did all the people have their hands folded when they walked back from where they had been kneeling?"

Well, why *did* they? Do *we* understand the importance of what is being done on Sunday? What is going on when Christians fold their hands?

Here's one explanation: "In the service the church gets its tank filled and its motor tuned up until it idles perfectly."

Is Sunday's service only preparation for the week's work? Is the Church's real service to God something different, done somewhere else? Some people seem to think so. Those things that happen on Sunday— lessons and sermons and sometimes sacraments—they should happen. But the Church, they feel, is really being the Church *after* that, *when it starts getting things done.*

Is the service only a way to get up enough courage? Or is the Church really "getting things done" when Christians *do their liturgy?*

"The service" or "the liturgy" means much more than a printed order in the hymnal. It is something

we *do* rather than "go through." In the first-century church, even during times of persecution, Christians would hurry through the streets to the place of worship where the Holy Communion service would be celebrated. "Dangerous or not," they said, "we must gather to *do our liturgy."* They thought of the service as *doing* something, and they knew it was important.

In ancient Greece the word liturgy meant a public work done by a citizen for the benefit of the state. If he had a ship built for his country at his own expense he was said to have "done a liturgy." In the Septuagint, the Greek translation of the Old Testament, the word was used for the offering of sacrifices in the temple. We Christians of the New Testament ought not lose the true sense of our *service* in *liturgy.*

The explanation of the worship service begins not with words, but with the *Word,* Jesus Christ Himself. He is present. He comes to church on Sunday. Through His offering of Himself we can offer ourselves to God. He is the Real Presence that makes all the difference. It certainly did at the home of Mary and Martha. If we realize that we "get together"

18

with God in the service, two things will happen. We will offer to God a "Mary mind" in order to receive from Him "the good portion"; and with "Martha hands" we will offer our service to Him and to our fellows. Then we are *doing our liturgy*. During the week we will be "getting things done," too, but they will be but an extension of our liturgy!

WORD AND WORK

I

In the service the Church "comes apart" in order to get together.

The King James translation describes many times when Jesus told His disciples to "come apart" for a while because He wanted to get together with them and have them get together with one another. *(Matthew 20:17ff.)*

Perhaps we should question whether that is still worthwhile in our modern times. *Matthew 18:19-20* ✠;

28:20b ; *Hebrews 10:19-25 (24-25).*

God commands, He promises, He invites. Reasons enough! But there is more. The church service pulls the Church together. Should our Head have to argue our legs and arms into getting together? *(Ephesians 4: 15-16)*

II

In the service the Church receives God in His Word in order to respond in our words.

"If Christ were really going to be there . . . or if the Spirit were really going to give out tongues of fire again, I'd never miss the worship service." People say that now — but they said it when Jesus was living with them, too. God gave Himself to men in Jesus Christ, died for man's sins, and rose again that all men could have everlasting life. But most people didn't realize what was going on. Is that true about us, too, and what goes on in the service? *(Mark 14:22-25; John 20:31; Romans 1:15-16 ; Galatians 2:20)*

Without God's power, grace, and forgiveness, we can do nothing. In the divine service we receive all this — in fact we receive Christ, the Word. By Gospel and by Sacrament we receive God into our lives. His Spirit is our power to worship. Because Christ dwells in us and we dwell in Him, we are able to worship. By the Word we respond in words. *(John 15: 1-10)*

III

In the service we give ourselves to God in order to offer ourselves to man.

Congregations sometimes figure out the average contribution given per member. Actually, "the average Christian" gives *an average Chris-tian* — himself — to the Lord. Giving ourselves to God is one of the big things we do in the liturgy. Our worship, our "adoring response," is exactly that.

Once we've given ourselves away to God, we don't object to being used by all our neighbors. Build a swimming pool just for yourself and it irks you to have the whole neighborhood use it. But build it as "a liturgy" for the community at your own expense, and you're delighted to have as many as can use it. When we give ourselves to God as we *do our liturgy,* we take the big step in offering ourselves to men.

20

Conclusion: When does a high diver make a dive? Is he diving when he climbs the ladder? Is he diving when he takes a deep breath? Or is he diving after he hits the water and is swimming back to the board?

It's all part of the dive. In that sense "doing our liturgy" doesn't stop in church. It includes everything the Church is to do. But *diving* is most specifically itself when a man leaps from the high board and flies through the air. And worship in the church service, doing our liturgy, is an exalted activity. We don't leave the earth, that's sure, but giving ourselves to God is like flying, like angels' work! *(Romans 12:1-2 ✠; Hebrews 13:15-16)*

woRship̄ing with the chuRch

Sunday

The third part of our discipline of worship is faithful *doing of the liturgy* each Sunday. Worshiping God with the people of God is the first and foremost activity of a Christian. God has set aside a whole eternity for us to do just that!

It is hard to do. But *begin* with that idea — each one of us must say, "Worshiping on Sunday is something *I do*. It is *my service.* I go *to do my liturgy.*"

Concentrating on these three aspects of the Church's worship can help us do a better liturgy: we come together because we *are* the Church and want more and more to *become* it. We are united with the Word, Jesus Christ, and so we are joined with Him in His service to the Father. We make a new beginning in offering ourselves in service to mankind as we offer ourselves to God in the liturgy on Sunday.

4

GOD WORKS WITH US

God comes to church on Sunday.

God *works with us* in the service. We must realize what He is doing for us so that we benefit from it all. It's not a partnership. By ourselves, without God, we are hopeless. We can never serve God by our own power. When a boy tries out for basketball—all arms and feet, just hopeless—the coach might shake his head and say, "I'll have to work with him." That's the way we are—even worse. But that's the way God is—even better! He became man for us. He took on our clumsiness, our sinfulness, and got rid of it by dying with it on.

When the Bible tells us about God's work for us it says, "The Word became flesh and dwelt among us . . ." *(John 1:14).* Jesus Christ is the Word made flesh. The work of God is done by the Word of God. The Word of God is God in action, God working with us. The Scriptures are the Word of God, because they are the power of God in action for man's salvation. The term "Word of God" includes God in Christ, God in water, God in print, God in our talk, God in bread and wine, God in the Church's fellowship and works and worship.

In all of these ways God works with us in the service. Since we are "hopeless," sin-filled, God really does all the work. Jesus took on our humanity and really lived for us. The Spirit of God takes us and worships for us. Christ offered Himself for us on the cross, and now Christ-in-us is in our worship. He joins us to Himself so that our worship is done in the perfection of His self-offering. That's how God works with us through His Word.

Each part of the outline of this lesson adds a new height and depth to our understanding of how God works with us by His Word. Many passages show what the Word of God *is* and *does.*

WORD AND WORK

I

The Word is God at work.

God speaks and it is done: *Psalm 147:15-18; Genesis 1; Psalm 33:6* ✠*; Hebrews 11:3; 2 Peter 3:5-7.*

God's Word changes our lives: *Hebrews 4:12-13; Romans 10:17* ✠*;* *Ephesians 6:17; 1 Timothy 4:5; 2 Timothy 2:9; Luke 4:4; John 8:31-32* ✠*.*

God's Word gives new birth: *1 Peter 1:23* ✠*.*

II

The Word is God at work in Christ.

Jesus Christ is called "the Word." In all eternity He is the Word. In the manger He is the Word. This means more than saying that He is God. Jesus Christ is God accomplishing His loving purposes in the world, by living, dying, and rising again. All of this can be called God's Word. *(John 1:1-4 and 14 ✠; 1 John 1:1-3; Hebrews 1:1-3)*

III

The Word is God's Spirit at work in Christ.

A cloud hid Jesus from the eyes of the disciples when He ascended so that they would realize His presence in the future would be invisible. God didn't want them to be like Thomas who said, "Unless I see . . . I will not believe." Many people missed the excitement of what God was doing in the Word-made-flesh, Jesus Christ. It

communicate with man God used material means. He had to make things happen in the brains of prophets before they could speak for Him. We say that He "inspired" them. When they spoke, God used men's ears to catch His Word. He had to use men's minds, arms, and hands when He wanted His Word written down. What they wrote was inspired. It was exactly what He wanted written, and it was full of power to accomplish exactly the things God wanted done.

God used other senses of men in order to work with us by His Word. He selected water and bread and wine to be the carriers of His Word in the sacraments. Holy Baptism and the Lord's Supper are in a real sense the Word of God. The Scripture and the sacraments are means of grace. *(Luke 24:25-27; 1 Peter 1:22-25; Titus 1:1-4; Romans 1:15-17 ✠; 2 Timothy 3:14-17 ✠; John 3:5-8; 1 Corinthians 11:23-26)*

would be too bad if we missed the excitement of the Word-Spirit working with us. God the Father and God the Son send God the Holy Spirit to work with us. The tongues of fire and the sound of a rushing wind were audiovisual aids to make sure people would know it. Now as the Word keeps growing and multiplying today we *know* the Spirit is at work. *(John 16:7-15; Acts 1:8; 2:4, 32-33; 6:7)*

V

The Word is God's Spirit at work in Christ through Scripture and sacraments in the Church.

All the different ways God works in His Word are here in this sentence. God works with us who are His Church, His separated people. We use the Scripture and the sacraments. We talk about God, we live the life of God, advertising how wonderful He is. Through us God works—and so we become "His Word" to our world. We gather together to do our liturgy and to worship Him; we use the Scriptures and celebrate the Lord's Supper. God is at work in Christ through the Spirit! If we are aware of how God works with us also when we come to the divine service, we'll "get the Spirit of the thing!"

IV

The Word is God's Spirit at work in Christ through Scripture and sacraments.

Electricity is a mysterious power. But the way it works isn't mysterious. It doesn't start humming over a rug and suddenly make the dirt disappear. It comes through wires to a vacuum cleaner. That sucks up the dirt.

People are made out of material. They live in a material world. To

24

worshiping with the church

"In the name of the Father and of the Son and of the Holy Ghost." When the words of the Invocation begin our morning and evening worship and when they begin our liturgy, we remember *God is working* with us. At the same time we should remember that *we are working* with God in worship.

We remember our baptism, for those words were spoken when we were born into God's family. We can make the sign of the cross placed on forehead and breast at Baptism. This reminds us of daily repentance for sins and how Christ the Word saved us.

But all these things remind us to *work,* too. His Spirit lives in us and we *can* work. Evening, morning, Sunday—worship is a task we discipline ourselves to do.

We can sometimes remember how *God* works with *us* in the worship service by noticing which way the pastor faces. His facing us reminds us that God's Word is at work with us and in us. His facing the altar reminds us that we are at work with God. God is faithful in His work. We should be, too!

5

GOD GIVING HIMSELF

God is at work in the Word. That Word of God was made flesh and blood in Jesus Christ. That was God giving Himself, giving forgiveness, giving life to the world. Are we aware that what He did then *He still does?* Jesus Christ took bread and wine, saying, "This is My body; this is My blood. Take, eat. Take, drink." That was God giving Himself. He told us, "Do this." As we do it, God gives Himself. As we eat and drink this Sacrament we receive the Word's body and blood. We show that we want God to work with us. And He does!

Whether we have been receiving the Lord's body and blood in many Communion services or are looking forward to our first Communion, this Sacrament is a holy mystery to ponder. God giving Himself! . . . *and we can have Him* . . . as we "do this in remembrance."

WORD AND WORK

I

The gift of the Word is Jesus Christ Himself.

It was the night Jesus was arrested. After three years the disciples were still not quite convinced that the only life worth living was the life lived with God. They had experienced it, living with Jesus for three years. But our Lord knew that at His arrest they would flee, showing they still felt that being alive, even without God's company, was better than not living at all. Jesus knew that at His death and when He would be in the grave, and even more, when He would be risen and invisible, it would be harder still for them to remember God-with-them. So our Lord instituted the Holy Communion as *the gift of Himself!* God wanted to keep giving Himself to His children, and wanted them to have Him! *(Mark 14: 17-31; John 6:47-51; the Small Catechism: the Sacrament of the Altar, Questions 1 and 2 ✠)*

II

What are the benefits of Christ's sacrifice?

It was Passover time. *(Exodus 12* tells how it all began.) Every Jew, including Jesus and His disciples, felt that by eating the Passover lamb he became more deeply a member of the chosen people, a partner with God. But too often the Jews felt that they had inherited their relationship with God and that they somehow *deserved* God's favor. God wanted to help His people realize how undeserving they were and how they continually needed His mercy. The people of Israel did not save themselves by painting the blood of the lamb on the doorposts. They were spared because God Himself was willing to forgive them their sin and deliver them from slavery in Egypt. Each Passover time they were to *remember* all this.

Jesus was God-on-earth come to deliver the whole world from sin's slavery. But in a matter of hours He would give His life as "the Lamb of God who takes away the sin of the world," and they would not even understand. Our Lord planned this Last Supper to help them realize His death was a sacrifice for the sins of all men. He made it a meal and celebrated it at Passover so that they would continue to realize they were eating with God and in that meal were made partners with Him. He wanted them to receive all *the benefits of His sacrifice:* "forgiveness of sins, life, and salvation." *(Luke 22:14-30; John 1:29 ✠; 1 Corinthians 5:6-8; 2 Corinthians 5:19 ✠; the Small Catechism: the Sacrament of the Altar, Questions 3, 4, and 5 ✠)*

III

He gives strength to remember and to live for God.

Jesus knew Judas would betray, Peter would deny, and the disciples would run. Yet He knew the future of His Church depended on His disciples remembering Him. He knew that forgetting would plague all His followers. Something was needed to keep them *remembering.* And that means *remembering something is happening*—present tense remembering! Just a slogan or a fight song wouldn't do. It had to be something with all the power that Jesus Himself had used to make them His disciples. He had come to give them life! Our Lord planned the Communion as a means of grace to share His life, the life of God with men. He gave them His body and His blood. He told them in words what it all meant and what He would do for them and what they should do for Him.

Add it all up:

It took people a long time to realize that the Child in the manger was God's way of coming into their lives. They had Jesus in person. But they also needed the Word in words. Jesus in the bread and wine is another way God has chosen to come into our lives. Wouldn't we have run to the stable to be with our Lord if we had lived then knowing what we know now? Realizing that God is giving us Himself in the liturgy, we'll come running!

It wasn't easy for the disciples to realize that the Crucifixion was the sacrifice of the Lamb of God to take away the world's sin. But when they understood, they believed it and they shared it! We understand that in the liturgy we receive the body and the blood that secured our forgiven-ness. We want to live as forgiven people, to have life and salvation! We eat and drink, and we "gladly hear and learn God's Word." We share in all Christ did for us.

The disciples thought theirs would be a sorrowful life when Jesus told them He was going to the Father. But when He promised to be with them always, it was like living again! When they understood that in the Holy Communion He was present with them in His very body and blood, they celebrated the Sacrament Sunday after Sunday and called it "The Eucharist," the Feast of Thanksgiving. The more we realize that Christ actually is with us in the liturgy, that we're surrounded by God's forgiveness, the more we'll rejoice. We have life with God in this Sacrament.

WORSHIPING WITH THE CHURCH

Everyday

Even if some of us are not yet receiving the body and the blood, we can know the joy of having Jesus Christ in our midst. We too are the Church.

Jesus, the Word, is with us in Scripture, too. Remembering means realizing that what did happen *is now happening*. In the reading and preaching of Scripture God is giving us His grace, giving us Himself. One of the most important things to remember about worship is that *we can have* the God who gives Himself! God gives us the responsibility to hear and learn the Scripture. As we do, we have God!

Our worship discipline requires constant practice—morning, evening, and Sunday! We also need one another's help to keep our discipline and do our liturgy. This week practice receiving God as He comes to us in Scripture. Use the words from the Sanctus (*L. H.,* p. 26) each morning as you wake up: "Blessed is He that cometh in the name of the Lord!" *(Matthew 21:9).* Christ comes to us! God still gives us Himself! If we remember it each day this week and on Sunday, we will really live!

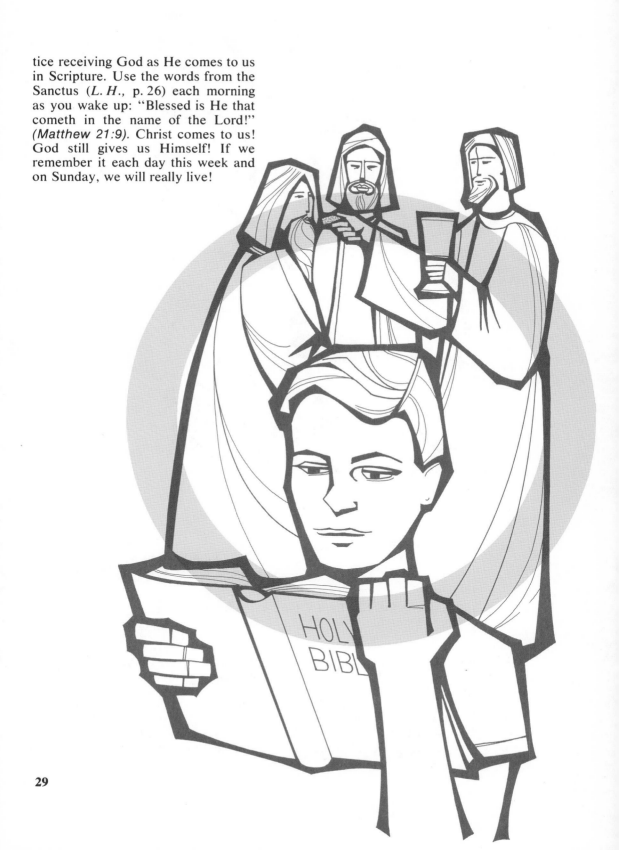

6

taking it all in

It is important for us to understand *our* part in the work of worship. It is our responsibility to *do* the liturgy. We want to *do* God's will in all our living. In the liturgy we take the high dive which thrusts us into a life of service. God offers us Himself so that we can rise to the heights of the service. We want to become skilled in the art of taking God into our living. The divine service is a good place for practice—there God gives Himself in both Scripture and Sacrament. We must learn to "take God in."

One of the reasons Jesus appeared to His disciples after His resurrection and lived with them for 40 days was to teach them how they should "take it all in." It was hard for the disciples to take in all the Lord had done, all He had been, all He had promised. Nor was it easy to take in the fact that Jesus would rule over all things "at God's right hand" and still be "with them always." That the Father and the Son would give them the Holy Spirit who would work in them and give them the strength of God—this too was difficult.

But one of the hardest things for us to understand is *how we are to take it all in*. It's hard for us to see how God gets through to us, how the Word can work on us and make us new men. It's even more difficult to know what *we* are to do, what *our* part is.

Imagine that we are with the risen Lord during His appearances after the Resurrection. Perhaps we too can learn how to take in all that God is doing for us.

WORD AND WORK

I

Take in the Scriptures.

Scene: The Upper Room, Easter Sunday night.

"The doors are barred and the windows bolted—but You came to us, Lord Jesus. Tell us—how will You come to us after the little while is over? Will there be a voice from heaven? Peter, James, and John told us about the voice on the Mount *(Luke 9:28-36)*. You explained to us in Your own words, but still we didn't understand *(Luke 18:31-34)*. We are still puzzled about Your dying. Why did You let them do all that to You? Even seeing You alive doesn't take away the horror of it. Even with You right here we're still frightened. How will we be able to 'take in' the Word of God, so that we understand, and so that we can be bold witnesses?"

We were not there. But God is here with us in His Word. The Scripture passages point us to where we will find God's explanation, and how it will become meaningful for us. But our task is to study Scripture. When we realize that His Word in Scripture is filled with the Spirit's power, we become alert to *our first big task in the liturgy*. We must hear and think. *(Luke 24:36-49; 24:13-32; 2 Peter 1: 16-21; Romans 1:16; 2 Timothy 3:14—4:5 [16, 17 ✠])*

II

Take in the Presence.

Scene: The Upper Room, one week later.

"The doors are still shut, Lord Jesus. We're still waiting for the promised power of the Spirit. But You are here. We're glad when we see You, Lord. At Your Word we do know peace! We could even leave the doors open when You are present with us.

"Will You always be present with us? Are You present even when we can't see You? We've been study-

31

ing and meditating over Your Word, especially about the gift of Your body and blood in the bread and wine. We recall how John called You the Lamb of God, and we have looked up Isaiah's prophecy *(Isaiah 53:7)*. Now we understand why all of this took place at Passover time. When we feasted on the Passover Lamb, we didn't just recall the Exodus — what happened was that *we became a bit more the chosen people (Exodus 12: 24-27)*. It all means that in this Supper You are really present. You give us Yourself. You make us God's people. But now, how will we take it all in? How will we receive You? You said, 'Do this in remembrance of Me.' Will You give Yourself each time we do this?"

If we take in the Scriptural answers to these questions, we'll find out how to take in His presence. Thomas discovered it was as simple as *being* there! St. Paul says that in the Sacrament we do become united with God and one another. His presence is real! But, of course, we must *do* it. That's as obvious as what Thomas learned. And we must do it *together*, really together, recognizing one another as the body of Christ. So Jesus said, "Do this — in remembrance!" — *our second task in the liturgy. (John 20:24-29 [29 ✖]; 1 Corinthians 10:14-18 [16, 17 ✖]; 1 Corinthians 11:17-33 [26-29 ✖]; John 14:22-24 [23 ✖])*

III

Take in the Spirit.

Scene: The Mount called Olivet, near Bethany 40 days after Easter.

"One more thing, Lord Jesus— this bit about the Holy Spirit. . . . You said we should be glad You're going so that He would be coming *(John 16:5-7)*. But frankly, we're having trouble taking it all in. It would help if we understood about the Spirit. You said we have known God the Father and seen Him because we have seen and known You *(John 14: 6-11)*. The Father will send the Spirit in Your name. You and the Father will be with us and the Spirit will be in us *(John 14:16, 20, 26)*. Are we right—there is but one God: Father, Spirit, and You? And You we will see no more until Judgment, yet You will be with us always through the Spirit? That having the Spirit with us is the same as having You? That's good. But—one last question before You part from us—how do we take Him in?"

We can get the answer from God as surely as could the disciples. It's as simple as asking! The Spirit is willing, always. Asking is important because it means we let Him in. There surely is no doubt of His coming— He has promised. And there's no doubt of His power. His presence makes all the difference in life and worship. *Our third task in the liturgy is very clear. (Luke 11:11-13 [13 ✠]; 1 Corinthians 12:3-13 [3b ✠]; 1 Corinthians 2:9-16; Romans 8:8-17 [16 ✠])*

worshiping with the church

Sunday

"Blessed is He that cometh" have been our wake-up words from God. Add now the prayer, "Blessed is he that receiveth—God help me take You in, in Scripture, Sacrament, and Spirit." Here it is more blessed to receive than to give!

In the liturgy on Sunday, we will surely receive the Spirit as we ask for Him. God will open our hearts to understand the Scriptures' Word to us. During the Communion we will be in union with God. Let's take it all in!

Worship is work—remember? If we don't work at it the Word won't even go in one ear and out the other. We must concentrate on what is read and said. We ask, "How does that apply to me? Does that Good News bring me forgiveness?" During the sermon we must hear it for ourselves.

response ability

Everybody ought to clap for God. He deserves applause. The angels realized it. When God placed His Son into the manger hay, they all sang, "Glory to God in the highest!" That's worship. That's *response*.

We have a *responsibility* to give God that kind of response. When the men on the assembly line have put together all the parts of a car, they expect it to run. That's what it was designed to do. God is the Creator, the Thrice-Holy One! Because of what He is and of what He made us to be, we have the responsibility to worship. There's more! After sin smashed the image of God in us, He remade us. He gave us Himself in Jesus Christ and gave us a new birth in Holy Baptism. Now our responsibility is something we *want* to do. We want to respond, to worship. God makes us able and willing. But God wants *us* to do the responding.

But do we have the response *ability*? Are we able to worship as we should? Or do we get bored? The fact is that we have a hard time putting ourselves into our worship. The angels have an eternally perfect response ability. Our worship response is something that has to be learned in time. There's no time like right now. Let's develop our *response ability!*

word and work

1

Before there can be a response, something must have been said.

God said a lot. God said *Himself.* God said *the Word.* God gave *the Word in flesh.* By that Word we know the *worth* of God. In faith we recognize His *worth-ship.* What we do about that worth, we call worship. If we merely admit that God *has* worth, we are not worshiping. To worship means to give to God the glory due to His name. Worship is always *action.* It is our doing something, saying something, thinking something *for God.*

The word worship includes everything we do in response to God's deeds for us. Just as a lens or a burning glass pulls in the rays of the sun and focuses them on one spot, so the word worship focuses everything the Christian does in *adoration.* Adoration is this recognition of God. When we—if we—get a report card with all A's, that's the teacher's recognition of our hard work. Adoration of God always means that we are recognizing God—that we are offering to God, not all that He deserves, but the best that we can give. Our response also includes confession, thanksgiving, and supplication. But adoration is worship's arrowhead.

II

The responsibility to worship is ours because God is God, but also because we are God's.

Words from *Revelation 14:6-7* help us see that. The responsibility to adore becomes more important as we realize how *living* our worship develops through *giving* God worship. In *Matthew 4:10* ✠ the two Greek New Testament words which may be translated "worship" are included in one sentence by our Lord. He is quoting *Deuteronomy 6:13* to defend God's sole right to adoration by men. As we study these passages we can discover:

1. How *giving* worship and *living* worship are related;
2. What it means to "fear" God;
3. That *adoration* is the beginning of our obedience to all of the Ten Commandments. (We can see that ten times over in Luther's Small Catechism as he explains the commandments' meanings ✠.)

The sun can start a fire when its rays are focused through a burning glass. When God's loving actions are focused in our minds by our adoration, our love begins to burn. We serve God more fervently. Can't we

see that happening in *Luke 2:15-20?* Isn't there another illustration in *John 21:4-7?*

The ways in which we act *for* God all have their beginning in the adoration we give *to* God. That adoration may not always be expressed in words. Sometimes it is not even formed in conscious thoughts. But it is always there. See how it works in this situation: Bill claims to be a Christian. He doesn't claim to be perfect—he claims God's forgiveness, Baptism's new life, the presence of Christ in himself. When he sees Beth (whom he can hardly stand!) left out of a game at league meeting and obviously most unhappy, he doesn't want to do a thing about it. But he remembers what God did for him, that Jesus gave His life "while we were yet sinners."

Now—there are two possible endings:

1. He realizes God deserves a lot of credit for what He did. He knows he ought to give God recognition for it all. But he doesn't. He doesn't adore God. And as a result, what does he do about Beth?

2. He thinks about God's attitude toward him. He says in his mind, "Well, God, I admit I don't want to, but after what You did for me, after what You made out of me, I guess I'd better." And then what does he do about Beth?

That's a pretty left-handed case of adoration—but it is, at least, a recognition of God. That is always the beginning of loving service. If we don't adore, we don't do. If we adore —well, we don't always do, but at least we have taken the first step in putting what we should do into practice.

III

God gives response ability.

It's not always easy to do the things we ought to do for people. But men and women to whom God has given His very self *can* love God. And as they adore Him, they do take a step toward loving people. That's the very point of each commandment, "We should fear—adore—and love God so that . . ." It's the very heart of our First Commandment responsibility, "We are to fear, love, and trust God above everything else."

Everyday

Faithful participation in the morning and evening discipline of worship and in doing the liturgy on Sunday should take on new importance for us. As we move into these acts of worship we get set to adore. *Adoration* is the first step in putting what we should do in all our life into practice. In our adoration God's loving actions are focused in our minds, and our love burns brighter. We are made more able to *do* our liturgy in life.

The *words* for our adoration are waiting for us morning, evening, and Sunday. If we just say the words, we are repeating words of Luther, or the angels, or the Church, or our Lord, but we're not adoring. We must fill those words with our meaning, with *our worship*. As we do that we adore, and we grow in our response ability.

37

8

the acts of response

We don't have to *wait* for God to make us into worshipers. He already has! That's what Christ's death and resurrection and our baptism have already done! We are worshipers! As a result we *can* adore Him. And most of the time we want to. But we are men not angels. We have the old human part of us that still doesn't think much of God and doesn't want to. When we sin we turn our backs on God. When we *confess,* we turn back *to* God. His forgiveness, and all His other gifts to us, call for our *thanksgiving*. Then as forgiven, thankful, adoring Christians, we can bring our *supplications* to God. That is worship's full response.

Adoration is the arrowhead, but the shaft we shoot up to God includes confession, thanksgiving, and supplication. Put the first letters of those words together and they spell ACTS. These are the things we *do* as we respond to God at home or in the service in church.

Our responsibility is to worship God every day—on our good days and our bad days. We need to work seriously at developing our response ability. The best way to become a better worshiper is to *worship*. Worshiping makes worshipers . . . it doesn't create them—only God can do that. But practice makes—not perfect—but *better* worshipers. Whenever we adore God, we preach to ourselves. Whenever we say words or think thoughts recognizing the "worth-ship" of God, we are preaching the Word of God to ourselves. It's as simple as measuring the distance between my mouth and my ears. God's ears are the only ones closer to our mouths than our own. That means that almost as soon as God hears what we say in praise of His love, our own ears hear it. Whatever we say about the love of God is the good news of the Gospel. And that's what saves us, changes us, and makes us into worshipers. When we worship God in our thoughts, the same thing happens. Our mind hears everything we are thinking in worship of God. As we worship we become better worshipers.

That's one reason it's so important to develop our *response ability*. And that's why the "Worshiping with the Church" paragraphs of this book are so important for us to do. As we give our response of worship in the service or in our homes, we not only fulfill our responsibility, but we also develop our response ability.

ADORATION

CONFESSION

THANKSGIVING

SUPPLICATION

I

Adoration

We can see the reflex action of worship taking place in *John 20: 24-29 (28 ✠).* Without Jesus in his life Thomas was not a worshiper at all. The presence of the Lord made him a worshiper.

How about Peter? As he jumped out of the boat he was putting his adoration into action. It helped him to put his adoration into words *(John 21:7, 15-19).* The *A* in our ACTS is the first in the sequence of all our worship action, and the stepping-off point for a life that is all offered as worship to God.

II
Confession

Matthew 26:69-75 points out another of Peter's ACTS that helped him to develop as a worshiper. Something he did did something to him. There are many passages of Scripture that describe what goes on when we confess our sins and receive forgiveness from God *(2 Samuel 12: 1-14; 1 John 1:8-10 ✠)*. The big job has been done by our God. He has taken into Himself the punishment of all our sins. But the responsibility to confess is ours. Confession is the *C* in our ACTS of worship. As we sincerely confess we accept forgiveness from God. When by faith we accept God's forgiveness we become saints and begin again to try to live holy lives.

III
Thanksgiving

Why did our parents insist that we say "Thank you" whenever we received something? Politeness is part of it. A greater part is the fact that *we become more appreciative people* as we express our thanks to others for what they do. God wants us to

give thanks to Him too so that we will recognize more and more that He is the Giver of every good and perfect gift.

(This would be a good place to look up some of the passages in the Bible which urge us to give thanks to God. Use a concordance.)

IV
Supplication

Asking for things for ourselves from God does not seem to be worship in the sense of response. Worship is something *we give to God.* In our supplications we seem to be asking God to give *us* things. But remember, our Lord showed us that we should pray, "if it be Thy will," and instructed us to ask in His name. That means we are acknowledging Jesus as the Son of God. We are admitting that God knows what is best for us. We ask God to give us only those things that will make our Lord's name more glorious. When our supplications are presented in that way, we are really offering adoration to God. The *S* in our worship ACTS deepens our adoration of God at the same time as it brings us answers from God. *(John 16:23-27 [23 ✠]; Colossians 3:12-17 [16 ✠]; the Small Catechism—the Lord's Prayer ✠)*

ACTS—the four parts of our response, our worship. All of them are focused adoration. As we offer each action to God, He gives to us more of the blessings that first equipped us with response ability.

woRshipinG with the chuRch

Sunday

It would be good practice in adoration to focus on the words of the *Gloria in Excelsis* in the Liturgy. If we work through the words we can spot places where we can give God glory, confess, thank, and supplicate. For instance, "we give thanks to Thee" is an obvious cue.

But what will you give thanks for? Getting the thoughts ready before the service makes it possible for us to fill the words with meaning when they come by in the chant.

The task of filling the words with our thoughts is most important. When we use the Creed and the Lord's Prayer, our thoughts must make *words* into *worship.* Only our thoughts can make the words of the Invocation into worship.

We could practice our ACTS in the words of *Psalms 29* and *96* or in the words of Sunday's Introit and Gradual. The Psalms are records of the worship of the Old Testament people of God. If we simply *read* their words, we only *hear* how they adored God. It's up to us to put *our* adoration into *their* words, our confession of our sins into their confession, and our thanks and our requests in place of the things they said.

9

take care of yourself

"I'm going to take care of number one first." Most of the time a person who says that counts himself as number one. But a Christian never is only one. He is always in the body, the Church. We are all members—arms, hands, legs—of one another. We must take care of one another.

WORD AND WORK

I

If a friend gives you a casual good-bye and says, "Take care of yourself," he usually thinks that covers the subject. He doesn't feel that he has to say to your right hand, "Take care of your friend there on the left." He doesn't have to say to your mouth, "Keep moving that food down the throat. Remember there are a lot of members depending on you." He takes it for granted that you stick together with yourself.

Shouldn't we be just as confident about the Church? *(1 Corinthians 12:12-27)*

II

We know who we are. We are the Church. Every other member is part of us. How do we take care of ourselves?

We may not always like what we see in the mirror, but we can't help liking *whom* we see. "You shall love your neighbor as yourself" *(James 2: 8)* is based on that fact. Who would "cut off his nose to spite his face"? Even when we don't like what we see and are a bit disgusted with whom we see, we "take care of ourself." Can we be as sure what taking care really means?

Love is a word that says it all. Is the meaning of love clear to us? Do we understand that it means *doing* rather than liking? *(1 John 3:16-18 ✠; Commandments 4-10 ✠).* God did not simply *prove* that He loved us by giving Himself into death for us. That *is* love, *to give yourself. Love is putting yourself out for someone.* That's what our Lord did—He put Himself right out of heaven for us. And we should put ourselves out for every other member in the Church. Since *we* are the Church, that's what it means to "take care of yourself."

Right after St. Paul pointed out to the Corinthian Christians who they were, he instructed them how to put themselves out for one another. His words tell us how to take care of oneself. *(1 Corinthians 12:27— 13:13)*

III

As soon as the Christians realized they were one body, they began to take care of one another's bodily needs *(Acts 2:44-47).* When the Church grew into thousands of members, they had to set up an organization to "take care of themselves," especially of the widows and orphans *(Acts 6:1-7).* But while all that was going on, they did not neglect taking care of one another's spiritual needs. They found that one of the best ways to do this was by gathering in groups *(Hebrews 10:24-25).* In the gathering of the Church they stirred one another up to love, to "put themselves out" for one another, to do good works. They did this by talking and learning the Gospel and sharing it in the Lord's Supper. In that sharing in the real presence of Christ they participated in building the Church.

Imagine we are the members of one of the early Christian groups. What would we say if someone made this proposal?

> We all know what our Lord wants us to do. But not everyone of us is doing what he should. There are some

around here who are doing practically nothing. I move we write into our constitution that every Christian has to do at least one good thing every day for someone else. And what's more, I move that we fine every person who fails to do his daily good work.

What is the only power that can make us love as God loves us?

We would not truly be members of the body of Christ if we did not help build one another up in faith and works. The Bible also calls that edification *(Acts 9:31; Romans 14: 19; Ephesians 4:29).* Whenever we help build up the body we are serving God. And in its larger sense that's worship. The worship service includes ways for us to edify one another. It's a way of starting to live for others *(Colossians 3:12-17; 2 Corinthians 1:3-7; Ephesians 4: 11-16).* When someone asks us, "How do you do it?" we say, "Here's how." After we've showed them how, we say, "Now *you* do it." *(1 Corinthians 10:16-17)*

Now you do it!

worshiping with the church

In its narrowest definition worship is our adoration of God. Since our confessions of sin, our thanksgivings, and our supplications are also offered to God, we include them in our ACTS of worship. We can do none of these things without the action of God for us, so we include the taking in of God's Scripture and sacraments as part of the service. Talking the Word to one another to stir up one another to live is so necessary that Christians also include it in their services of worship. Our actions speak as loudly as our words. When we eat and drink the Lord's Supper we "proclaim the Lord's death." *(1 Corinthians 11:26* ✠*)*

When the Church gets together to stir up one another, they don't all talk at once. They elect someone to do the talking for them. Think about the sermon this Sunday as *your* words. It takes the place of the mutual conversation that went on in the small groups of early Christians. When the lessons are read, all of us are really reading them to one another. After we have done our liturgy in church, we keep the conversation — and our liturgy — going. We talk about the message of the lessons and the sermon to one another.

We sing hymns to God as adoration. But the message of the hymns includes the Word to be sung to one another. Think about the members of the body of Christ as you sing the hymns of the Church.

Remember them in Holy Communion. We share Christ's strength with one another as we share the bread and wine in which He gives us His body and blood.

It's easy to know when we should help a fellow member of the Church with his bodily needs. We can see he is hungry, so we feed him. If we remember that all of us need strengthening by the Gospel all of the time, we will always welcome the chance to edify, to build up, our brother. Look for ways to edify this week. Sunday's Bible class, catechism classes, and home devotions supply chances to edify. So does ordinary conversation. Instead of saying, "Good luck," we could say, "God bless you." Don't be content with "Keep a stiff upper lip." Say, "That's one of the good things about being a Christian—you can ask God for help and be sure He will answer."

Remember to care, and you will take care—of yourself.

10

the offered life

"God so loved *the world* that He gave His only Son . . . !" That's what our Lord said about the heavenly Father *(John 3:16 ✠)*. "As the Father has sent Me, even so I send you." That's what our Lord told His disciples. And we are His disciples. *(John 20:21)*

We need to be aware of the fact that our lives are to be lived for the world. We are to edify the Church but also to sanctify the world. From the very moment that the Word and water power of God was caught by our lives, they were directed toward God and God's people. Each time we give to God the response of adoration, we commit ourselves to living our lives as worship. We share with one another the Word that edifies in order to stir one another up to the life of commitment. All this is a part of the liturgy and the life of the Christian.

Before we complete the study of our part in the liturgy we should see the difference between a "good" life and an "offered" life. The Christian is not simply concerned to "behave himself." He works to take every action and deliberately transform it into an offering of worship to God. He prays for the mind of Christ so that he may live in self-forgetfulness and self-sacrifice. But day by day he tries to transform the things he "ought" to do into things he offers.

This is the life we would live — the Christian life as worship. We who catch the grace of God, give the response of adoration, share with one another the Word, go on to transform all we do into the offered life.

word and work

I

There ought to be no doubt in our minds that good works are essential in the Christian life. It should be clear to us that we are not to live unto ourselves, but unto God and for people. *(2 Corinthians 5:14-15 [15*

✠]; Matthew 7:21 ✠; Luke 6:46; James 2:14-20; Matthew 25:40)

But there is an essential difference between "good" lives and "offered" lives. The difference is seen in the way our Lord lived His life on earth. The difference should be visible in the way we live our lives on earth. *(Matthew 4:1-10* and *Deuteronomy 6:13; Philippians 2:4-11* *)*

The devil was not tempting Jesus to do things that weren't "good." Jesus might have become famous overnight if He had followed the devil's advice. In this way He would have been able to do a lot of "good" for many more people. But our Lord knew that the only good way is God's way. He resisted the devil because He had come to give His life as an offering to God. His whole life was to be an act of worship to God. That's what He meant when He added "Him *only* shalt thou serve" to the passage He quoted. It's that kind of a mind, that attitude, that we should have. All our acts of self-forgetfulness and self-sacrifice are to be offered as worship to God.

II

It is easy enough to see how some of the things we do can be offered up to God *(Matthew 5:16* *; 1 Peter 2:11-12).* Some of the things we do are simply following orders which our Lord left us to obey. Doing them will surely glorify His name. *(Matthew 24:14* and *28:18-20)*

47

But some things seem so far removed from God that we are apt to miss the connection. What a pity! That would be like carefully making a valentine for your best girl and then not mailing it. She'll never know! The good things we do for others, when we offer them to God, become acts of worship which please Him. He knows the loving deeds we do whether we deliberately bring them to Him or not. But the jobs we have to do become much more pleasing to *us* when we do them for God's sake. The real secret of the offered life is to practice offering every single action to God as worship. Just to wash dishes is not any fun, and not very dignified. But dishwashing to the glory of God becomes an act of worship, part of our liturgy! And when we love the Lord as much as we do, everything we do for Him is fun! *(John 13:12-17; Matthew 10:42 ✠; Acts 9:36-42)*

worshiping with the church

Don't try to change your life overnight. Take one thing at a time and offer it to God. Take one thing a day and shine it up as a worship offering to God. One of the best ones to practice is doing the dishes.

Nothing is more boring than doing the dishwashing and drying. Nothing seems to bring out the selfishness in us more, if we have brothers or sisters. Nothing seems further from being an important thing to use for worship. But we can use the fight about "whose turn it is" as the chance to serve God through our brother or sister; and we can offer the whole job to God as a token of our offered life. But be happy doing it. Perhaps you can use the opportunity to witness, too. Let your brother know why you're so peaceful about the "turn" argument. But do be lighthearted about it!

Can we put together our *four kinds* of action in the liturgy this Sunday?

We see the Lord! *Catch* the vision — Father, Son, and Holy Ghost!

Give the response — We adore! We confess, thank, supplicate. "Holy, holy, holy is the Lord of hosts! . . . I am a man of unclean lips. . . . My guilt is taken away. Thank You, God! . . . Help me be the kind of person You want me to be."

We *share.* Tell one another about the Lord. Share the vision!

We *live!* Hear the Lord's question: "Who will go for us?" Let Him hear the answer, "Here I am! Send me." The offered life!

Don't miss what is happening in the Holy Communion. Our Lord tells us what He gives us — "This *is!*" But He also tells us, "This *do!*" That's one of the first steps in the offered life which we can take as we do our liturgy.

If we are to "catch" the power of the Word in the Sacrament we must, of course, participate in the Supper. We give to God in all our ACTS of response as we kneel at His altar.

We are actually sharing the life of God with one another in the service, but also with the whole Church.

As we receive Him we also participate in the offered life He gave up to God. We remember and make present His death with which He worshiped God. As we eat and drink His body and blood He joins *us* to *His* offering. By the assistance of God the Holy Ghost we "earnestly purpose to amend our sinful lives" and day by day to offer them to God.

49

makinG time christian

We want to live the offered life. That takes time — a whole lifetime of time. But the trouble with us is that we wear out in time; we die down in time. In some ways it seems easier to die for God than to live for God. It would take courage and God's grace to die as a martyr. But it takes courage and grace — and a lot longer — to live as a saint! That's what we want to do. We need a way to get God's help — in time!

God set men into time. Our life may be long or it may be short. But it begins in time. It ends in time. It is measured by time. From the time that "there was evening and there was morning, one day," man has had to come to terms with time. At first time was not a problem — the more days, the more time for God and man to be together. But after man sinned all this was different. Every time God came near, man felt like hiding. Even as God's children we have some of this problem.

Out of our situation in time, we Christians are to worship the eternal God. Our problem is to keep time from holding us back. Our goal is to make time Christian — to make time be a help to us in our worship.

worD anD work

I

We can get started on thoughts about time by wondering what it would be like not to be controlled by seconds and minutes and hours and days and weeks and years. Actually, we can't get free from time's limits. We are suspended in time, almost like a pendulum which hangs and swings until the clock runs down and stops.

God is completely outside of time and time's control. What a difference that makes in the way He looks at men and the world and the way He operates in our lives. Take an important thing like God's love. He has always loved us. He always does; He always will. He doesn't change. The very idea of change is something that has to do with time. But for us to understand about God's changelessness, about His steadfast love, God had to make it real for us *in time*. He had to do something. He had to make something happen that we could experience. Without that we could only keep asking, "God, do You really love us? When did You begin to love us? Will You keep on loving us? Prove it. Show us. Count out the amount of Your love on Your fingers so we can see it." Man, who is covered by time, can't get an eternal idea unless the eternal God enters time and fills it with His love. So *that's what He did.* That's the way He made time Christian. He gave us Christ in time! *(Galatians 4:4-6* ✠*)*

II

He did; *we can* make time Christian, too. If we want to make the love of God real to our understanding, we can't do better than God did. We fill a piece of our time with one of the acts He did.

Take Christmas, for instance. We don't know exactly *when* our Lord was born of the Virgin Mary. But we know that He *was* born. After many years the church generally accepted December 25 as the day on which to observe His birth. Every year we agree to fill that piece of time with the remembrance of the incarnation of Jesus Christ. Then we live in it! It's almost a kind of holy pretending. We sing "Christ is born today!" Actually it was hundreds of years ago—in time—that He was born in Bethlehem. But we have filled Christmas Day with this great act of the love of God, and so it is happening *today.* God is still loving us, no matter what the time. That becomes real to us as we celebrate the gift of a Savior as though it were happening on *this* Christmas Day. Once the piece of time is filled with a great act of God, we live in it. We anticipate the Nativity on Christmas Eve. We observe it on Christmas Day. We celebrate it on Second Christmas Day and on the Sunday after Christmas.

Of course God has actually filled all of time with His gracious acts. But to experience His love we fill a day of *our* time with the remembrance of one of His acts and then live in it. It's something like the way a rainmaker works. The rain clouds are already in the sky. The water is there. But the earth is dry. He seeds some of the clouds with chemicals; suddenly they release their rain and sprinkle the whole county. As we live in a day we've filled with an act of God's love, the goodness of God bursts all over us with blessing!

That's the way we make time Christian. We fill time with the remembrance of His loving acts. We keep putting Christ in our time.

III

"That would take years!" It would, too. After all, He lived for 33 years. His ministry was about 3 years long. And the things He taught are as important to remember as the things He did. Then there are all the things He did through His Spirit in the Church! "It would take a year just to go over the important things."

So the early Christians *took* a year. And that's the way the church year developed. And we celebrate the great acts of God and the great Word God spoke and the great power of His Spirit working in us. We do it year after year, filling the weeks and then living in them. In that way the whole year becomes God's year, and as we live in it God's grace showers us!

It's important that we "make the most of the time." God can use our celebration of the church year to make *our* time Christian. *(Ephesians 5:15-20* ✠*)*

There are two parts to the church year: the half year of our Lord, and the half year of the Church. The first half celebrates the great events of our Lord's life. The second half helps us focus our lives on the things our Lord and His apostles taught us. Pages 54 to 94 in *The Lutheran Hymnal* list all of the Sundays and holy days of the church year.

worshiping with the church

Our biggest problem in living the church year is that we can't step out of time. We must do it mentally. It's almost like pretending. We could try it tomorrow. If we take the Gospel for last Sunday and decide that from the morning to the evening we will pretend that it *is* the day on which that event happened, we will be working at making time Christian.

Before we go to the service next Sunday, let's look up the Gospel for the day. Remember the secret of "Christ *is* born today." Say of the event described in the Gospel, "Today this *is* happening in our congregation." As we live the day, we make time Christian.

12

filling in the time

"Just filling in time" is usually a description of doing nothing. But when we live the church year we fill in our time with the most important thing ever, God's Word and work. As we think of Him, our prayer is answered by the Spirit's presence. As we love Jesus Christ, we keep His Word, and the Father and the Son come to us. *(John 14:23)*

Living the church year gives us the time of our lives.

wORD anD wORK

Filling in the Feasts

The first Christians were Jews, just as Jesus Himself was. It was natural for them to celebrate the Passover when it came at the spring full moon. But their observance the first year after the resurrection of Jesus centered in the Lamb of God that took away the sins of the world. He was the Paschal Lamb, and they were the New Israel, the Church. They were celebrating Easter. This was the first feast to be celebrated regularly. It began the development of the half year of our Lord.

It's natural for people to say, "Just a year ago today. . . ." The Christians said that about Pentecost's gift of the Spirit and about Ascension and about the events of Holy Week. By the 4th century these times were fixed and most Christians observed them as special times. Between the 3rd and the 5th centuries the celebration of Christ's birth was introduced into the church year. The Church had many Gentile members by then. Their pagan festivals at the winter solstice filled time with sinful acts. The Church set a different reason for celebrating. By remembering the birthday of the Lord, they made the day Christian.

Not till the 10th century was the Feast of the Holy Trinity added. Everything God has done for us is summed up in the celebration of His being and nature.

The church year was not worked out ahead of time. It just grew in time. As we *live* it, the cycles of the festival half of the church year fill the days to overflowing with the Gospel, and we grow in time, too.

II

Filling in the Seasons

The boy Jesus must have looked forward to His birthday celebrations just as we do. Mary probably helped Him *anticipate* them. She may have told Him of the prophecies of His birth. We do the same thing during Advent—we *anticipate* Christmas. After we have observed Christ's birth, we celebrate it for 12 days to the Epiphany and throughout Epiphanytide.

The Feast of the Resurrection has a period of *anticipation,* too— Lent and the pre-Lent days. Easter's observance doesn't stop with the day but continues through the *celebration*

days of the Sundays after Easter. Some of those Sundays seem to anticipate the Ascension. At the same time Ascension is part of the anticipation of Whitsunday, the Feast of Pentecost. The Feast of the Holy Trinity is the octave of Pentecost and at the same time a feast in itself. All of the "after Trinity" days are also "after Pentecost" days. They make up the half year of the Church. They are days in which we remember that we live in the strength of the Holy Spirit.

The half year of the Church does not have a chronological sequence. One suggestion for division is this: The call to the kingdom of grace, reminding us of how God begins the new life in us and makes it strong (I to V); The righteousness of the Kingdom, describing how with the new life must come a new way of living (VI to XI); Christian faith and life in the Kingdom, which are shown in love and service (XII to XVIII); The consummation of the kingdom, urging us to be ready for our final salvation (XIX to Advent).

III

Filling in the Sundays

The first Christians continued to worship with their Jewish brethren on the Sabbath, but at sundown Saturday they went to one of the Christian homes for the Eucharist. Saturday evening and on into the dawn of Sunday was the fixed time for the service as the Church became mostly Gentile in membership. The connection with the synagogue was lost, and the Resurrection was the event that gave meaning to the liturgy. Each celebration renewed the Church's communion with the Lord and one another.

The Christians took from the

synagogue the custom of reading from the Law and the Prophets. When the New Testament books had been written, readings that later became our Epistles and Gospels were chosen. The Psalms became the hymnal of the New Testament Church just as they had been in the Old. The Introits and Graduals are psalm verses we still use today.

If anyone asks us on a Sunday, "What's new?" we could answer, "The propers." The lessons and the psalm verses chosen for each Sunday make each Sunday "new." But to "fill in" the meaning of the Sunday, a person would have to fit the "proper pieces" together.

IV

Filling in the Days

The pattern of the church year can be seen as a great wheel. God's work in Christ is the center. The Sundays are the spokes. Each one is specially carved—like those on medieval coaches. The propers are the carvings. The saints' days and holy days surround the year like carvings in the rim. All those things are beautiful and necessary—but what holds it all together? and what meets the bumps in the road? The rim itself. Those are the days of the weeks that hold the Sundays together. Those are the days that each Christian must live out in his vocation. We celebrate the Sunday past and anticipate the Sunday coming. If we use matins and vespers each day, or if we have morning and evening prayer, we are working at our worship to fill in the days.

woRshipinG with the chuRch

Everyday

All during the week we celebrate what happened last Sunday. It's not only the Gospel that gives meaning to the Sunday, but the other propers as well: the Introit, the Collect, the Gradual, and the Epistle.

Sunday

Before we attend the Sunday gathering of God's people, we prepare to celebrate by finding out "what's new." We can usually find an accent for the day in the propers. Not all of the propers will make this point. Sometimes the Introit will simply urge us to "praise the Lord." Some of the propers remind us we are sinners; some preach the Gospel. They would fit any Sunday. When the theme becomes clear we fit the other facts together as Law and Gospel. Then our task is to "catch" and to "give" and to "share" when the propers come along in the service. Each time we must work at filling the words with our meanings as well as getting the meanings from the words.

13

we've got a date

A date may be fun, but it can be quite a strain. Here are some sample speeches by teen-agers—a girl, then a boy . . . then a voice that seems to be talking about something else. None of us will have trouble understanding the fellow or the girl. What about the third speaker?

Girl: "Hair, face, dress—I've got to look my best. I won't admit that I care very much, but I do hope he likes me."

Boy: "Shoes shined, car shined, face shined—I've got to make a good impression. On her. And on her folks."

Voice: *Speaking of dates—every Sunday is the Lord's Day.*

Girl: "What are we going to talk about? For hours? What if he talks about things I don't know anything about? What'll I do?"

Boy: "What if I say the wrong thing? And what if after everything I say there's just a hollow silence?"

Voice: *Speaking of the problem of conversation—there's a "proper" solution. The give and take of Sunday's conversation is all laid out. A person can get ready in advance.*

Girl: "When I'm with other girls, it's no problem. We don't even have to finish sentences. We know what we mean. But it's harder to talk to a boy."

Boy: "There are some things I want to tell her, things I want her to know about how I feel. But—how do you say things like that to a girl without getting tied up in your own tongue? I'll never get them out."

Voice: *Speaking of how to say what you mean, extraordinary things are very well said in the "ordinary."* [The parts which are the same in every service we call the "ordinary." They seem ordinary to us when we use them so often.] *The words for what one wants to get said are all ready. Just add thoughts and serve—God!*

Girl: "Where will we go? Why doesn't he tell me where we're going? Flats or heels? Party dress or shorts? I've got to know."

Boy: "She knew it was a picnic. So why heels? You ought to be able to *expect* a girl to know what's going on!"

Voice: *Speaking of what's going on—for years and years we've known in advance what all the celebrating is about. It's a banquet. And the Speaker is the greatest!*

Girl: "Wonder if I'll like his friends? Some boys are so funny. . . . What if they insist on doing something I don't want to do?"

Boy: "In some ways it's easier to double-date like this—but when you don't know the others, it can be worse. Maybe we won't be able to get together at all!"

Voice: *Speaking of harmony and unity, the Church fits together like one body. Whoever has the same Head, fits. It's never hard to get started. The program's already under way. There's a regular pattern, so that everybody can get together. Just begin, and pay attention—study a bit—you'll catch on.*

59

WORD AND WORK

The conversations we hear from three different seats on a bus are seldom worth trying to figure out. But this conversation could be worthwhile. A class that has worked through the 12 lessons of this catechism could overhear the conversation and connect it to our whole worship life as the Church.

I

Get ready on Saturday.

There's no problem of God's liking us. God *is* love. He has loved! We can't make a good impression, actually. The best we can do before God is to recognize the worst we have done. *(Matthew 18:1-4; James 4:1-10 [6-8 ✠]; Luke 18:9-14; 14b ✠)*

We can get ready to "catch," to "give" and to "share" on every Lord's Day date. Much of God's part of the conversation can be checked ahead of time. We can decide just what we will say in reply.

If we know our lines, we can watch for the cues that help us worship together.

II

Get started on Sunday.

The life of the Church is already going on. It's up to us to make the beginning of "living." We make sure we know what time it is, what *He* has done already, what *they* are doing. Then we can do our part. God has made His power available for us. He gives us *Himself*. What more could one ask for?

Nobody would insist that a game be changed to be played just the way *he* likes it. The Church has been at its Sunday work for years. We want to find our place. The Church helps us do what we've always wanted to be doing, in good style, the way we've always wanted to do it.

III

Keep going on Monday.

A ring is only metal going around in circles, until it is given as "a token of wedded love and faithfulness." The way to start giving our lives to God is to give Him one day sincerely. That's a token. It means we resolve to stop going around in circles. Then give Him every day. We do it with the token again—begin with moments that are His alone as each day begins.

What we *said* we'd do for one another on Sunday, gets done on Tuesday and Wednesday. Better than a souvenir pasted in a scrap book is a good memory. We can remind ourselves of what we did in remembrance by remembering every day.

worshiping with the church

Sunday

It's polite not to interrupt when another is speaking. But we can talk back to God while He is talking to us. It's one of the best ways to make sure you're really hearing Him. Let's try it with Sunday's propers. When we've *caught* what He will say, we can plan the response we will *give* and the thoughts we will *share*. We hear and respond at the same time.

Everyday

Things God says are so profound you hear new things each time you listen. A way to try it is to read the Epistle each morning, the Gospel each evening during the next days. Listen for new things spoken from God. And talk back! The Evening and the Morning Prayers could give us the words; we supply the thought or make our own sentences.

61

PROGRAM NOTES

The stage is set. We know that we, together with all the other members of the Church, are included in the cast. As worshipers we know we are already caught up in the action of the play.

Before our roles at center stage begin, however, we will watch the Prologue, followed by three acts in each of which there are five scenes. The Epilogue brings the action up to the times in which we find ourselves. Then we will recognize ourselves taking over our roles in God's drama of redemption.

"Get your program here! Can't tell what's happening without a program."

That's to be expected in this drama. The plot is God's, and it happened over thousands of years. It takes the 66 books of the Bible to record the details. But the story line is simple.

The great Creator made a world and placed men on it. They were to be His people and He was to be their God. That's the way He designed them. The center of their life was to be the worship of the God of love. But mankind didn't want to be His worshiping children. They wanted to "be as gods." They were not interested in admitting they were less than God. That's the way His commandments made them feel. They felt that to worship God would be too humbling. They were too proud for that. They turned their backs on God.

(Up to this point the verbs have all been in the past tense. The pronouns have all been saying *they.* But this is about *mankind.* That includes *us.* And all this describes us today—present tense. Every human being is born with this same kind of rebellious pride. It is only by the grace of God that some men are changed back or converted into worshipers. All of the action in the Prologue and the three Acts is about us, too. We rebel. The grace of God that worked out man's salvation through Jesus Christ must be in the present tense, too, if we are to be worshipers. Think of this, then, in the present tense. Change the pronouns to include *us.)*

Because God's love is so great He is not going to let us walk away to our death without trying to bring us back into His family. The Bible is the dramatic account of all that God has done to turn us back into worshiping children. It is much more than that, however, because what God *did,* He is also *doing.* What *happened* is *happening,* right now as we ponder God's Word. His Word is also God at work. We must keep looking at the drama both as the history of what God *has done* to make men into worshipers and also as the work of God—God's Word—shaping us *right now* into true worshipers.

We look at the plot, therefore, in order to follow it better—but (and this is the whole point of our study this year) also in order *to follow God better,* to worship Him more truly. In order to focus our attention on the present tense of the drama, a second title is given for each act as well as for the Prologue. That title reminds us that the same power of God is working on us now. It describes what is happening in terms of *the Word of God.* The Word of God is with us at this moment, and God is making happen now by His Word what He made happen then. In the Word *God* is *at work.* And God is at work—on us!

(The titles of the Prologue and the Acts are taken from Luther's Explanation of the Third Article in his Small Catechism.

There are five scenes in each act. To remind us that all of the scenes actually involve our own lives, the scenes are based on the passage of an average human life from birth through marriage with its ups and downs until finally death comes and then the resurrection. In each act these events are repeated with different characters. What God worked to achieve with Israel, He repeated in the life of the True Israel, Jesus Christ. The process repeats itself in the life of every one of us, in Act III, from our baptism to our resurrection.)

The Prologue: *God Calls a Worshiping People* (Lessons 14—16)
The Creation; the love that remained true when men proved false; the saving of the human race through Noah.

The Word Was God. This is not dry history. It is living fact. God is directly involved with each one of us. During the time of the Prologue, however, God did not use prophets or written records to reach men with His Word. God met man face to face. The Word was God!

Act I: *God Gathers a Worshiping People*
(Lessons 17—21)
God changed His approach. He decided to gather a special people to be His own, a people in whose lives He could demonstrate His love for the world. Their worship would reveal God's greatness and urge other men to follow Him. He was not only gathering a people but gathering *by* them.

The Word Is in His People. Through them He spoke to the world. Through the record of His mighty acts for Israel He still speaks to us and to all who read the Scriptures.

Act II: *God Enlightens the World for Worship*
(Lessons 22—26)
Israel failed God. God took over the task Himself. Jesus Christ, the Light of the world, became God's

demonstration of how true men should live. He showed the world. But He did more—by His dying and rising again He saved the world.

The Word Made Flesh. He is with us always. Even though we do not now see Him, He is in charge of the universe. The record of who He is and what He does for men still changes the lives of men who hear and believe.

Act III: *God Sanctifies Us to Be Worshipers*
                (Lessons 27—31)
                We are on stage in this act. God separates us from the world, makes us holy by forgiving us, and now depends on us to bring the Word to the world. We are the new Israel who are to live such worshipful lives that men may see our good works and glorify God.

                The Word in His Church. By His Spirit He creates us as His body. We bring to fruition His sufferings, continuing the work He did to bring God's love to everyone in the world.

The Epilogue: *God Keeps Us Living Worshipful Lives*
                (Lessons 32—62)
                All the while we are studying the acts of this drama we are facing up to the problems of the Epilogue. Our whole life is to be worship, and it isn't easy. That's why we need the Word. *The Word is in Scripture and sacraments.*

14

In the Beginning God!

As children on a playground merry-go-round, we are never content just to sit and go around in circles until everything comes to a standstill. We study just how fast the merry-go-round is going and study its relation to the earth which is standing still. Then we swing off, help give the merry-go-round a running push, and jump on again. We become a part of its action.

The Church was already in motion when we got in through our baptism. It's a going concern. We study its history and its movements in the Bible and learn about the world in which it moves in order that we might do our part to keep it going. We use the Bible to show us where life and action is. That's the way we ought to undertake the rapid overview of the whole Bible in the Prologue and first two acts. We're not only trying to satisfy historical curiosity; we want to be made a part of God's action.

We admit that much of the time we would prefer simply sitting on the merry-go-round and letting someone else push. Certainly we'd often rather be *in* the Church than *be* the Church, people pushing for God. That is the other reason we study the Bible record of the great things God has done for His Church. We want more than the facts. We study the Bible because in it we find that *God acts!*

We discover that from the very beginning God was at work in the world. He spoke and it was done. That's the big reason for considering what went on "in the beginning." We find that God dealt face to face with men whom He had created. In different ways His Word came to them, but it was always a *moving* Word. It moved them to action. That's what we need. We want a moving Word from God that will put us into action.

There is no way of "proving" that the Bible is God's Word for us. It does have a power to convince those who study it. But we have a different starting point. We have been brought to faith in God through Holy Baptism. We have come to know Him through Jesus Christ, who lived with us on our world. By His Spirit we are persuaded He *is,* and He *loves,* and He *speaks* His Word, and He *acts.* It is this Bible that testifies to all the things we are convinced by the Spirit are true. We are sure that just as He uses water in baptism, so He uses the print of the Bible to work on us with His Word. He uses the record of all that He *has* done for the Church to *do* things today to the Church—to each one of us. That's why we should give our best efforts to this overview of the Bible. As we study the record of all that God's love did for men we will experience His love doing things for us.

We can understand how God's working Word reaches us through a thing as common as words and print when we compare it with ordinary relationships in life. When we hear that somebody likes us, we begin to notice that person, too. When we read about God's loving care for men, we are changed into people who love Him, people who love Him more and more. Ordinary words do things to us — think about a big Thanksgiving dinner: turkey with crisp, crackling skin, tangy cranberries, steamy, rich gravy. The words can make our mouths water.

The words do more than state facts. They begin to *act* on us. The Bible words do that — and much more. They are a means of grace — a way that God uses to give us His undeserved love, and by His Spirit He gives us His power to become His people and to live His kind of life.

As we study how God worked to make men into worshipers, our own worshiping life will be strengthened.

WORD AND WORK

I

All creation centers in the God we worship.

If we were to attempt to picture God by a diagram on this page, He would be the entire sheet — in fact we would have to think of Him as pushing out beyond the borders of the page and both up and down into infinity. He fills all things. We can't limit Him to a "Lo, here!" or a "Lo, there!"

We should always remember that our worship of God is not simply something we are ordered to do. We are not like clever dogs that can be taught to sit up and "speak." God is central to all life. Everything that is created simply *must* bow down and worship Him. *(Psalms 66:100 ☩; 150)*

II

God created the world, a stage for worship.

Read *Genesis 1* and *2* as stage directions for worship. When we read it that way, not only looking for details on the world's construction as scientists might, the account keeps reminding us, "Worship!" If even God saw that "it was good," what must man have thought? "Three cheers! Oh, come, let us worship the Lord!" *(Psalms 95; 104; 148)*

III

God set man upon the stage to be a worshiper.

God didn't need people for companionship. *We* collect friends because of what they can do for us, because they can make us happy. God created friends because of what He could do for them. What He did and what He does is summed up in THE WORD. He spoke His creating Word and man came to life *(Psalm 33:4-9)*. It was His Word, too, in "face-to-face" encounter that taught men what it was to be really *living*. To worship God and to serve Him in daily work is to live. To make *self* central is to die *(Genesis 2:2-3; 15-17; Exodus 20:8-11; John 1: 1-4 ☩)*. The Word that created man a worshiper continues to work with us to re-create us as worshipers. *(The First Article ☩)*

nor to an "out there" or an "up there." He is! Everywhere. Always. Almighty!

But when He created a world He established *space*. The world was a place, a limited space. That we *can* picture. Surround space with a circle and we draw a symbol of the world, the universe, and all it contains.

Mankind can also be drawn in. They are creatures of body as well as spirit. They occupy space and are limited by time.

Since our God deigns to keep in touch with the human beings He created, He reveals Himself in the place where His people live. Now it is possible to draw God in— because He counts Himself in. We can place His mark—the creating Hand, revealed in Trinity, within an eternal circle. God is the center of His whole creation.

worshiping with the church

Everyday

We work at learning how to worship because we want to be the kind of men and women that God originally designed. But we didn't create ourselves and we can't re-create ourselves. God must do that. Since what God *says* is *done,* His Word makes it possible for us to *do.* When, therefore, in the worship service and in our devotions we "catch" the Word, we are enabled to "give" God adoration and to go on to "share" and "live." In practice we "catch, give, and share" all at once. The psalms in this lesson, or the verses in Sunday's Introit and Gradual, help us practice. They not only teach us about worship, but are God's Word to make us worshipers. They are also channels of worship. As we say the psalmist's words we can express our own worship in thoughts of our own. As we do them *together* the Word draws us together. But it is up to us to *use* the Word in all three ways. Good food smells good, but unless we eat it, it won't be good *for us* and unless we *share* it, it won't do others any good. Work with the Word!

15

in the second place, man

Here's a puzzle for us. If a good God created all that exists, how did things get into such bad shape? Why did man stop being a worshiper? If he was created to control the whole earth, why is is that he can't control himself?

That concerns us. It's important that we all be philosophers and historians and ask these questions because we are in as bad a shape as the world. *We* don't control *our* selves. If we don't realize the condition of our human nature, we won't be interested in having anything done about it.

That's why God Himself wants us to be interested. That's another reason God caused the Bible to be written. He wants us to know what man has done to spoil creation. He wants us to realize that we continue to make the same wrong choice Adam and Eve made. He wants us to grasp the solution He has worked out.

When we use God's Book, we must also use His Table of Contents. There's no point arguing that it should have been written differently. Take the first chapters of Genesis, for instance. We aren't the first people to wonder about the beginning of the world and of evil. Some account of what had happened was probably passed along by story-tellers. (The same thing is happening in every one of our families. Our parents tell us over and over again the things that happened when we were children.)

But a special thing happened with the Hebrew people. God chose them to be the means through which He would remake the spoiled world. God acted in a special way in the history they were making and in the history they wrote. Some of the men in other tribes had forsaken the true God and their accounts gave a false picture of God and a false picture of man. God wanted a truthful account: it would also be a transforming power to act on all who would read about His acts. This is His WORD.

God accomplished this by a mysterious process which the Bible calls "inspiration." We don't know just how, but the Spirit of God guided men to speak the truth God wanted written *(2 Peter 1:21 ✖)*. And God made their writings a power to change men

(2 Timothy 3:16-17 ✖). But we must remember that God did not change the writers into 20th-century historians. He was perfectly willing to have them use their own history methods. Ancient historians may not have been so anxious to decide exactly how everything had happened or to put everything down in chronological order. They seemed to like the story form. It was a good way to put a point across. Just as God guided St. Luke when he studied various records before writing his Gospel account, so God guided the Old Testament writers so that they recorded the truth. They could use different forms of writing, different records, different accounts of the past, as historians ordinarily would. But by the inspiration of God their words were the Word of God.

It is our task to make sure we understand God's truth. Sometimes we do not distinguish between what they are telling us and their way of telling it. Sometimes people interpret the Scriptures differently as a result. But certain truths are very clear in Scripture's accounts of the beginnings. In the first place, the truth about God is made very clear: *He is in first place!* Now — in the second place — let's study about man. About us.

71

word and work

Man, the creation of God, is "number 2" *(Genesis 1:26-27).* That is no insult to have God above you, to be made only "a little less than God" *(Psalm 8:3-8),* unless in pride one begins to think he should be as a god himself. It is almost beyond understanding how man-in-the-image-of-God could begin to imagine himself man-the-equal-of-God. God's Word reveals that it was an evil power outside of man that corrupted him *(Genesis 3:1-8).* The Church has always seen Satan in the serpent *(Revelation 12:9; 20:2),* and recognized all the devilish beings as fallen angels *(2 Peter 2:4).* But that still doesn't wholly answer the question of how evil came into existence in a good world. Nor does it solve the problem of why God permits evil to continue and even permits it to mar the happiness of His own children.

Here are things we *do* know:

About God:

1. God is in control of the universe *(Genesis 1:1).* But it is *His* control. He directs it as He sees fit. Omnipotence means that God can do anything He *chooses* to do.

2. God chose to limit His exercise of power by giving angels and men a free will. With that free will God also made it clear that His creatures must accept the result of their choices. *(Genesis 2:16-17)*

3. But God retains the right to shape events to His purposes and promises only good for His called children. *(Romans 8:28* ✠*)*

About man:

1. Man is the climax of all creation. His highest distinction is the privilege of fellowship with God. His call as a creature is to worship God and serve his fellowman.

2. God would not compel man to love Him. Man was given freedom to choose. In arrogance and pride man used his free will to choose life on his own, rejecting fellowship with God and refusing worship.

3. Life apart from the presence of God is death. Man no longer has the power to choose anything but to live in selfishness.

4. Fellowship between men and God can be restored, therefore, only through an act of God Himself.

5. All this is true about us. *Mankind* fell. We are born in Adam's image. We, too, have repeatedly chosen the option of death:

72

About God and man:

1. That God means what He says and carries out what He threatens is terribly clear. *(Genesis 3:8-24)*

2. That God is consistent with His promises is seen in that He did not spare His only Son from the effect of evil but gave Him up for us all. *(Romans 8:32)*

3. That God is faithful to His promises is seen in the resurrection of His Son, the redemption of the whole world, and the gift of the Holy Spirit through which we are adopted as His sons. *(Romans 8: 32-34 ✠; Galatians 4:4-6)*

worshiping with the church

Sunday

The five propers of every Sunday have been selected from the Scriptures to create a harmony. It's our task to make the different propers harmonize. Usually one of the propers sounds the theme. If we can decide on a unifying theme for next Sunday, we can help one another fit the other propers into a helpful harmony. (Look for the notes that remind us that the justice of God condemns all sin. Find every place in which you can hear the descant of the Gospel: God's forgiving love in Christ Jesus. Don't miss the rhythm sections—they urge, "Worship Him who delivers us from evil.")

Everyday

When a new tune really becomes popular, we find ourselves whistling it at odd moments throughout the day. If the theme for Sunday really clicked with us, we could help ourselves live the church year by remembering the idea each day of the week. We don't have to whistle it or chant it, but saying the theme quietly to ourselves will help us remember God's message for this week.

WORSHIP HIM WHO DELIVERS US FROM EVIL

16

the world is baptized

There are three ways of looking at the Flood. One is from the inside of the ark looking out. Another is from the outside of the ark, unable to get in. The third is the viewpoint of God.

The destruction of the whole created world is terrible to consider from either of man's points of view. Those in the ark were helpless to do anything for those who were drowning. Those outside who were drowning had an even greater despair in the realization that they had brought destruction upon themselves by ignoring Noah's warning.

We must try to see all this from God's point of view. God's thoughts are not our thoughts, and God's ways are not our ways. But God had not taken a new position when He permitted the Flood to destroy the wicked. God is love. He is unchanging. He always desires man's good. We can accept that—after all, we have the point of view of those who were saved. All men living have descended from the passengers in the ark. But we can't quite forget all who were drowned. Didn't a God who is love consider them?

Think it through from the beginning. Time and again Adam and Eve must have regretted that they were put out of the Garden of Eden. But from God's point of view, it was the best thing that could have happened to them, once they had disobeyed Him and become sinners. When we read of God's point of view about that exile in *Genesis 3:22-23,* we get a totally different picture from that of Adam and Eve. God did not want men to live forever as sinners. He hoped for better things for mankind. He did not want them to eat of the tree of life and to live forever as only half-men, men who were no longer what the initial creation had designed them to be. He wanted them to be worshipers forever. Man had eaten himself out of house, but God saved him from eating himself out of his eternal home.

Doesn't that give us a clue as to the way God was thinking at Noah's time? The Scriptures were written for our learning. We don't need instruction in feeling sorry for ourselves. So the Scriptures don't dwell on the tragedy of the dying rebels. But we do need to be instructed by God to understand how His love was at work even in this catastrophe. God caused the account of the Flood to be written to teach us how mercifully God was salvaging the human race out of the wreck man had made of himself and God's whole creation.

The Flood was not only a great destruction but also a great baptism. It was water sent by God to save mankind—to give mankind another opportunity really to be God's kind of men, worshiping men. Many were lost, but by this baptism everyone who has since come to faith was saved! Eight people were carried to safety by the waters of the Flood which held up the ark. All the faithful were in that ark. That is why it still stands as a symbol of the Church. The mystery of why some were lost and only a few were saved is hidden in the mind of God. We know that those who were lost had refused to accept God's salvation. But only the grace of God saved those who were saved.

We ought to try to look at the Flood from God's point of view. We should marvel at the greatness of the patience and mercy of God toward His children. God acted in redemptive love through the Flood. Out of the death of so many God raised up a small group of people to new life. God worked a salvation by water to enable mankind to return to their status as worshipers.

word and work

I

God's hope that sinners would turn from their sin and live again had been frustrated. In justice and divine wisdom He resolved to destroy evil men in order to give mankind another opportunity to live. *(Ezekiel 33:11 ✠; Romans 9:20-24; Genesis 6:5-7 [5 ✠]; 11-13; 17)*

II

In His mercy and grace God resolved to establish a small group of worshipers in a new world, men who would know Him as the true God and recognize Him as the focal point of all life. *(Genesis 6:8-9; 13-22; Genesis 8:1; 20-22 ✠)*

III

God followed through on His promise to rescue mankind. He made a covenant with the family of Noah and declared that the rainbow was His mercy-mark over the world. The stage was set for God's redemptive drama in a world born anew. *(Genesis 9:8-17; Genesis 3:15-16; 1 Peter 3:18-21; Hebrews 11:7)*

woRshiping with the chuRch

Everyday

Noah and his family must really have gotten down on their knees when they saw how the Flood destroyed everybody on earth. The whole family must have worshiped God fervently when they saw that the ark floated and God had saved them.

God must make us realize our sin, too. And God reminds us of His love over and over again. The Law is preached to make us realize that like Noah all of us sin and deserve what the world deserved. Did you hear it Sunday? Do you remember it as being true about you?

Surely Noah did not have to be threatened by another flood in order to recognize its seriousness. But he did need to *remember* it. Our need is the same. We need to examine ourselves and recognize our sin. We need to get down on our knees and acknowledge our guilt before God. That is an important part of worship. It is hard work. We'd rather avoid it. The discipline of worship holds us to our confession as each day closes.

But recognizing sin's seriousness didn't keep Noah from sinning. Nor is it the answer to our problem. We need a power only God can give.

Our solution is not a matter of "trying harder." That wouldn't have kept Noah dry—he needed the ark. So do we—we need God's Gospel. That is the Good News that God has sent His Son, and in the ark of His Church all who repent and accept His forgiveness are saved. Did you hear the Gospel? Remembering it is also a power of God to save us!

We preach the Gospel to ourselves each time we say "for Jesus' sake!" We should be sure we listen to our own sermons!

the BIRTH OF ISRAEL

God deliberately limited His control over men by giving them a free will. He did not want a forced worship, He wanted worship that grew out of love. But a free will meant also that men would have to bear the results of their wrong choices. When they turned away from God, they left the Father's house. But God did not stop loving men. He offered to adopt

them as His children again. Generation after generation rejected His offer. Then came the Flood and a new beginning. But the Tower of Babel showed that man was still not ready to be a creature that worships God.

Act I of the drama of redemption now begins. God seemed to say, "Perhaps men don't understand what 'adoption' means. They're unwilling to come back into My family because they've never known anyone who was adopted." God decided, "I will adopt a man and his family. I will love them as My children. All the world will see what life is like when one is a child of God. Then they will return to Me and love Me and worship Me."

That helps us understand how Abraham, Isaac, Jacob, and the children of Israel came to be the chosen people. God chose this people to be the ones in whom He would act out His Word. He would *do* it to show mankind, rather than just *say* it. He would love Israel in action. Then Israel would *be* His Word to the world. *The Word was in a nation.*

Act I begins. We'll cover the whole Old Testament in five scenes. We won't try for detail, but to help us remember what happened we'll call the scenes *Birth, Marriage, The Ups and Downs, Death*, and *Resurrection*. We'll use the same divisions for Acts II and III. Remember, we describe the scenes in this way to remind us that they all involve us and our way of life.

WORÒ anÒ WORK

I

God conceives the plan and prepares for the birth of a gathered people.

God began to gather His people *(Genesis 12 to 50)*. It was all *God's* plan *(Genesis 12:1-3)*; Abraham didn't think it up. All of a sudden, all undeserving, Abraham was chosen. That's *grace!* But God was thinking of the whole world, too. *(Genesis 35: 9-15; Exodus 4:22-23; Hosea 11: 1-2; 12:1-6; Malachi 1:2-3; Romans 9:4-18)*

This is how a man becomes a worshiper of the true God. God reveals Himself as a loving God. When a man "catches on" that God is his Father, he can make his response in worship. True religion requires a response. "So Abram went, as the Lord had told him" *(Genesis 12:4)*. A willingness to listen to God and a continually worshiping obedience to God is what God must create in us if we are to be His children. Martin Luther sums it up in his explanation to the Third Article: "I cannot by my own reason or strength believe in Jesus Christ or come to Him; but the Holy Ghost has called me by the Gospel."

II

The nation of Israel was like a child, born in pain and suffering.

The first 11 chapters of Exodus tell of the birth of Israel as a nation. *Exodus 3:13-17* and *4:21-23* tell us something about the child and about

the Father. (Instead of the usual "Both mother and child are doing well" something should be said about the father.) The pain and agony of the birth of Israel as a people should teach them that they were completely dependent on God for life and for deliverance.

III

The child Israel learned to know its Father.

God's Passover made the Exodus possible. The celebration marked the final deliverance of God's child, Israel, from bondage. The continued celebration of the Passover taught Israel to know God and helped them realize they were God's gathered children. *(Exodus 12:21-27, 42; 13:6-10)*

IV

The children of God learned they had been chosen for special service.

Abram got the Word at once *(Genesis 12:2)* and repeatedly during his life *(18:17-18)*. His son, Isaac, got the Word *(26:4)* and also *his* son, Jacob *(28:14)*, who was given the name Israel by God *(32:27-28)*. They got the Word, but frequently they did not get the picture *(Isaiah 6: 9-10* and *Acts 28:23-28)*. They were to accept the grace and fatherhood of God so completely in His covenant with them that they would *be worshipers,* His people. They were to come out from the unbelievers and be a separated people, thereby preserving the true faith and at the same time *making worshipers* and attracting others to serve God.

(Look ahead—we can see in Israel the pattern of life for the whole Church. God's salvation has been sent to us. Do our lives mark us as a separated people? Are we making worshipers?)

worshiping with the church

Sunday

It is important that we remember *we* are adopted sons of God. Important for one thing because we must never forget that we bring our old inheritance with us into the family of God. We are sinners still. Important too that we remember God has made us new men and by His Spirit makes it possible for us to live as sons of God.

God is giving us *the Word* while the pastor and people are speaking their lines in the Confession and Absolution. Our task is to hear God at the same time we are *telling* God.

"We poor sinners confess unto Thee that we are by nature sinful and unclean." "I, a poor miserable sinner, confess unto Thee all my sins and iniquities." In those words God speaks His law to us, if we will but hear and understand. Our task is to lay the Law down to ourselves. "Miserable" does not mean that we must somehow try to "feel awful." It reminds us that we are "people who need mercy." We should *hear* that Word each Sunday in the service.

God's other Word that we should hear comes through loud and clear in the Absolution. Through the pastor the grace of God is announced to us. "In the stead and by the command" of our Lord Jesus Christ he gives us the forgiveness of God, the Father, Son, and Holy Ghost. That's the Word of the Gospel. "To them that believe on His Name, He giveth power to become the sons of God and hath promised them His Holy Spirit." It's God "calling us by the Gospel" each time we hear it, calling us to live as His people.

> **Adore** Him in the Invocation.
>
> **Confess** your sins in the Preparation.
>
> **Thank** Him as He grants His Absolution.
>
> **Serve** Him—service begins in Supplication and is exercised in all of life.

18

ISRAEL WED AT SINAI

It wasn't easy for the Children of Israel to remember all that God had done for their ancestors Israel and Isaac and Abraham. They had never learned to be very good children. During the slavery in Egypt Israel had forgotten what it meant to belong to God *(Exodus 6:2-9)*. Israel needed a strong reminder that she was God's own. She needed a strong reminder that she was to recommend God to all the world by the way she herself worshiped and served Him.

God prepared to dramatize His relationship with Israel. He decided by a formal ceremony to establish His covenant with the generations He had freed from Egypt. With some of the Bible authors we can describe what happened at Mount Sinai as a marriage ceremony between God and Israel. God established His covenant with Israel to keep her pure and to demonstrate in her His love for all the world. He would so richly bless her that later on all the nations of the earth could be blessed through her. He did this all "out of fatherly goodness and mercy without any merit or worthiness" in her. "For all which it was" *Israel's* "duty to thank and praise, to serve and obey Him." *(The First Article of the Apostles' Creed and its explanation* ✠*)*

WORD AND WORK

I

God picked a nobody to become a somebody.

It was God who chose — not Israel who deserved. It wasn't a 50/50 love affair. God was the lover — Israel was only unlovable.

Wouldn't we agree that was true right after the Exodus? *(Exodus 15:24; 16:2; 17:2)*. And still true from then on right through the conquest of the Promised Land? *(Deuteronomy 9)*. And true much later during the times of the prophets? *(Ezekiel 16:1-14)*. But God made her a somebody! *(Exodus 19:3-6)*

The chosen people often got it all backwards. They claimed that they deserved to be the sons of God because they were the children of Abraham. They thought that God liked them because of the way they observed the Law. Actually it was the other way around. They thought that

God had rejected the rest of the world in favor of them. Actually God had favor on them not only because of His grace but because He wanted through them to win the rest of the world back into His family.

This is important for us, because we are still tempted to mix up His love and His law. His love has made us "a chosen nation, a peculiar people." *(The Third Article of the Apostles' Creed and its explanation ✠)*

II

Israel was to be somebody for everybody.

It was not only because the Lord loved Israel, but because of the oath He swore to her fathers that God saved her *(Deuteronomy 7:8; Genesis 12:2; 22:16-18; 26:2-4; 28: 13-14).* She was to be God's showcase *(Exodus 19:5-6; 34:10)* and be the means by which God blessed all the nations of the earth.

III

God was to be all in all.

The Ten Commandments were given after God reminded Israel who He is and what He had done *(Exodus 20:2).* God didn't say, "If you'll do all these things, I'll take you as My bride." He had already called Israel and gathered her out of bondage in Egypt. Long before that He had called Abraham and made him the father of a great nation. His love and mercy had been given time and time again before the Law was given. The commandment-giving at Sinai was the 430th anniversary of the promise *(Galatians 3:6-9, 15-18).* The Law was given to remind Israel — and us — how unworthy man is and to keep them remembering their need for God's mercy. God entered a covenant with Israel out of His steadfast love and continued it by daily forgiveness. The Law kept reminding them of their need for mercy until that mercy would be living with them in Jesus Christ. *(Galatians 3:11-29)*

To celebrate their anniversary a husband and a wife often exchange gifts. God had given His bride a great gift — the exodus from Egypt. In the Ten Commandments He told Israel that she should give Him *herself in loving obedience (Deuteronomy 5:29-33).* Israel's best gift was just that — to stay married, not to leave her God, to keep on trusting His promises.

The most detailed directions God gave to Moses were for the worship in the tabernacle. Only people who gave God the glory could truly be His people. But it is clear that these forms of worship are also designed by God as a way to help Israel remain true to the covenant. Worship is the first step in living all of one's life to God. Human beings are helped in their worship by the use of things that remind them of God. Worshiping develops better worshipers. *Exodus 25 — 32* and *35 — 40* show how God's plan worked out. *Exodus 32* shows what happened when the people turned away from the true God.

worshiping with the church

Everyday

Giving God the glory that is His due is the first step in giving God the life we owe Him. This is a most important principle in worship. It is not only vital to let God be God, but to make sure we keep man man. We too are nobodies, undeserving of being made somebodies. Unless we in honesty humble ourselves, we won't come to God to be exalted. We move from the Invocation to the Confession in the worship service to accent this. Similarly we move through an act of adoration to a recollection of our sinfulness in our daily devotions.

Another principle — since sinful man is no self-starter, we need the Law to show us again and again how dead we are in our "flesh" without the Spirit. Then the good news of God's love in Christ moves us into the faster motion of faith again.

One more principle — since we are creatures of time and space, we are helped in our worship by a schedule, by worshipful surroundings, and by actually doing things. As Advent begins we can help ourselves in our regular family worship by constructing an Advent wreath.

The end of the church year is a time to take stock of how we are using these principles in our discipline of worship in the evening and the morning and on the Lord's Day.

19

ISRAEL A FAITHLESS BRIDE

We are at the close of the church year. With the ending of the old year we remember the fact that the whole world will end.

The United States Thanksgiving Day comes at the end of the church year. The Christians everywhere can look forward to Judgment Day with thanksgiving because the days of the new heavens and the new earth will then begin for them!

God had very little reason to rejoice over the people He had gathered for Himself. But He found all too much reason for judgment. This is Scene 3—"The Ups and Downs" in the marriage between God and His fickle bride. When a marriage made on earth breaks up in divorce, there seldom is "an innocent party." It takes two to make a quarrel.

But in the marriage made in heaven between God and His chosen people (and between God and us) no one need look far for the guilty party. In the end time of the church year we ought make no mistake about who that guilty party is. He's right under our nose, and from there to the top of our head, too.

Together with the Old Testament people, however, we should keep looking forward to the innocent party—the Christ, whose Advent we soon celebrate. The wickedness of wayward Israel makes ever more clear the steadfast love of God that never stops seeking to bring back His Bride.

WORD AND WORK

I

It was a short honeymoon.

The ups and downs of this marriage began right away. Moses was up on the mountain talking to God when Israel was down on the plain worshiping a golden calf. We can read *Exodus 32,* or skim through the chapter headings in Numbers to remind ourselves of that discouraging history. After 40 years in the wilderness Moses summed it up again for Israel in *Deuteronomy 9:6-24* and *8:1-10.*

II

Things weren't any better in their new home.

The warning God gave Israel before she entered the Promised Land *(Deuteronomy 8:11-20; 29:9-29)* was ignored. The Books of Joshua and Judges record one damnable thing after another. They didn't live happily ever after. *(Judges 2:1-4)*

III

But God kept on wooing His wayward Bride.

He didn't flatter her by telling her what a lovely Bride she was. He made it very clear that He wanted her as His Bride *in order to make her lovely (Deuteronomy 30).* God has to work the transformation *(v. 6).* His working Word was in their hearts to enable them to serve Him *(vv. 11-14).* Israel seldom knew what was good for her—that God was good to her! *(Romans 10:1-13* records Saint Paul's grief over that.) Read of the deeds of the judges, of Deborah, of Samson, of Gideon. What they did, they did for the Lord, and they did it to bring Israel back to the Lord. Not everything they did was good—there was wickedness among the judges, too. The record does not hide that. But the thing we ought not miss is that God kept using every means He could to hold Israel as His own.

IV

As times grew better, things went from bad to worse.

Israel's discontent with God's rule was highlighted by their desire for a king. More than anything else this showed the seriousness of their frequent sinning. They wanted to get away from God. They didn't trust Him to manage their lives *(1 Samuel 8:4-22).* Israel's malady was that they refused to admit this reality of sin. The prophet Ezekiel gives the horrible description of how Israel slipped further and further into unfaithfulness and adultery *(Ezekiel 16:14-34).* Remember—this is recorded for *our* learning. Whenever people think they are pretty good, they expect God to think them pretty good, too. God pleads with us to see what a mistake that is! A man who thinks he is something can never be anything. Only one who knows he is nobody will turn to God to be made into somebody by His grace.

If the season of Advent is to be helpful to us, we must remember that it is a penitential period. The paraments are violet, and the Gloria in Excelsis is dropped, just as in Lent. We resist the department stores' attempt to begin celebrating Christmas before the Nativity. Just as you plan to go easy on breakfast on Thanksgiving morning so that you will be really ready for turkey, so we hold back in Advent, postponing our joy, so that our Christmas celebration will be a great climax. "It's more fun that way," and we are the more helped to think through our need and God's solution in the gift of His Son.

With Advent's new year's day we could resolve to deepen our worship life as a family. Remember the principles: 1. Take the first step in living for Him by making a definite point of offering Him worship. (The suggested devotion in the next lesson will help.) 2. Set a definite time—we are helped by a schedule. 3. Construct an Advent wreath—we are helped by what we see and do. 4. Let God start us off with His Word. (The daily Scripture selections suggest prophecies of the Messiah.)

On Saturday we remember to make our own study of the Sunday's propers. The "stir-up" words in the Advent propers set the pace. On the first Sunday in Advent we pray our Lord to "stir up His power and come" that we might be rescued from "the threatening perils of our sins." That was the whole point of His first advent—and of Advent I.

20

ISRAEL PURGED BY DEATH IN BABYLON

A forest ranger's job is to *protect* the forest. He likes trees. But during a forest fire he will sometimes deliberately burn up acres of trees to make a firebreak, a burned-over section to stop the progress of the forest fire. It's worth sacrificing some trees to save more. We have no trouble with that. But to do something like that to *people* is somehow different.

Worry that thought a bit. This is Scene 4, the death scene. God permitted the chosen people to be carried off to Babylon and into captivity. How could a living God permit the death of Israel? How could He make it happen?—for that is the way Scripture speaks of it.

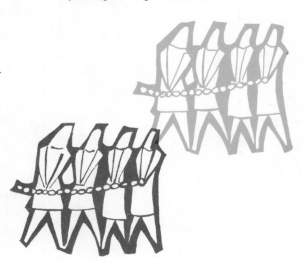

Let's work through the history. Death was a blessing to Adam and Eve. If they had eaten of the tree of life they would have lived on and on as sinners. God was not the cause of their sinning, but He shaped the result into a blessing. God did not *cause* the kings and people of Israel to drift away; but when He saw they were turning away from Him, His steadfast love operated even in His wrath to purge His people. When their pride and idolatry was going to be the death of them, He shaped the division of the kingdom and their captivity in order to work out a net result that would be a blessing. Even their death in captivity would be a blessing if through it they could be raised again as true worshipers in His covenant.

But even more was going on—the captivity-dying of Israel was used by God to keep eternal life alive for us, too! The nation of Israel was part of God's plan to keep faith alive in the world until the Savior should come. It was for the Gentiles as well as for the Jews that the captivity was permitted. Remember, this is not just the history of a tribe of Palestinian nomads. It is the history of the Church, of the Church to which we belong.

WORD AND WORK

I

God wanted His Bride to have the best of everything.

God used the kings Israel wanted as blessings. Under Saul the throne became a rallying point for all the tribes, so the Israelites were united as one people. David's rule brought about a greater unity in the practice of the true faith. His rule brought just protection. Solomon's temple dramatized the truth that all Israel's prosperity depended on God's blessing. He brought Israel into contact with the world which Israel's Savior was to bless.

But when the kings began to consider *themselves* the real power in Israel, when they forgot they were servants of God and His people, disaster was certain. God guided it so that His blessing could reach the people even in catastrophe. *(1 Kings 1:9-13; 26-40; 12:1-24)*

II

But the hopelessness of God's unfaithful Bride became obvious.

Jeroboam had God sculptured as a golden calf *(1 Kings 12:25-33)*. Ahab conceded there might be other gods by permitting Baal worship *(1 Kings 16:31-33)*. The affair of Naboth's vineyard showed that kings were using their power for themselves instead of for God and His people *(1 Kings 21:1-16)*. The voice of Elijah is a symbol of the protest all the prophets of God raised *(1 Kings 21:17-26)*. The Second Book of Kings tells the bad-to-worse story. Jeremiah reminded Israel that she had been the Bride of God *(Jeremiah 2:1-5)*. Amos lamented all the evil

that came as God's punishment to the fallen virgin Israel *(Amos 4:6 — 5: 2)*. Ezekiel's account dramatized how evil Israel had become *(Ezekiel 16:35-58)*. The details are numerous, but the result was simply death.

III

God gave Israel up in order that He might really have her.

In *2 Kings 24* and *25* we read of Israel's terrible end and the exile to Babylon. Some of the people who were left fled to Egypt *(Jeremiah 41:17-18; Hosea 9:3 and 11:5)*. *Lamentations 5* puts the whole bitter story into a prayer. It must have seemed the end of the hope of Israel. Were these the people through whom God was to fulfill His gracious purposes among men?

He was showing His love for the world even then. We all need to know that it is only the grace of God that can make a people become God's people. His love was so great that even death could be used for His gracious purpose.

worshiping with the church

Everyday

This is a new church year. We make our resolution to live with the Church during the year. Use the following order of family prayer during Advent.

Leader: In the Name of the Father and of the ✠ Son and of the Holy Ghost.

Response: Amen.

Leader: Make haste, O God, to deliver me.

Response: Make haste to help me, O Lord.

All: Glory be to the Father and to the Son and to the Holy Ghost; as it was in the beginning, is now, and ever shall be, world without end. Amen.

Leader: (Reads the prophecy for the day:) Eve of Advent I: *Psalm 24:* First Sunday in Advent: *St. Matthew 21:1-9;* Monday: *Genesis 3:1-15;* Tuesday: *Genesis 12:1-5;* Wednesday: *Genesis 28:10-15;* Thursday: *Genesis 49:10;* Friday: *Numbers 24:15-19;* Saturday: *Deuteronomy 18:15-22.*

Leader: O Lord, have mercy upon us.

Response: Thanks be to God! (Now one of the family lights one or more candles on the wreath, according to the number of days or weeks that have passed in the Advent season.)

Leader: Let us pray. (The collect for the week is prayed.)

Response: Amen.

All: Our Father who art in heaven. . . .

Leader: The Lord bless ✠ us, defend us from all evil, and bring us to life everlasting.

Response: Amen. (Then let each member of the family pray silently for the others, for the Church, for our parish, for our pastor, and for all the faithful in Christ.)

(Following the close of prayers the candles may be extinguished.)

> — From "Advent in the Home" (New York: Una Sancta Press, 1957).

21

ISRAEL RAISED
through a REMNANT

The natural thing in the world is to "make yourself comfortable." That's why Advent is important. It reminds us that in the world we are *not* to be comfortable. We are pilgrims, sojourners, exiles. We are God's people, *in* the world but *not of* the world and planted here by God to do His job. What we need to keep us going is not the comforts of the world —they will make us settle back and relax. What we need is the continuing comfort that comes from knowing God is using us; God plans great things through us and promises great things for us.

Our gracious God was doing something like that for Israel in Babylon. He did not want them to "get comfortable," but at the same time He sent His prophets to "speak comfortably" to them. He didn't hold them under the Babylonian captivity just to punish them or to mark time until the next act in Palestine was staged. He was purging them. He was raising up their dead hearts as much as their dead nation. What He promised He did; He raised up a remnant to be a new-born people of God, destined to bring light to the world.

WORD and WORK

I

God brought His Bride back to life.

A person must know he is sick before he will call a doctor and get help for health. Before Israel could come back to life, she needed to know how dead she was. We can see how the prophets drew pictures for Israel so that she would understand. Ezekiel reported his vision of Israel in the Babylonian graveyard *(Ezekiel*

37:1-14). The same prophet had compared Israel to an unfaithful bride. *(Ezekiel 16:59-63)*

II

God restored a worshiping heart to His people.

The dry bones needed more than flesh. The Spirit of God must fill Israel if she were to live. God

like *Ezekiel 36:16-28.* It was like the exodus from Egypt all over again! *Isaiah 10:20-27* and all of chapter *11* give us the feel of it. We would not want to miss *Ezra 6:3-5* and *15-22* as a description of how the heart of worship began to beat again in the remnant that returned.

IV

Israel became more sure of the Day of the Lord and the kingdom of God.

From the beginning of God's choice of Israel to be His people, their eyes had looked forward to the time when the election would be made sure as God's kingship was made plain. They waited for a "Day of Yahweh." It would be a time of judgment, but it also would usher in the Kingdom. Just as at the exodus and the deliverance from captivity God had suddenly filled all of time with His power and goodness, so there would come a day which would

breathed into the remnant just as He did into the dust-shaped Adam. But He did it, not only to move Israel but to get His plan for the world's salvation in motion again *(Ezekiel 36:22-38).* This was the work of God's Word. It was moving in the remnant all during the Exile. There is so much written in the prophets! We can feel God's moving love recreating His people in *Isaiah 43: 1-3, 14-28* and *44:1-5.*

III

A remnant returned to begin a new life of worship.

The Books of Ezra and Nehemiah tell the story of the Return. But some of the thrill of it shows up in chapters be full of His kingship and in which Israel would completely be the people of God. The prophets worked hard to keep people from thinking the Day of the Lord would only usher in a time of independence and national power. But even the prophets couldn't see the whole wonderful truth; each one saw the coming of the Day in the crises of his time. But by God's Spirit the prophets also revealed new details of that great day, in "the fulness of time" when God Himself would be born into the world and the kingdom of God would really be "at hand."

Some of the difficulties the prophets faced, and some of the joy they revealed we can share in these passages: *Isaiah 7:10-17 (14* 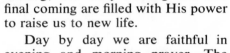 *); Isaiah 53; Jeremiah 31:31-34 (33* 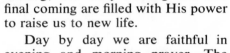 *); Joel 2:28-29; Micah 5:2; Zechariah 9:9.*

WORSHIPING WITH THE CHURCH

Sunday

We prepare for the Day of the Lord in our generation, too. We must do it day by day. (The First Sunday in Advent reminded us that we need the Lord's "coming in power" to save us from "the threatening perils" of our sin.) He came as the Word made flesh. He comes in the Word— in worship, in wine and bread, in water, in family relationships, and in print.

The Second Sunday in Advent, especially in the Holy Gospel, reminds us of our Lord's second coming. His daily coming and His final coming are filled with His power to raise us to new life.

Day by day we are faithful in evening and morning prayer. The Advent prophecies bring Him to us with life and power. He unites our family. Sunday by Sunday we gather the propers together so that the Word is clear to us. He unites us as the family of God.

The keynote of Advent II is the prayer, "Stir up our hearts to make ready the way of Thine only-begotten Son." At His return He should be greeted by a people prepared—His Church. The Epistle reminds us that God's promises were to the Jew and the Gentile. If we claim His promises, we must strive to be a part of His program—"living in harmony with one another in accord with Christ Jesus." In the liturgy He gives us Himself "to enable us to serve Him with pure minds." Through the whole worship service we "lift up our heads, with joy for our redemption draweth nigh."

the true

ISRAEL IS BORN

This is Act II. Remember the theme of the whole play—"God is forever God and longs for all mankind to be His worshiping children." The Prologue described how God *called* all people to be worshipers. He tried to invite men—*God to the whole human race.* Then in Act I He gathered a people. He made Israel a kind of demonstration group and invited man, *men to mankind.* The nation of Israel never quite accepted God's adoption and never quite adopted God's accepting attitude toward the rest of the world. They did not want to be saved, nor did they want to be saving. They did not really want to be worshipers nor to make their lives worshipful.

In Act II God begins another approach, with a "new Israel." He shows His love—*Man to men!* Another Israel, the fulfilled Israel, is born to bring the light of the love of God into the world. Jesus Christ, the True Israel, is born as "a light to lighten the Gentiles and the glory of Thy people Israel." The Word is made flesh! God enlightens the world for worship. The five scenes are repeated as Jesus Christ fulfills all the assignments the old Israel failed.

Scene 1 of this new act is the Nativity scene—the birth of this true Israel. To restore mankind to worshipful obedience God Himself takes on our human nature. Jesus Christ will live the perfect life to *perfect* man. By being true Man, He enables man to be a new man. Christ will be a true worshiper and by His life atone for all man's idolatry.

The Advent and Christmas days are a good time to be thinking about all that Jesus Christ did for us. Advent especially reminds us to be conscious of time. All our time is connected to our Lord as we live the church year. Remember we are already acting out Act III. By now, *the Word is in His Church* — and we are the Church. There is a cosmic game of "follow the Leader" going on here. While we watch Christ, our Leader, being "It" in Act II, we remember that we today are in Act III in which He is Lord, and at the same time *we're* "it." We follow Him but at the same time "lead" the people we know and who know us.

We can't study the life of Jesus as though it were just a biography. We are connecting ourselves to a power. He is the Word of God: God working in the world. The Word is made flesh, and He is with us always. We study the things that are written about Him in order that we may believe more strongly and live more worshipfully *(John 20:30-31* ✠*)*. To have faith means more than to have knowledge. It means to *be faithful:* to be a son. It means that God is present in our lives as our Father. By God's action we are born again as His children. *(John 1:12-13* ✠*)*

The question we must answer is this: "What do *we* mean when we say, 'I believe?' 'I believe in God, the Father . . . and in Jesus Christ, His only Son, our Lord.'" Luther's explanation of the Second Article sums it up in four words: "He is my Lord!" *(The Second Article* ✠*)*

WORD AND WORK

We already know so much about the nativity of Jesus Christ that we are in danger of not really thinking about it. Make this lesson a "think session."

Think about it this way: The stage lights go on for Act II. The New Testament curtains part. It's the setting for the Nativity. *Who is going on? What is going on? Is all this still going on?*

I

First read from one of the last books written in the New Testament, the Gospel According to *St. John — 1:1-14.* Then take *Luke 1:35; Matthew 1:20-23;* and *Mark 1:1.* Try *Hebrews 1:3; 1 Peter 3:15.* Read St. Paul in *1 Corinthians 8:6; Colossians 2:9;* and *Philippians 2:9-11* ✠ The Christians called Christ Lord — *Kurios* (the Greek word we still use in the Kyrie). For Greek-speaking Jews this was the word used for the God of Israel. That is *who* is going on!

II

There is more going on here than we might think. Compare *Mark 1: 2-3; Matthew 1:1* and *17; Luke 3: 23-38;* and *John 1:17. Acts 10:43* and *Romans 1:2-4,* joined with *1 Peter 1:10-12* and *Hebrews 1:1-2,* make the point very clear. The whole Old Testament plan of salvation is still going on — that's *what!*

If we have any doubt as to what the Scriptures want us to think about Jesus, St. Peter's sermon sums it all up in *Acts 2:36* ✠. Notice that he had first quoted from the prophet Joel a passage that used "Lord" as a word for "God." This is the same accent that the early Church in Jerusalem included in their greeting in the Aramaic language, "Marana tha" — "Our Lord, come!" which St. Paul uses in *1 Corinthians 16:22* and which he seems to be thinking of in *Romans 10:9.*

III

Something new was happening as the New Testament began, but it was "nothing new" in one sense. Remember, the Word of God is *God at work saving His people.* The same Word that came to the prophets and to Israel is now the Word made flesh. The climax of God's activity for us men takes place in the coming of the Messiah and in the deeds He performed for our salvation. But the Word's action as *Man to men* is still going on. But the same event, the same Word at work, is going on right now as our Lord comes to us in the bread and wine, as God's Spirit works in water, and as the Scriptures bring us the power of God unto salvation!

Here are passages for the second week in Advent to use in your family prayer: Sunday: *Psalm 2;* Monday: *2 Samuel 7:12-17;* Tuesday: *Isaiah 7:13-14;* Wednesday: *Isaiah 9:1-6;* Thursday: *Isaiah 11:1-9;* Friday: *Isaiah 40:1-11;* Saturday: *Isaiah 42:1-9.*

Everyday

The liturgy becomes exciting the more we realize the *who* and the *what* that are still going on. The *Kyrie* dramatizes it for us. When we sing "Kyrie," we are confessing that Jesus is *both Lord and Christ,* who is present always and with the two or three and more of us gathered in His name. All the mystery of the Christmas truth that God was manifest in flesh is in our cry of "Kyrie — Lord!" And when in the Eucharist Jesus Christ gives us His body and blood, our prayer, "have mercy upon us" is dramatically answered. "Have mercy" — *eleison* in Greek — beseeches God to continue to keep His covenant with us and to extend His patient forbearance with us in spite of our faults. He is *the Christ,* the promise of the covenant fulfilled. The body and blood of our Passover Lamb is our deliverance, our partaking in God's rescue of His covenant people.

Remember to "lift up your head with joy" every day. "Your redemption is drawing nigh." The thought should fill our heads as soon as we lift them off our pillows.

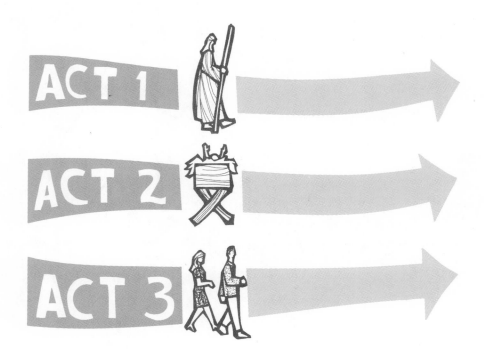

23

the true israel

is god's beloved

Ever read a serial in a magazine? One section of the story is printed each issue. Sometimes it's hard to remember what went on before. When we take up a new chapter we need a synopsis of the preceding chapter, a "what's gone on before" summary.

The Children of Israel living when Jesus was born had that kind of problem. For thousands of years God had been using their nation as His pilot project for saving the world. But it had been hundreds of years since

a live prophet had preached to Israel. They needed a synopsis of the preceding chapters if they were going to understand what God was beginning through *the Word made flesh.*

It was even harder for the Gentile converts in the first centuries of the New Testament Church. It was like trying to get in on a conversation that has been going on for a long time before you got there. This was a conversation between members of a family, all of whom had known each other and each other's relatives for years and years. Things they took for granted were strange to Gentiles. It wasn't just the Hebrew and Aramaic language. The thought patterns were sometimes different. They weren't the logical, reasonable, "scientific" approaches Greeks and Romans were accustomed to. The conversation was going on between desert nomads and Orientals. It was full of traditions and prophecies, promise of a Messiah, and of a Christ who would be the Savior. The Gentile world had to be briefed on the Old Testament way of thought and on God's way of dealing with men, before they could understand Christianity.

We need a synopsis even more than they. Everything that God has said and done before must be understood if we are to realize what He is doing right *now*. That wouldn't be necessary if God had dropped all the Old Testament patterns, the temple and priests, lambs for sacrifices, and the idea of a Savior, and begun a new story in the New Testament. But He didn't. In fact, in the life of Jesus God began to repeat some of the Old Testament happenings. In that way He helped people review His Old Testament *Word,* and at the same time He made clear the real meaning of the New Testament *Word made flesh.*

Thus we can call Jesus the True Israel, and compare events in His life to Israel's birth, her covenant-marriage, her ups and downs, her death in exile and the resurrection of a remnant, because that's the way God taught the Jews and Gentiles what important things He was doing through Jesus Christ. We can find the comparisons in the books of the New Testament. Remember that God

caused those books to be written from 30 to 70 years after Christ's resurrection. They helped new Christians see the connection between the work of Jesus and all that God had begun in the Old Testament.

Sometimes we think it's a chore to catch up on all that past history. A boy might like to be an atomic physicist without boning up on the molecular table, but he simply can't. So we study the New Testament books. They help us new Christians understand that God Himself was making the sacrifice for the world's sins. God's own Son took on human nature and on the cross became the one sacrifice for all men, the Lamb of God that takes away the sin of the world.

WORD AND WORK

I

St. Matthew's account of the Gospel was written especially to help the Jews realize how Jesus Christ and all He did fit right into the Old Testament. If we check the first three chapters of Old Testament quotations and look them up, we'll see how true this is.

II

Especially in the accounts of our Lord's baptism can we see that God identified Jesus as His beloved Son (*Matthew 3:13-17* [*17* ✠], *Isaiah 42:1,* and *Psalm 2:7*). All the evangelists make sure we don't miss the point. (*Mark 1:9-10; Luke 3:21-22;* and *John 1:14-18*)

III

Just as Israel was intended to be a blessing to all nations, so Jesus is shown to be the Savior of the world (*John 1:29-34* and *Isaiah 53:7*). He, like Israel, is a Light for the Gentiles. (*John 1:4-13; Luke 1:67-79; Isaiah 49:3* ✠ *and 5-6*)

Remember we're in this, too, as Act III. The call of Abraham began Act I, 2,000 years before Christ. By the time Act II began with Christ's birth, Israel had been a failure. Now it is close to 2,000 years after Christ. Are we fulfilling something of God's hope for us?

worshiping with the church

Sunday

The Third Sunday in Advent reminds us there is a third coming of our Lord which is going on right now. He comes in the Scriptures and the sacraments. He is working through the Church's ministry. Catch that in the Epistle. Doesn't all that fit right into this lesson? How about the Gospel? It's a Matthew lection; it quotes the Old Testament connection. The Introit, Collect, and Gradual have connections with this lesson, too. The important thing is not simply to find them — but to *think* them and so enrich our worship in Sunday's liturgy. In the same way we should use the parts of the liturgy that reflect the Old Testament to connect us with the people of God throughout the centuries. *Psalms 124* and *32,* from which the versicles and responses in the confession are taken, were prayers Israel prayed; they have been used in the new Israel, the Church, for 2,000 years. We pray them earnestly as in the Collect we remember "the darkness of our hearts." Note that the "stir-up" prayer is in the Gradual on Advent III. Make the Kyrie work for you, too. We save the Gloria in Excelsis for Christmas, but when we do sing it, we join the angels' chorus!

the true israel is tempted, yet never estranged

The game of charades goes much faster when the players have agreed on signals. Pulling your ear means "sounds like." A frantic "come-hither" gesture with your hands means "Keep guessing—you're getting warmer and warmer!" Similarly some of the events which the evangelists report in the life of Jesus Christ are simply things that happened. Others are events that "signify." They are not only marvelous miracles that show the divine power of Jesus, but they reveal Him as the One through whom God is working in the New Testament time. Just as God used Israel the nation as His means to show the world His saving power, so He uses the True Israel, Jesus. God was *enlightening* the world through Him.

Jesus the Man is both Lord and Christ, and many of the things He did prove not only His deity, but also His connection with the saving acts of God that began in the Old Testament times. The Jewish people should have recognized the signs. Many times they didn't. Sometimes they refused to accept them when they did recognize them. The evangelists wrote about them so that the Gentiles too, who had been learning what had happened before they got into the story, would be more sure that Jesus was the Savior. *John 20:30* and *31* tells us, too, that these things have been written so that we might believe and that believing we may "have life in His name."

word and work

I

What connection can we draw between Israel's testing in the wilderness and our Lord's temptation after His baptism? *(Matthew 4).* What would the selection of 12 disciples signify? *(Luke 6:12-16).* Sometimes the people understood the signs *(John 6:14* and *Deuteronomy 18: 15-18).* But they did not always go in the direction toward which the signs pointed *(John 6:15; 25-66).* Some did —are we among them? *(John 6: 67-71; 67-69* ✠*)*

II

Since Jesus was true man as well as true God, we perhaps imagine that it must have been a struggle for Him to realize He was the Son of God and the Messiah. The temptations He endured were very real. But He never faltered. Israel had failed God time after time. But Jesus lived a life without sin—and He lived that life for us! *(Hebrews 3:1-6)*

The devil's temptation for Jesus to doubt His Father and His mission went right on during His life on earth. And it wasn't just Satan but others who urged the temptations on Him *(John 6:15; Mark 8:31-33; Luke 22: 47-54; Luke 23:33-39).* But at the end of the struggle, He could say, "Be of good cheer, I have overcome the world." And *Hebrews 4:14-16* ✠ makes it clear how important this is to us!

III

Jesus fought off the temptations. He knew that He was the Messiah of God. He knew that His task was to bring God's redemptive rule to men. He realized that He was to be the True Israel, taking up the task that Israel had failed to accomplish. Through all the ups and downs of His life He showed that He knew what He was doing. Not until the close of His ministry did He openly acknowledge that He was the Messiah *(Mark 14:61ff.),* but God always seems to teach men that way. He wants us to discover the meaning— He doesn't just give us the answers. That is why Jesus often revealed who He truly was in an indirect way rather than by direct statements.

For example Jesus showed the connection between Himself and the Servant of whom Isaiah prophesied and the Son of Man of whom Daniel spoke. In *Mark 10:45* and many other places Christ called Himself "Son of Man" and said He had come

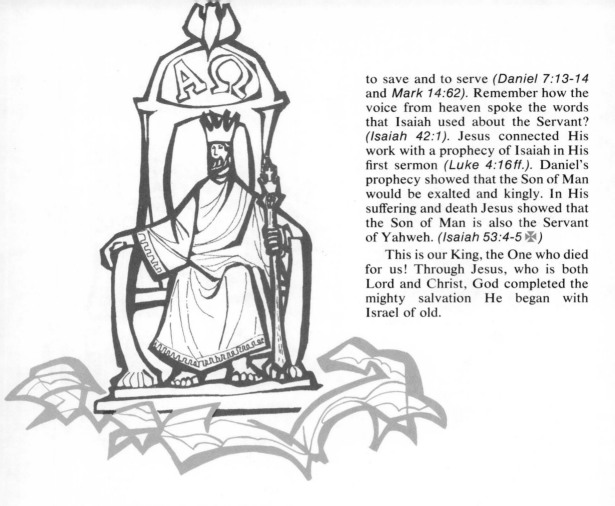

to save and to serve *(Daniel 7:13-14 and Mark 14:62).* Remember how the voice from heaven spoke the words that Isaiah used about the Servant? *(Isaiah 42:1).* Jesus connected His work with a prophecy of Isaiah in His first sermon *(Luke 4:16ff.).* Daniel's prophecy showed that the Son of Man would be exalted and kingly. In His suffering and death Jesus showed that the Son of Man is also the Servant of Yahweh. *(Isaiah 53:4-5 ✠)*

This is our King, the One who died for us! Through Jesus, who is both Lord and Christ, God completed the mighty salvation He began with Israel of old.

worshiping with the church

At Christmas we should be prepared to fill the Gloria in Excelsis with our worship. That is always our task with the words of the liturgy. To claim "We praise Thee, we worship Thee, we give thanks to Thee" is not worship. Worship is something we do *as* we sing the words. A good way to help ourselves concentrate on adding our worship to the words is to think of specific things we praise Him *for* and thank Him *for* or to think of specific aspects of "His great glory" that impel us to adore.

In the celebration of the Nativity the great contrast between the Kyrie's prayer and the Gloria's triumph is highlighted. We plead with God to continue His steadfast love: *Eleison!* A pause, then: "Glory to God in the highest!" He has continued His steadfast love!

And in each service we live through the Christmas miracle again!

Everyday

The passages suggested for use during the third week in Advent—Sunday: *Psalm 72:1-15;* Monday:

Isaiah 55:1-9; Tuesday: *Isaiah 60:
1-3;* Wednesday: *Isaiah 61:1-11;*
Thursday: *Jeremiah 23:3-8;* Friday:
Jeremiah 33:14-22; Saturday:
Zechariah 9:9-12.

the true israel gives his life

"To you is born this day in the city of David a *Savior,* who is Christ the Lord" *(Luke 2:11).* When the angel made that announcement at the nativity of our Lord, the Christ Child, the God-man in the manger, didn't know what was involved in being the Savior. It was God's plan—and Jesus is the Son of God.

But when Christ was born "only God knew" what it meant to be the Savior. As man the Christ Child had to learn—He had much to learn. And learn He did. He accepted the task the Father set before Him. Israel had been called to offer itself in worshipful obedience to God and to give its life for others, but it failed. Now the True Israel would offer His life to God—as Man and *for* man.

We are the children of God by adoption. We too have much to learn. We are to live worshipful lives, offered lives. We are to be slaves of God and servants of men. But a miracle must happen before we can live that way. Jesus Christ worked that miracle. Scene 4 shows Christ's death. It is a good story for Christmastide. In Jesus Christ God gave us the gift of life and the power to live.

This is the very heart of our Christian faith. Let's start right in on:

word and work

I

Real living is self-giving.

When God created the world and humankind, He was giving Himself. He was saving the world from the very first day of creation. Only in Him could man live and move and have being. God is love—and love always means "putting out" for others.

God created man to live *the offered life.* He made him in His own image. Man was created to be a wor-

shiper—"to glorify God and to enjoy Him forever." God created Eve as a "helpmeet" so that man could really live by devoting his life to others.

Even before the creation of the world God knew what sin would do to it. In His love He was ready to "put Himself out" for man. *(1 Peter 1:18-21 [18-19 ✠]; Galatians 4: 4-5 ✠)*

II

For man, self-giving involves obedience.

Obedient man is really alive. His life is centered in God and moves out to others. The power of choice came along with the image of God in which man was created. He wasn't *forced* to offer himself to God or to devote his living to others. God *wanted* him to live the offered life; but obedience or disobedience was up to him.

But disobedient men are dead men. Adam and Eve found that out *(Genesis 2:17)*. All men who ever lived were in this sense dead. Remember the Flood? Babel? The nations destroyed by Israel? Israel herself? And think of every one of us! *(Ephesians 2:1-3)*. Jesus Christ is the one Man who ever really lived! *(Luke 2:49; Luke 22:42; John 13:12-15; Mark 10:45)*. He made clear that giving up one's life for others is really living. What we might call "losing our life" He called "really living." *(Matthew 10:39 ✠)*

III

Jesus Christ gave Himself as man's representative and sacrifice.

He offered His life *as* man. We read *Philippians 2:5-8 ✠* remembering that Jesus Christ was true Man, one who truly had the image of God. We can compare Him with Adam who lost that image in disobedience. *(Genesis 1:27—Philippians 2:6a; Genesis 3:11b—Philippians 2:8b; Genesis 3:5—Philippians 2:6b)*

His was an offered life. He lived His life as our representative *(Romans 5:13-19; Hebrews 2:9-18)*. He offered His obedience in place of our disobedience.

He offered His life *for* man. He claimed the title of Servant and of Son of Man and foretold His suffering and death *(Mark 8:31)*. The disciples had a hard time realizing what it meant for Him to be the world's Savior *(Luke 18:31-34)*. We could explain it all more clearly to them today. *(Romans 3:24-25; 1 Peter 2: 19-25)*

The last chance Jesus had to make it all clear to His disciples before He offered His life was in the Upper Room at His last Passover. While they remembered that with the blood of the lamb sprinkled on the door posts God had saved Israel, Jesus took bread and wine and said, "My body . . . My blood." While they remembered how by the covenant God had made them His people, Jesus said, "This is My blood of the covenant. . . ." *(Mark 14:22-25; 1 Corinthians 5:7b; Hebrews 9: 15-28)*

IV

By this sacrifice we have been made perfectly able.

We see the beginning in *Hebrews 10:14-18*. The end is not yet with any of us! *(Hebrews 10:19-25; Mark 10: 43-45; Philippians 2:1-5; 1 Peter 2:21; The Second Article ✠)*

worshiping with the church

Through the Holy Days

It is the Holy Eucharist that associates the Nativity with the name Christ Mass. He offered His life for all men. We who receive His body and His blood share in His life and share life together. Baptized children and confirmands, who may not yet commune, are all in this together.

Ponder the Epistle for Christmas Day, *Titus 2:11-14:* "The grace of God has appeared"—(Gloria in Excelsis! at Christmas and Good Friday and Easter, and each time we do the liturgy!) "training us"— (Let the Collect for Advent IV with its "stir up" set the pace for our training by grace—"speedily" is the word!)

The final passages for Advent devotions—Sunday: *Malachi 3:1-6;* Monday: *Micah 5:2-4;* Tuesday: *Luke 1:5-25;* Wednesday: *Luke 1: 26-38;* Thursday: *Luke 1:39-66;* Friday: *Luke 1:67-80;* Eve of Christmas: *Luke 2:1-14.*

the true israel's victory

Remember how the nation of Israel went down into captivity and almost disappeared? Remember the tortures, the killings, and the slavery? There was no question that wickedness was real in those days.

How real is the evil that made it necessary for the Christ Child to be born? Surely we can't think of it merely as the thoughtlessness of an innkeeper, or even as the murderous bungling of Herod. Sin is such a damningly serious thing that Jesus Christ came into the world to lay down His life for His people. God so loved the world, and God so knew the desperate state of sinning men, that He gave His Son into death to save them. To kill evil the Son of God had to be killed. That's how real sin is.

Now, what about the evil that surrounds us — the evil in the world and the evil that still plagues our sinful nature? We dare not forget how real it is *(John 17:14-15)*, but we don't want to lose sight of the fact that makes all the difference *(John 16:33)*. The nation of Israel went down into captivity's death, and only a remnant survived to keep hope alive.

But Jesus Christ was victorious over death, devil, and world. Jesus Christ still lives and reigns. From the right hand of God the Father, our Lord governs His Church and controls the whole world. The True Israel, Jesus Christ, lives in us through the Holy Spirit. Through Him we can worship and live worshipfully every day.

word and work

The grave was opened by the earthquake force, not to let Jesus get out, but to let men look in. We still have the chance to look into the resurrection event to learn what God wants us to realize.

I

Realize that Christ Jesus is triumphantly alive!

What does it take to convince us?

Forty proofs? *(Acts 1:3)*. How about eyewitnesses? *(John 20* and *21* and *1 Corinthians 15:6-7)*

But the final evidence is given by God within us. When we call God our Father — imagine that! God, our *Father* — we show that God has raised us up to life *(Romans 8:14-17* ✠*)*. God does that for disobedient man, because He raised the obedient Man. *(Philippians 2:8-9* ✠*)*

II

Realize, then, that our Representative reigns as God with the Father and the Holy Spirit!

If we elect a representative to Congress, we can't expect very much help just for ourselves. But Christ is our Brother! And He is God! He lives and reigns as God the Father's right-hand Man!

The Ascension does not mean that Christ has gone away. He promised to be with us always. It is a dramatization of the fact that He will be with us *in a different way. (Acts 1:9-11)*

What this means for us St. Paul tries to write in one long sentence in *Ephesians 1:16-23.* Ours is one long, unending triumph, because we are continually represented before God. *(Hebrews 7:23-25)*

III

Realize that God lives and rules in us through the Holy Spirit.

God is very kind to us. He knows we can't really catch on to things very well unless we *see* them. That's why He showed us Himself in the Christ Child. That's why He showed us how His Presence would be different at the Ascension. And that's why *Acts 2:1-4* took place! Don't miss the point! There has been a new kind of incarnation and we're involved. *(1 Corinthians 3:16* ✠ and *6:19-20* ✠*)*

worshiping with the church

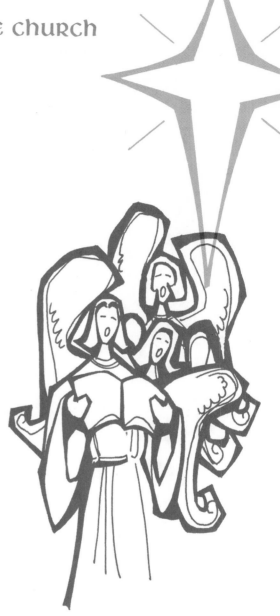

Everyday

These are the days in which the celebration of Christmas takes place ... Advent for *anticipation,* the Feast for *observation,* but the Twelve Days of Christmas and Epiphany for *celebration.* Whenever we remember the Incarnation—God coming into our humanity—let's remember that He has come to live in us, too. All that Christ did for the world, the Spirit brings to us each day!

January 6

We don't want to miss preparing for the Epiphany. We needed all the help we could get to realize that God could become the Child. Now we take all the help we can get to realize that the Child *is God.* Wise Men set the pace! They came to worship Him. So do we. We worship because we know He is God and because we remember that He is with us always.

In the liturgy, the Salutation, "The Lord be with you!" is another Old Testament phrase in which we share in our worship *(Ruth 2:4; Judges 6:12).* It keeps before us the great news included in *"Emmanuel—God with us!"* But it also helps us remind one another of the divine Presence with us always since our Lord's Ascension *(2 Thessalonians 3:16).* Such a small phrase can easily be lost—but if we fill the words with worship they both express much and teach us much. When the pastor "salutes" us and we reply, "And with thy spirit," we repeat our commissioning of him as our pastor. His words, "Let us pray," remind us again we are all the people of God. We are all in this together. We who have seen the Daystar come to worship Him!

117

27

BORN INTO THE CHURCH

This is Act III: "God Sanctifies Us to Be Worshipers" — "The Word is in the Church." We aren't forgetting that we are characters in this drama. We wrote ourselves in as we were "Setting the Stage." But now, with the curtain going up on Act III, *we're on!* Of course, in a way we've been on all along, and we've been trying to *do* our part. But now we ourselves are the subject for study. We're in the spotlight. These lessons should be easy. Don't we know more about ourselves than anything else — and than anyone else?

Let's try a new approach in this act. Let's write the chapters ourselves — about ourselves. On this page there will be notes to give suggestions for the outline and the ideas. But the subject is *yourself*. So *you* cover the subject. Write up an introduction, and then develop Parts I, II, and III.

WORD AND WORK

Something should first be said about the connection between Act III and what's gone before. Remember that the titles of the Prologue and these acts have been taken from Luther's explanation to the Third Article: "called, gathered, enlightened"—and now—"sanctified." Luther's words begin in the singular—"I" and "me." Better figure out how the *us* gets into the title of this act: "even as He calls, gathers, enlightens, and sanctifies the whole Christian Church. . . ."

There's another connection to be made. Act I was about Israel, Act II about the True Israel. Are we in the Church the *new Israel?* Try *Romans 4:16-25; 9:6-8; Galatians 3:6-7, 27-29;* and *6:14-16.*

One more thing: the explanation of the Creed talks about what God does *to* us. The old Israel and the True Israel were God's way of getting things done for others, for the world. Does the title of New Israel imply that God want to do something *by us?*

That's enough for an Introduction. Here are notes for Part I. It could be titled: The Church is a family and the body of Christ.

". . . the whole Christian Church on earth. . . ."—isn't that simply a collection of individuals? It's "I" and "you" and "you." Does the "we" or the "us" mean anything more than the plural of "me"? Nicodemus was thinking about himself when he came to Jesus *(John 3)* and Jesus spoke about "one" being born. But at once He talked about "the kingdom of God"—God's ruling over *people.* And He talked about God loving the *world.* How about this? "Born anew" tells us that each one of us is involved as a person. We were born of flesh. We need to be born again of water and the Spirit. Everyone (even twins) is born one at a time. But everyone is born into a *family.* The Church is always *us.* In *Ephesians 2:11-22* St. Paul shows how Gentiles and Jews have been made one body,

and all of us "members of the household of God."

The Church as the body of Christ —that's another figure, a *"singular"* figure. We are *one,* not just many *ones.* (*1 Corinthians 12:12-14* and *27; Romans 12:5; Ephesians 4: 4-6* ✠).

Jesus also talked about Himself as the Vine and we as the branches *(John 15:1-9).* He is the whole thing. As branches we are part of the whole! A branch surely isn't a grape vine, nor are all the branches piled up together a vine. But His is the Vine. And in Him we are the Church.

"Born anew"—we'll need more on that. Part II could be titled: Born anew means a new kind of life.

"Born." Being born is a miracle. It's like being a new creation. What does "born anew" mean?

Try "Romans, chapter 6." "Baptized into His death" and "buried with Him by Baptism"—do we *die* in Baptism? "The old Adam must be drowned and die . . . ." Forgiveness is not an operation to remove sin—performed while we sleep under a kind of anesthetic and feel no pain. Jesus paid. He felt our pain. With Him we die and are buried in Baptism. What happened to us must keep happening all over again, day after day. We must drown the old Adam. We must die to sin. Dying daily—is living our baptism. That's the new baptismal life.

There's another thing: All this happened so that "As Christ was raised from the dead, we too might walk in newness of life." That's the continuing miracle of our baptism. We're given a new life! *(The Catechism: Holy Baptism* ✠ *)*

Old Israel came into being by God's doing. Remember how Abram was called by grace? Our new life is all God's doing. We are saved by faith. Faith is the presence of God in our life as our Father, because of Christ, through the Spirit. It is not something we do. We live with God because He begins living with us in Baptism. It couldn't happen too soon to any child!

Nothing much is expected of a baby. But grown up, he's expected to do his share in the family. Part III: Life means service.

"Chores! Every family has 'em. I certainly don't need more. But what if I think about the Church as 'body'? It's no chore to feed myself! . . ." Try that angle with *Romans 12:3-9, 15:1-6* and *1 Corinthians 12:14-18*.

If we're going to take seriously our call to be the new Israel, there's a good bit of follow-through that's expected. *(1 Peter 2:9-10 and 11-12)*

worshiping with the church

Everyday

The miracle of Christ's birth in the flesh! The miracle of the Spirit's entrance into ours! The Christ Child serving in the Father's house. Our daily service! Think it all through with the sign of the cross and the Invocation (just the things used at our Holy Baptism!) each morning as you "come forth and arise." Remember the old Adam got up with you. Drown him. Live before God in righteousness!

Sunday

Our daily service—our Sunday liturgy! All part of our new life. We are to be *epiphanies*—revelations—of His grace. Catch the Epistle for the First Sunday after the Epiphany from *Romans 12*. It builds what we should do on all that Christ has done for us. It makes clear that we are one body: members one of another. The Gospel is the second example of the "epiphanies," the revelations, of the glory of the Child. We can put our joy and gratitude for all He is and has done into each Sunday's liturgy at the responses to the Gospel: "Glory be. . . . Praise be!" And the Collect is just the thing for our praying!

made fellows in the church

"I believe in the Holy Ghost, the Holy Christian Church, the communion of saints . . ." Just what do we "believe in" when we say "Church, the communion of saints"? Scene 2, remember, describes "marriage." We know ourselves—right? Then we should be able to describe how our fellowship can be compared to marriage: our fellowship with God and our fellowship with one another. We never forget that all this is more than definitions. A man who says, "I believe in marriage," *gets* married and tries to make his marriage work.

The notes below can help you. It's your life. Write it up!

word and work

An introduction is necessary. . . . What's a good start in thinking about our fellowship in the Church? We need help. When a child is born into a family he is only concerned about himself. Everything is "mine, mine." Gradually he learns about "thine." For some "we" and "us" don't become real until nearly the teens. But "husband and wife" expresses an even deeper fellowship. That's the Bible picture of the Church and Christ *(Revelation 21:2 and 9; Ephesians 5:25-27)*. The fellowship between a husband and a wife in a good marriage is a good bit more than the fact that there was a ceremony and a wedding certificate. What does the Scripture mean when it compares our fellowship with Christ to that of a bride and bridegroom? Better dig. . . .

I

The first thing to do is to describe the fellowship. *It is a union with God,* which He created through Christ and which the Holy Spirit makes strong. (It wasn't love at first sight, not between us and God. Who proposed to whom? . . . [*John 15:16; 2 Thessalonians 2:13-14; 1 Peter 2:9-10* ✠]. But what a love from God to us! [*1 John 4:9-10*]. And what a change it's made in us! [*1 John 4:19*])

Do we know we're loved by

God? Can we tell? Some married couples never seem to talk, seldom seem to appreciate one another. Does God's friendship die down? Does He continue to love us and to be with us? . . . *(John 14:15-29, [26-27* ✠*]; Romans 8:26-28)*

It is possible to take a love for granted, or to forget how great a blessing it is to be a member of a family. What a fellowship we have with God! What will help me to remember it always? How can I express my love? . . .

II

People with God are certainly a different breed from people without God. Can you tell the difference? Show the difference? Remember it? Time for a second point. What does the fellowship we have with God do for the fellowship we have with one another? Some people have a hard time keeping up a conversation. Then they find a topic in which they are both interested, something they have

both experienced. That does it. What kind of a common experience have Christians had? Does it make for a fellowship, one that they can experience with one another? *(Ephesians 2:11-16; Galatians 3:23-28)*

Mathematicians feel kinship with other mathematicians whom they have never met. They have read something of their experiments. They know where they are and what they are doing. They think about them. What about the Church's fellowship? Do I have to see Christians in other countries to have fellowship with them? . . . Some Christians have died—but still they live. What about them?

The Church is a fellowship of all those who know Christ as their Brother and their Savior. But this is not so much a matter of the head as of the heart. With our Brother we share a common life. He shared ours. That's great. But He *gives us His.* That's the greatest! We share the life of God *(Romans 12:4-5).*

"Let us pray," the pastor says in the liturgy. Who is "us"—each one of us individually?

III

Fellowship seems to go up and down and in every direction. What keeps it alive? What makes it grow in strength? Here are some notes for a third point. It's your life. Do the notes fit into your life?

"The Holy Ghost . . . the Church . . . the communion of saints . . ." If "communion" means "fellowship," what is meant by the "fellowship of the saints"? The punctuation in the catechism suggests something—semicolon after *Ghost,* comma after *Church,* and semicolon after *saints.* Is "the fellowship of the saints" a description of the Church? *(The Catechism: The Third Article* ✠*)*

But is it more? Some scholars say "the communion" may also have meant "the sharing, or taking part with his fellow Christians in the holy things, the gifts of grace, which bind them into one body." It sounds like "doing the liturgy" and sharing in Word and Sacrament is important enough to get into the Creed. Can I say, "I *believe* in that?" Does believing mean more than knowing?

How about a conclusion? *It's one thing to write about your life. It's another thing to live it. But best of all is to live it up the way you write it down.*

worshiping with the church

Everyday

We are born by the Word of God. We are *wed* by the Word. We remember it is "our" marriage, never "my" marriage. It is "our" fellowship. We catch on as we keep on *catching* the Word. We *give* adoration to God so that it is continually clear who is the Head.

God does not want our worship of Him to stop with what we do for Him. We are to move out to everyone else in the fellowship. We are to *share*. Epiphany I's epistle urges us to be living sacrifices to God and calls that our spiritual worship, our reasonable sacrifice. But at once it reminds us that we are in this *together*. We *share* in our worship and in our living with all those who are members with us of the body of Christ.

You can't help but be conscious of *schoolmates* who are with you in the same classrooms every day at school. We need to make a special point of being conscious of church-mates. At wake-up time, we remember "the communion of saints" together with Baptism's Invocation and sign. Each time we confess the Creed we can picture all the others in the Church Catholic [universal] who are members of the body whose Head is Christ. Then we begin the day, "being about the Father's business," with the host of the redeemed.

wayward,
but forgiven in christ

"My, but how you've changed." People say that to other people after some years have passed. What would we have to say to a person like Adam if we actually saw him before and then after *his righteousness* had passed? There are actually two human races in the world. One race has lost the true relationship to God and to one another. It is our imperfect race. But there is another race. Since Christ has lived a life of a perfect relationship to God and all men, the perfect race has been recreated. It is a *perfected* race. All those who have Christ as their Head have received through Him a right relation-ship with God. They are sons of God. Because the Spirit of God is in them, the purposes of God can be realized in their living.

". . . the communion of saints, the forgiveness of sin." If ours is a fellowship of saints, of people made holy by the love of God, why do we need to add "I *believe* in *forgiveness?*" Is it because when we sin over and over again, it is almost unbelievable that God will continue to forgive over and over again? Partly. But we remember that *believing* includes more than *knowing*. It means having.

WORD AND WORK

Start to think about yourself. Aren't you mixed up? Don't you contradict yourself? Sometimes you want to do good. Many times you actually want to be bad. Why is that? It's your life. Can you work it out? The notes below will help you realize again how real is the evil in our nature.

I

It helps to know I'm not the only one caught in contradiction. How about St. Paul? He was a saint! But he admits he's a sinner. I'll work through *Romans 7:14-25* (18 ✠) . . . try different translations . . . see if I'm not a brother to Saint Paul. Just like Paul, I *want* one thing but *do* something else. Is there a difference between the real "I" and the "me" that sin has made? . . . It's like belonging to two different races — the earthly race and the new humanity. I am "God's willing servant" but I'm also "an unwilling prisoner to the law of sin and death."

Perhaps it's not so strange. Let me think about it. . . . If I had been sick for a long time, and in bed with a high fever so that I could hardly eat, could I expect to jump up and run around as soon as my fever had been cured? What if I were a prisoner in a dungeon for years and years: not able to make decisions for myself, forced to do what others made me do, having no light, and being completely out of touch with the changing world? What if I were suddenly freed and put out into a modern world to live in the light and to make up my own

mind about things? How would I do?

II

All this is probably quite clear to you. It is fine about us, the Church. But if Christ has overcome the world, why aren't we more victorious? What's going on? What on earth is going on? What in heaven is the idea?

Some days I wish I weren't in my teens. I wish I were back in the fourth grade . . . But some days I wish I were a 20-year-old. Some days I'd like best of all to be little and get toys for Christmas again. Some days I know I'm so adult that I can't understand why my parents don't realize it. I live in two ages at once. Is the world like that: the sinful world and the saved world? I could look more closely at *Romans 8:18-25* in different translations. *Galatians 4:1-7* describes the whole world. Without Christ the world is subject to evil. In Christ it has been freed. But we must learn to live like freed men.

God teaches us. He makes me *want* to live in Christ, not *have* to. That's the way He's acting all along. That's why Jesus came so "incognito" into the world. And God's Spirit still hides Himself in the Church and the means of grace.

III

What's the score in your life? Who's winning? Who will win? Does it all depend on you? This is a life

or death matter! It is God's idea that we live *together*.

(*Romans 7:24* to *8:4,* and *8:31-39).* The victory is already ours. We are cured! We are out of the dungeon! There's no doubt of it. I need never doubt it! *Psalm 73:21-26* is a good hymn. The only bad thing would be if I lived as though I were sick, or preferred to be in chains, or didn't care to be a freed man.

That means every moment I must decide whether to be led by the "flesh" or by the "Spirit." And since the Spirit dwells in me, I can decide. *(Romans 8:5-17* [11 ✠]; *Galatians 5:16-26* [25 ✠]; [*the Third Article* and *Sixth Petition* ✠]) All the while I must remember the other members of the body. We depend on one another. *(Romans 12:10; 14:13; 15:1)*

Sunday

Jesus' miracle at Cana was one of the signs that God was in Christ. The Epiphany season is one sign after the other that God has won the victory. The service is full of cheers for the good God who has put us on the winning team. Catch that Epistle — it tells us to be good team men on the winning team. Live by the Spirit! Live in the body! Live for the brethren!

Since it is *our* fellowship, all temptations are also *ours*. We share the powerful Word together as we strive for victory. That's the way we should see the sermon on Sundays. That's the way we should *hear* it. From the man who speaks in the pulpit comes *our* voice. We call the pastor to speak the Word for us. When he speaks, therefore, we are all talking to one another to help overcome our temptations and to build up the fellowship. The Word we speak to one another tells things to us, but its most important value is that it *does* things to us. The Word made flesh made all the difference in the world! The Word in the sermon and the Word in our conversation with one another after the service, can make a world of difference!

when we die, we live

People don't usually say, "I'm going to throw away my life." If they do—and mean it—they're probably contemplating suicide. When a man does throw away his life that way, it's over and done with, as far as this earth is concerned. But some men's lives are just killing time. Then they really are throwing away their lives, a day at a time. A man who goes on day after day with no reason for living is dead while he's breathing.

Take a deep breath. What does it prove? You can breathe. Can you live?

There was a man who loved his Cadillac so much that in his will he asked to be buried in it. His request was granted. The men who shovelled the dirt on top said, "Man, that's living!"

Do you know the difference between living and life? Can you point to things and say, "That's living!" and to others and say, "This is life?" It's your life. Live it!

word and work

I

God chose the nation of Israel to show His love and forgiving grace to all the world. He set them apart so that men would see them and see through them to God. But Israel was content just to sit apart—just to be by themselves. They didn't want to sanctify the world. Were they living? . . . When did they really die?

Jesus Christ, the True Israel, lived and died, too. When did He live? . . . In what way did He die? . . . God chose to take on our humanity in Jesus Christ and then to set Him apart so that men could see God in Him. In His death on the cross He really showed God to men. That was why He had begun living on earth. *John 12:23-33* gives a different definition of glory from the ones we're used to. Dying is living, and there is no death. Does that make sense? . . .

Really living, then—what would it be like? Would it mean being filled with ambition to get to the top? *(Matthew 20:25-28; [26b-28 ✠])* . . . Would it include collecting attractive people to love, people who were friendly and could be helpful? *(Matthew 5:43-47)* . . . Would it also try to keep itself alive, even at the expense of others? *(John 15:12-17)* . . . The biggest example of real living is that of our Lord. *(Philippians 2:1-11 [5-11 ✠])*

"Follow Me!" our Lord said. The disciples died with Him that they might live with Him.

II

That may be what life is like— but to have that kind of life, a person would have to stop "living." . . . God suggests about the same thing: *Romans 6:6; Galatians 5:24; 6:14.*

It is not a simple thing to die that kind of death. In fact none of us can. That's why our Lord died that kind of death for us. That's why Holy Baptism is so great a blessing. We "get in on" this dying He did for us when we are baptized. *(Romans 6:3-4✠)*

But the God who knows the "old Adam" must die is the God who raised Jesus Christ from the dead. Can't He make us live, too? *(Romans 8:9-11; Galatians 2:19-20).*

Baptism is a death to sin—but this dying is a daily dying. It must be a deliberate dying. It's a matter of putting self to death, making decision after decision, and letting the Spirit rule. *(Romans 6:1-2; 5-14; Galatians 5:16-25; [Baptism IV ✠])*

III

"I believe in the resurrection of the body. . . ." That kind of new life is a bit different, of course, but if we really do believe in the risen life that is ours through the risen Savior, we'll live our lives for others. That is in line with God's plan. He wants to sanctify through us, the Church! Are you part of His work?

Man's big mistake was to think that the way to be free was to be independent of God. Jesus showed us that real freedom was to be perfectly at one with God. Who is most free in a basketball game—the one who fights the rules, or the one who knows them so well that he doesn't have to think about them, and follows them? . . . How free can you be? *(Romans 8:2)*

Here's one man's list of freedoms . . . am I that free?

Freedom:

from my own past

from dependence on the good opinion of others

from personal ambition

to achieve new goals by the Spirit

to regard every man as a brother

to be no one's master and everyone's servant

to share the secret of life in Christ with everyone

131

worshiping with the church

Everyday

The Christian is free to get up in the morning under the sign of the cross; to use the sign of the cross and the Invocation to remind himself of his baptism; to adore, to confess, to thank, to supplicate; to die to self; to rise to newness of life. Each morning we *start to live!*

But living means serving. The Christian is *not* free to refuse "this reasonable service." Not to live for God is sin. Not to do the good God wants done for the world is sin. We who died to sin cannot still "live in it" by not living for God. But we do. For that reason we must continue

to *catch,* to *give,* and to *share.* Through those actions we make the beginning of our action for all of God's world.

To *live* remains our task. We are a chosen generation who are to show forth the praises of God who called us out of the darkness. We know He wants us to. There can be no true worship of God that does not try to do what God wants. And no one who asks for God's gift of the Spirit will fail to receive Him. With God's Spirit living in us, we can live for God!

133

31

LIVING HIS RISEN LIFE

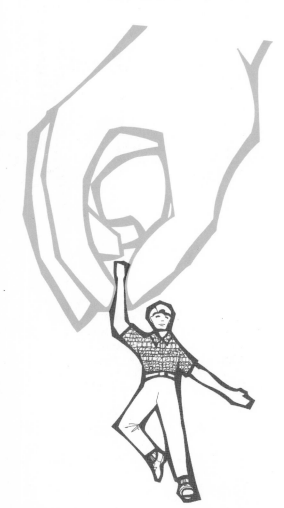

"I believe . . . in the resurrection of the body and the life everlasting." A novelist wrote the phrase, "the great perhaps of the hereafter." What is it for us? Is it "perhaps" or is it "hope" or is it "the great *certainty* of the hereafter?" If a girl thinks "perhaps" she'll be invited to a party, what does she do? If she "hopes" she will be, she acts a bit differently. But if she's *certain* she will, because she has already been asked and accepted, she will be a totally different kind of a person.

And so will you, if you've been asked by God to live everlastingly with Him, and if you've accepted. This is one of the most important things you've ever talked about or studied about in your whole life. No one can give you the answers. You've got to work them out for yourself. Perhaps—only your prayer and your study can make it "certainly"—the notes below will help you!

WORD AND WORK

I

With my body, I will live forever. . . . That's what I confess when I recite the Creed. I *believe* it, I say. What *is* my idea of heaven? God hasn't told men very much about what happens after death, but is my idea at least in line with what He *has* said? . . . Let me think first what I *do* think. . . .

Now I'll check up on what God has revealed about eternal life.

134

It's one of the wonderful things Jesus told us about: *John 3:15; 4:14; 10:27-28.* The apostles knew and looked forward to life after death: *Romans 6:22-23; Philippians 1:21-23.* Job asked the question one way *(Job 14:14),* but the way Jesus spoke, it came out like this: "Can a man to whom God has given the new life ever die?" *(Luke 20:38).* Jesus' own resurrection supplies the big proof! *1 Peter 1:3; 1 Corinthians 15:12* and *20-22.*

But now—what will I be like? I know something about decay and death, about old age and dimming eyesight, and about heart attacks and hardening of the arteries. Yet Jesus promised that those who believe in Him shall never die. Look at Him after His resurrection! The disciples did and touched Him and ate with Him, too *(Luke 24:39).* Other people have asked the same question about the resurrection body. I'll work through St. Paul's answer: *1 Corinthians 15:35-37 (51-52 ✠).*

What will heaven be like? How can I even imagine it? Everything on earth I measure in three dimensions: length, breadth, and height. Nearly everything I think about comes in dimensions of space and time and matter. "Heaven"—being with God—is beyond all that. But I can only think of it as the best, the most perfect—everything! No sin, no sorrow, no separation! We shall see Him as He is and know all our fellows who are "in Him"—forever!

II

But "life everlasting" is right now. The end never comes, but the beginning has already passed.

I'm *in* everlasting life! *(John 5:11-12)* When I die, I shall still be I. That means I'd better face up to the fact that I shall go on living with myself. With God's grace I'd better work on myself to make myself a better companion! *(2 Peter 3:11, 12; [1 John 3:1-3 ✠])*

For God's sake too we ought to grow up. We surely should not think of God as an indulgent father who follows us around all our life mopping up our spilt milk with His forgiveness. Our parents waited for the day we would stop tipping over the glass at the dinner table. Our God wants us to "grow in the grace and knowledge of our Lord Jesus Christ" *(Ephesians 4:15-16)*. He gives us His Spirit so that we can mature and manage our lives properly.

III

With my body, then, I must live for *everybody*. We should see all men as people who have died and are waiting to be helped to arise to repentance and new life. Christ did the dying for everyone. He left us to share the new life so that all men could begin living again *(2 Corinthians 5:14-19)*. God sanctifies by us, the Church. He could do it some other way, but He does not choose to. Who am I, then, not to choose to?

What to do? Help and service to the whole human race, wherever it is in need. . . . The good news of what God has done in Jesus Christ proclaimed to everybody He did it for . . . and most important of all is it that the Church should be itself! *(The Third Article ✠, Holy Baptism ✠)*

worshiping with the church

Sunday

The Sundays of Epiphanytide go on and on proving that the Child, the Man, is God! The greatest of all the epiphanies is the Transfiguration. Remember through all these Sundays that after the disciples saw our Lord's glory on the Mount of Transfiguration, they went down with Him to the plain. Because He suffered for the world, they could carry on His loving service for mankind.

If we are not careful, we can make a mistake in the Offertory that is very much like Peter's on the mount. Christ was not looking for an offer to construct three booths. The vision of God's glorious Son set to redeem

the world should have resulted in a better offer. The Word from heaven, "Listen to Him," expected greater understanding.

What kind of offer are we making when after the sermon we sing the Offertory? A new accent in the service begins at this point. We concentrate on offering our whole selves to God. We offer our money and our prayers and our thanksgivings— our eucharist in this sense. As we receive the body and blood of Jesus Christ, we "earnestly purpose with the assistance of God the Holy Ghost" to "listen to Him" and to live for Him!

program notes

The Epilogue — God Keeps Us Living Worshipful Lives

What God has done has really been great. But there is no reason for us to fall into the trap of thinking that the best has already been. The best is yet to be!

Join the Future

Isaiah expressed something of that anticipation *(Isaiah 64:3-5)*, and St. Paul quoted him *(1 Corinthians 2:9-10)*. In the King James version the words seem to describe our future: "Eye hath not seen, nor ear heard, neither have entered into the heart of man, the things which God hath prepared for them that love Him." We should live by the Spirit in that spirit.

In the past much of God's activity in the world was limited to a family, to a nation, and to certain areas in the world. But now all nations are God's field. And we are His harvestmen.

What marvelous tools He has made available! Jets and rockets put the whole universe within reach of the hands that administer the water of Holy Baptism. Radio, TV, and the new marvels of communication bend the whole world's ear toward the words of the Gospel. And — best of all — He has given us His "always"! "Lo! I am with you always!" No matter how long the future, we need never fear running out of His "always"!

Join the Ministry

We join the Church by Holy Baptism. Is there a continuing confusion about the fact that we have all joined the ministry? Jesus Christ came into the world not to be ministered to but to minister. Just as the Father sent Him, He has sent us. We are all ministers. There are special tasks we have assigned to men who are then ordained to their clergy role in Christ's ministry. But all of them and all of us are laity—the people of God—and all of us have been given the tasks of ministry.

Obviously we are not expected to serve where we are *not*, nor to do what we *can't*. But that means we are to serve where we are and in what we are able.

Join the World

Do we need a rite through which we can deliberately join the world? In a sense that is what confirmation is. Young Christians confess again their faith in the Christ, whom the Father sent, and determine to live by the Spirit who comes from the Father and the Son.

This life is to be lived in the world. The Church is not *of* the world; that is true. But it is *in* the world. Redemption does not cancel out creation. It is still God's world. He made the whole thing, and He redeemed the whole thing. The Church is in the world to reclaim it for God.

That means there is no part of the wonderfully changing civili-

139

zation that is not God's. The city is God's. The country is, too. Space is. Music is. Atomic power is. Dancing is. Fun is. Work is. Sexuality is. School is. Families are. People are. All people are God's.

We've always been a part of that world. If we've ever had the idea that the Church is a place into which we go to get away from the world, let's change that idea once for all. The Church is the people of God—not a place. The Church is the people of God reborn in the world to be God's agents in reclaiming the world for Himself.

It has always been and still is a good idea for God's people to come together to gather God's power from God's Word. He gives it to us through the Scripture and the sacraments. We "go to church" in that sense. But we are *the Church* and we are in the world. God's Word to the world is in us. We carry the power of the Scripture and the sacraments within us. We share it, it is true, with one another in the Church. But that power gets God's work done fully only when we are active in the world.

Join Your Liturgy to the Liturgy

In the rite of confirmation the congregation gathers to hear young Christians give their confession of faith and express their determination to live that faith in the world. The congregation prays for the special gifts of the Spirit to be poured out on them. The confirmands are welcomed into the fellowship, the Communion, the regular offering of thanks, the eating and drinking of the Lord's body and blood. The confirmands are ready for their part in doing the liturgy.

The liturgy we do is part of our service of God. He always does more for us than our service can ever reflect. What God does for us in Jesus Christ is beyond comparing with what we do for Him. He gives us forgiveness, life, and salvation; He moves us by the Scripture and strengthens us by the Lord's body and blood.

But our first task as we do the liturgy is to receive those gifts in faith. We *catch*. We then offer our ACTS of worship. We *give*. The liturgy goes further. In it we also serve God through people. We consciously *share* God's gifts with all the others of God's people who gather together with us.

But there are even more of God's people who are not in the church building doing their liturgy with us. The whole world is God's. He has redeemed all people. When the body of Christ leaves the church building and encounters the world, it is still the body of Christ. We are still God's extension of Himself into the world.

We have more work to do for God. And in this work each one of us must do his special part. *The* liturgy we do together. Out in the world we have *our* liturgy to do. No one else can do it for us. If we don't do it, it won't be done—until God sets someone else at our job. (He had to do that to fill in for Judas, remember?)

This is what the Epilogue is all about. Its aim is to help us discover the special tasks that God has assigned to us—our liturgy. In every lesson we will keep in touch with the Sunday's liturgy. Some of the lessons will take their entire point from the propers of the day. It is in the liturgy that *God keeps us living worshipful lives*. There we receive the *Word in Scripture and sacraments*. But we are the letters of Christ to the world. We want to join our liturgy to the church liturgy.

my Response to God

A teen-ager can hardly wait to get his driver's license. Christians don't all seem to be that eager to qualify for the kind of living their membership in the Church calls for. Even some of us have one excuse after the other to delay our getting into the thick of the Christian life. We stall. We'd rather question than act. We'd rather discuss than respond.

But everything God has done for us demands our response. Worship is man's response to God. Our whole life should be a form of worship. When we were children and someone gave us a present, our parents would urge us with a little reminding shove, "What do you say?" And after we said our thanks we were expected to *use* the gift *appreciatively, thankfully.*

What *do* we say? What do we *do?*

This is the beginning of the Epilogue. In the Prologue and in Acts I, II, and III, we have studied the great acts of God. Now we study our acts, the ACTS of the disciples. In the liturgy, we receive what God has done for us, and through Him we express our worshiping response. We share with the rest of God's people. Now to the liturgy in the worship service we add our liturgy. We live our liturgy out in the world and in the lives of others. By His Word in Scripture and sacraments God has given us a new kind of life. Our concern is that we now *live worshipful lives!* Our lives should be like sacraments for the world: the means of bringing God's Word to the world.

woRδ anδ woRk

I

God's great acts make us Christians and therefore worshipers. Do we agree?

Our Christian life comes to us from God *(Romans 1:16-17)*. All that we have learned has been taught by God *(John 14:18-26; 2 Timothy 3: 14-17)*. By Holy Baptism God makes it possible for us to live a new kind of life *(Romans 6:1-11 [1-4 ✠]; 1 Corinthians 10:31)*. This life we live together as the Church *(Ephesians 4:4-6)*. Each of us has particular gifts to use in his ministry. *(Ephesians 4:7-12)*

What *do* we say? What do we *do?* What do you say we *do?*

II

"Now what is our response to be?" St. Paul asks this at the beginning of *Romans 6*. In the translation by J. B. Phillips, the answer Saint Paul gives goes like this: "Shall we sin to our heart's content and see how far we can exploit the grace of God? What a ghastly thought!" In the King James Version that suggestion brings the response, "God forbid!"

What is *our* response?

Many of the verses of *Romans 6* warn us about what our response can not be. We certainly can not just go on sinning as though nothing that God has done makes any difference. It would be simple if God were now to spell out just exactly the things we are expected to do. But the last thing He wants from us is an attitude that says. "O. K. so I'm in. Now tell me what I have to do and let's get it over with." By God's grace we have "entered the service of righteousness." "So, now give yourselves to the service of righteousness —for the purpose of becoming really good." *(Romans 6:19b ✠)*

A person who has fallen in love keeps looking for ways to show how great his love is. God has first loved us—and now we love Him. People who are changed into worshipers will be looking for ways to respond to the love of God.

God is worshiped not only by words but also by acts. He is worshiped through the things we do for other people. Do we agree?

Our Lord made it clear Himself

(Matthew 25:40, 45 *).* His prophets and apostles agree. *(Micah 6:8* *; James 1:27)*

The Bible has many passages that help us think through the ways God's worshiping people are to go into action. Almost every instance is set in a situation different from the ones in which we will find ourselves. It's good practice to see if we can think of the problems we will meet and decide how we ought to act when we do. *(James 2:1-9; 1 Corinthians 10:23-33; Ephesians 5:1-3; 5-8; Titus 3:1-2; Acts 4:13-22 [19-20* *])*

God isn't pushing us. He doesn't force anyone to love Him. But He is helping! His Spirit makes it possible for us to say "yes." It's up to us— we're old enough to have a "license" to love Him. What do we say? What do we *respond?*

worshiping with the church

Life as Worship

We qualify for the Church; we have our license. Shift into high gear. Pick one thing out of our discussion to do this week as an act of worship — something to do for God through a fellowman. Offer it to God in a prayer as you decide. Praise God with it as you do it!

The Worship Life

God's Word reaches us through Scripture and sacraments. God uses them to keep us living worshipful lives. So important is God's power in all we do that in the very beginning of the part of the liturgy in which we offer ourselves in response to God's love, we pray for God's creative and renewing power. "Create in me a clean heart, O God, and renew a right spirit within me."

The pre-Lenten Sundays urge us on to the living out of our liturgy, but the propers stress how much we must depend on God's power. Yet the power must be *caught.* The Epistle for Septuagesima *(1 Corinthians 9:24 — 10:5)* gives a sharp warning to any who think it is enough to "belong" to the people of God. With many of the old Israel who were saved by water and fed by God He was not well pleased. They began to think of themselves as saved by race, instead of by grace. The Gospel *(Matthew 20:1-16)* has something to say about that. They thought that as long as they were in the right race they did not need to strive to win the race.

We who accept the grace of God, are we striving for the prize as though everything depended on us? Then in the liturgy in the church service we will be alert to *catch,* and in our daily liturgy we will strive to *live.*

145

what are you doing now?

All of us heard that suspicious question time after time while we were growing up. Often what we were doing turned out to be what we shouldn't be doing. Some of the things were evidently too babyish. "Why don't you grow up? Are you going to be a baby all of your life?" Most of the rest of the things were too grown-up. "You're not big enough yet. You can do that when you're a little older." Sometimes in desperation we would feel like asking, "What can we do *now?*" Teen years are often a time of catching up. Once a body has grown inches taller and broader, the person who lives in it has to do a lot of eating and a lot of resting just to fill it up. But the cry that shakes us out of the hammock is,

"Why don't you get up and *do* something?"

The Sundays in pre-Lent demand that we ask these questions of ourselves. We are down on the plain now, after having seen the Lord in glory on the Mount of Transfiguration. In the Lenten season we're getting ready to view our Lord's "ministry" for us. Since we are "growing up" in Him, we consider also our ministry for Him and His "least brethren." Pre-Lent tells us that we can't phrase the question in the future, "What are you going to do when you grow up?" We must ask it of ourselves in the present tense, *"What are you doing now?" (Mark 10: 42-45* ✠ *; 1 Corinthians 7:17 Phillips)*

word and work

I

The Proper Point

The propers we used on Septuagesima give us power from the Word of God to examine and to remold our lives. The Introit, Collect, and Gradual give us helpful patterns to review our past life. We could have done that just from the point of view of Christians entering Lent. But there is room for additional meditation if we think of our past record in terms of following through on our Christian *vocation*. What *have* we been doing up to now—we who are called by God to serve?

The Epistle and the Gospel are full of God's push for our future. All

that we have is a free gift from God. By His amazing grace we have been given a first place when we deserve only the last. In Christ we all have received the prize. But we are to run as in a race in which only one can win. We are to discipline ourselves as athletes who are in training for a hard fight. We can no more be content to be mere "church members" than could the Israelites be content to have been part of the chosen race who were saved in the Exodus. They were baptized in the sea, and they ate the heavenly food. We have been baptized and we eat and drink the body and blood of our Lord — but that is no guarantee that we please God. *1 Corinthians 10:12* is a good summary of the day's warning to us.

But after all the warnings of Septuagesima, what we need most is its power. It reminds us that God Himself gave His life for us. "The Lord is my Rock and my Fortress." "There is forgiveness with Thee, that Thou mayest be feared." "We who are justly punished for our offenses" have been and every day are "mercifully delivered" by His goodness for the glory of His name.

II
The Right Reaction

"Who am I?" Boxer, track star, vineyard worker. . . . But many other things: student, member of my family, friend (both to fellows and to girls), odd-job worker, extracurricular participant, and always Christian and member of my congregation.

To all these, the question is not, "What are you going to be when you grow up?" but "What are you doing now?" If each one of us were to take on a certain character, one of the many roles we play each day, we could discuss some of the passages of Scripture that talk about the way of life of the "called" man. Pick your role!

1 Corinthians 1:1-9 — We can all get together on this. We have been called just as surely as the Bible people were *(Ephesians 4:1-3* and *12-16)!* If a basketball player isn't a "team man" he'll soon be a bench warmer. There's no bigger team than the Church, and no team that needs the help of every man more. *2 Peter 1:3-11* — Every one of us must work at his own skills, too. The warning of Septuagesima is that many are called — few chosen.

woRshipiNG with the chuRch

Life as Worship

The Epilogue's "life as worship" accent is very clear in this lesson. It is a helpful reminder to pick out a chore that we know we have to do no matter what, and to decide to do it as an act of our Christian vocation. Try it on studying for a social studies test . . . or on your share of the household jobs.

The Worship Life

During pre-Lent we take a closer look at the ways and the places in the liturgy in which we have the opportunity to "catch" the impetus of the Word. Today we reviewed the propers of Septuagesima. How much of the power God packed into the propers really reached us on Sunday?

Power can be generated if a river is dammed, a waterwheel constructed, and *the two are brought together.* If the water doesn't hit the wheel, there's no chance for the creation of power, no chance for the grinding work to be done. We have to move ourselves into position so that the power of the Word is "caught" by our attention and our meditation. Only then will it move us and start us out in the grinding work of life to which we have been called.

If we wait until the propers are being chanted or the lesson's being read, it may all be water over the dam—and no power. It's vital for "doing our liturgy," especially for the "catch" work to study up on Saturday for the work we're going to do Sunday.

It is just as necessary for living our liturgy to keep remembering Sunday's Word during the week. If we wake up with the Introit's words: "I will love Thee, O Lord, my Strength," we will be off and running as soon as our feet hit the floor. (Or better still, our knees.)

34

my ministry in my home

When our Lord said to the fishermen by the Sea of Galilee, "Follow Me," He led them into the world to do *extraordinary* things. But when He took a towel and began to wash the disciples' feet, He gave them an example of how they should do *ordinary* things. God has called us, too. Our *vocation* is not only to take a part in the extraordinary work of Christ's Church, but to follow His example in the ordinary things of life.

That's hard. In many ways it is

a good deal easier to give money for worldwide missions or to attend a rally for the building drive for a new church than it is to do dishes with your brother to the glory of God. The disciples felt that way. None of them was about to pick up the towel. Jesus had to do it. Imagine what Jesus might do in our homes when selfishness has started a good quarrel. "It's your turn!" "It is not—I did them last time." Would our Lord pick up the towel? Can we?

word and work

I

The Proper Point

The coming of Sexagesima reminds us that only some sixty days remain before Easter. In Lent we try to look closely at our way of living. We ask God's help to repent and by His grace to turn back to God's standards of living. What we want is to be well prepared to celebrate Easter in God's way.

Before Sunday give your way of life at home a careful look. There is probably no other place where we take things quite so much for granted. Regarding home, Robert Frost put into Warren's mouth in *The Death of the Hired Man:* "Home is the place where, when you have to go

there, they have to take you in." But Mary answered, "I should have called it something you somehow haven't to deserve."

Isn't that what St. Paul tells us in Sunday's Epistle? There were false leaders trying to lure the Corinthians away from Paul's leadership *(2 Corinthians 11:4-5, 13)*. Paul shows that he could brag himself up as much as those men did. But he calls himself a fool for doing that kind of boasting. If there is anything he should be proud about, it is his weaknesses *(2 Corinthians 11: 30-33; 12:5-10)*. Not that he felt it was good to be weak, but God had

150

taught him that only those who know their weaknesses look for God's strength.

St. Paul's words do not apply only to our home situation, of course, but if we take a specific situation like that we can examine whether we are aware of our own weaknesses. Perhaps we need to make a list to make sure we will be specific.

After a bit of honest peering into ourselves, we can surely make the words of the Introit and the Gradual our own. The Collect is just the kind of prayer we need. Surely we don't dare put our trust "in anything that we do." But can we be sure that God will use "His power" to defend us? *Verse 9* of *2 Corinthians 12* will help us with that answer.

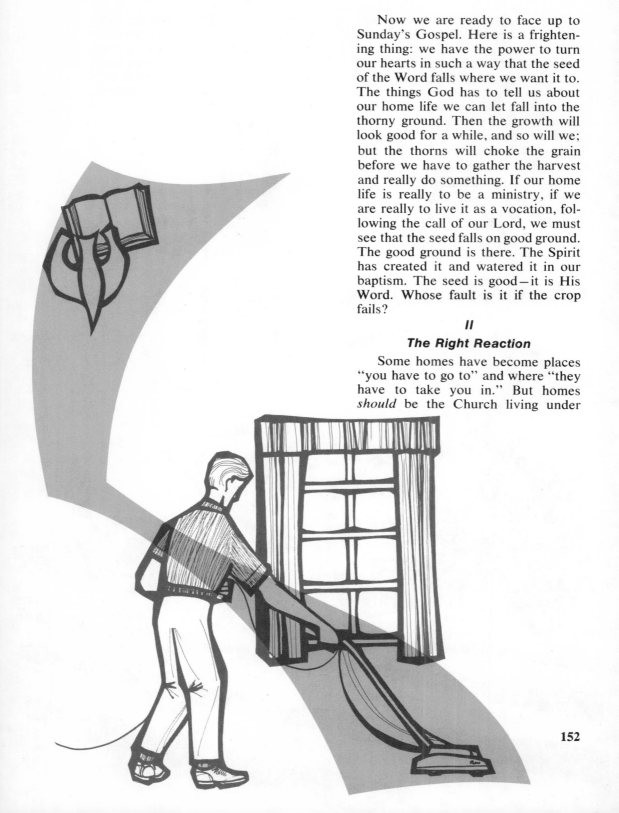

Now we are ready to face up to Sunday's Gospel. Here is a frightening thing: we have the power to turn our hearts in such a way that the seed of the Word falls where we want it to. The things God has to tell us about our home life we can let fall into the thorny ground. Then the growth will look good for a while, and so will we; but the thorns will choke the grain before we have to gather the harvest and really do something. If our home life is really to be a ministry, if we are really to live it as a vocation, following the call of our Lord, we must see that the seed falls on good ground. The good ground is there. The Spirit has created it and watered it in our baptism. The seed is good—it is His Word. Whose fault is it if the crop fails?

II

The Right Reaction

Some homes have become places "you have to go to" and where "they have to take you in." But homes *should* be the Church living under one roof. *Ephesians 4* begins with a reminder of our vocation, our calling. It tells us that we are one body. Then begins a long list of duties in the Church. By the time we read to chapter *5:21* and on to *6:4* we have found out how all of us ought to act in the Church at our house *(Ephesians 6:1-4 ✠). The Fourth and the Sixth Commandments (✠)* help us summarize some of these tasks. In *Colossians 3* St. Paul begins by reminding us that we are risen people. *Verses 12-14* and *18-25* cover the ground again, telling how we ought to live with other resurrected people.

1 Peter 2 begins by reminding us we are newborn people. *Verses 9-10* call us God's people and make clear why He chose us. In Chapter *3:1-12* the kind of life that should be found in our homes is described *(8-9 ✠).* Those children whose homes are not like this, whose parents do not try to live as Christ's Church under one roof, have a special calling. They need to do *extraordinary* things as well as the ordinary ones!

The seed of the Word has been sown. Check the ground of your heart into which you've let it fall. Check up again on Sunday!

worshiping with the church

Life as Worship

Every day at home should show some harvest from the seed of this Word. Our honest examination of how we have been living should suggest one thing: start easy. If you try for a bumper crop right away you may get discouraged. Harvest something and offer it to God at the end of the day as your worship.

The Worship Life

Every Christian must preach the Word to himself in the service. That is always true—but it is a special responsibility when a person knows ahead of time what the lessons will be. Two things must happen at the same time: we hear the lessons read and the sermon preached, but we also *infer* lessons for ourselves. When we hear the Epistle, we'll remember what we found that was *good* in our analysis of our home. But we'll remember with St. Paul that we haven't earned this. In our weakness God gives

strength. That's good, because we'll be remembering the bad side of our home life as we pray the Introit and the Collect. We hear of the power of God, then, in Collect and Epistle. And now, our biggest task—we must *catch* the power. The Good News is not spelled out—we must think through all that God has done through Jesus Christ. He "so loved." But we must be one of the "whosoever believeth." We must catch the power and raise the harvest.

The liturgy from the Offertory on is filled with Gospel power for us to catch. Take the first paragraph of the General Prayer, for example. And look at the prefaces—especially the one for Lent. In the midst of the Sanctus are the words "Blessed is He that cometh in the name of the Lord" reminding us of Him who comes to us in His body and blood in the Sacrament.

35

my ministry at school

It's easy for us to dismiss something as unimportant. "That's for the birds," we say. Is this what we have said about certain of the things God wants us to do? "It's for the birds," we say and so we let the seed fall on the trodden path where the fowls of the air will devour it.

It's difficult to live as a person whom God has called out from the group in school. It's tough to be odd. Some of us know that by bitter experience. When we don't have money for the "right" clothes, when we don't have the "right background," when "we don't have it" (whatever "it" can mean), we know the feeling of being left out. Then, usually to compensate,

we try to be "in" on all that we can. We imitate what those who *are* "in" say, what they think, and the way they act. We try to be as much like everyone else as we can, so that we feel part of the group.

The question we need to ask ourselves is whether ministers of Christ in school can take that approach to life. If the fishermen who were told to follow Jesus had wanted to stick with the group, they would never have caught men. Of course, they would probably not have been killed for being disciples of Jesus, either. Which do we want to be (or must we be), ministers who might be martyrs, or just one of the gang?

woRd and woRk

I

The Proper Point

What difference does Sunday make on our Monday? If we are at all serious about the church year, we try to make the seed sown on Sunday spring up to some kind of harvest on Monday. If it doesn't, it is not the fault of the seed; the seed is the Word of God. God is working in that. His power is strong enough to get things done. The fault can only be with the soil, our heart; or with the farmer — that's us. There is such a thing as

a curious gardener who digs up seeds to see if they're growing. There are Christians who simply look curiously at the seeds sown on Sunday. They don't give them any chance to take root.

We ought to wake up each morning of this week thinking about getting in shape for Easter. The way we get in shape is to let the seed of the Word grow. The particular seed we're con-

centrating on is that which tells us what God calls us to be and to do. The field in which we should bring forth a harvest is our school life. Our Christian vocation is a call to be doing things for God through Christ right now. Since much of our "right now" is in school, part of our vocation is to be God's person toward our classmates.

155

II
The Right Reaction

Remember who you are — beyond being a student in school. *Matthew 25:14-30* should remind you. If this seed takes root, we should be looking at our classroom work and homework a bit differently.

Or try *John 17:18-21*. Our Lord didn't enroll in our world with the thought of what He could get out of life. His idea of life was what He could put into it. It wasn't only what He said and not only what He did; a great deal of His witness lay in what He *was*. Does that give us any ideas for our role in school?

John 15:1-17 is another familiar story that says something about students. It's not that Jesus Christ is the stem and merely supplies power to the branches; He is the Vine, the whole thing. As branches we are extensions of Him. That says something about branches that plan to stay green but refuse to bear grapes. But it says even more about what has happened to us through Jesus Christ. His dying for us has made it possible for us to be living for Him.

Think about what you can do — you're always planning your day anyway. Each one of us could take *Romans 12* and find some specific suggestions about *what he could do* this week as a called disciple in school. Our Lord did not limit His love and concern to those who believed. He came for the world. All the world belongs to Him. Our concern should certainly not be limited to people we like or to people who are Christian.

We can't miss the fact that God depends on us to *say* something. *Acts 26:22* and *20:17-24* are illustrations. We *can*, too. *(John 15:26-27)*

And all the time we must *be* something. There's a purpose to how we act. We're "good on purpose." *(1 Peter 2:11-17; Matthew 5:13-16 ✠; 1 Peter 3:15-16 ✠)*

worshiping with the church

Life as Worship

Whatever harvest you gather of the seed God has sown is worship when it is offered to Him.

The Worship Life

We have a particularly difficult job to catch the Word when it is delivered in sermons. You know from school that it is hard for any one to say something that interests us every time he talks. The preacher has to aim his words at an even broader audience than a classroom. If he's going to hit the target that is your life, you'll have to move it into his range. You'll have to *want* to get hit. That's *catching!*

We can try getting in range by remembering three words: point, problem, and power. The preacher has the *point*—something he wants us to do or to believe. Catch it. He tries to help us diagnose *our problem,* why it is we've been acting the way we have. That's preaching the Law,

and the Law always condemns us. If you think of it simply as a little slap on the wrist, *you moved!* The sinner cannot stand before God. That's our problem. Then he preaches *power,* the power of the Gospel! The Law or admonition that simply urges us on toward the point won't move us. That just irritates us. The Law makes us want to rebel even more against God. But when the sermon tells us again what God did for us in Jesus Christ, that is God's power. What God did once-for-all through the Word made flesh, He does once again for us right now in the Word made words in the sermon. When that happens to us, *Mark 5:18-20* should become true in our lives. When we tell others "how much the Lord has done for us" and "how He has had mercy on us," we set the power of the Word to work in their lives.

36

my ministry

in my leisure time

"I've just got to have some time for myself!" Most of us will automatically agree with that. But ought we? For *2 Corinthians 5:14-15* ✠ and *Mark 8:34-37* ✠ certainly seem to suggest a different approach. There is no time off. We're always on duty.

The Mark passage comes immediately after our Lord described His own approach to life — *Mark 8:31-33* — a deadly realistic one. When Peter protested that He should arrange His life differently, our Lord told him "get behind Me, Satan!" But even though the apostles described themselves as "slaves of Christ" they insisted that His service was perfect freedom. If we really want some "free time," then, perhaps we'll find it only in serving God through our fellows.

word and work

I

The Proper Point

Quinquagesima — and now it is 50 days until Easter. At Easter we hope to stand before the risen Christ as His risen followers. He does the

raising, we must do the following. Beginning now.

The Gospel for Sunday's liturgy is another example of how our Lord made clear to His disciples how His life was really to be *lived* by moving steadfastly ahead to His *dying*. The disciples didn't really understand that kind of talk nor can we. When we pray the Collect for Quinquagesima we are apt to have a different definition of evil. We want to be defended from all the things that we find unpleasant. Our Lord saw as the greatest evil anything that would keep Him from dying for others. Now that He has "set us free from the bonds of sin" are we ready to see as evil everything that keeps us from *living* for others?

The Epistle is St. Paul's wonderful song praising the greatest of virtues: charity, love. It would be an interesting experiment for us to write a paragraph on love. Without looking at

St. Paul's description, in which he gives 16 things that love is or that love is not, we could try to describe our idea of what it means. If we use simple sentences like, "Love is—" and "Love is not—" we could find where we agree and where we disagree with St. Paul. It is vital that we understand love—and even more vital that we love. St. Paul says that love is even greater than faith!

The point of the combination of this Epistle and this Gospel is that loving is really a kind of dying. For us it may not mean the kind of dying our Lord did upon the cross. It will mean, however, the kind of dying to self that He illustrated in healing the blind man. He might have felt that three years of healing the sick and dealing with the beggars and sinners along the world's streets were enough. Now He was pushing on toward the cross and the end of His work of saving mankind. Surely He could be excused for devoting His spare time to Himself. But He simply didn't think that way. He had entered time to give Himself for men. "In time" He was just as completely committed to the will of the Father as "in eternity."

Since He wanted to give Himself for others, it made no sense at all to try to save some of Himself for Himself.

It's a good thing we get the Gradual between the Epistle and the Gospel—we need the chance to praise Him!

II
The Right Reaction

Doctors make it clear to us that our bodies need rest. To what extent would we say that God agrees with them? The Sabbath was to be

"a solemn rest"—was its purpose really *rest* or was it worship? Could it have been a reminder that the two need not be far apart? *(Exodus 23:12; 31:15; 34:21; 35:2; Leviticus 23:3)*

Two things are quickly apparent about our Lord and leisure time. He recognized His own need for it and sought it—for example, *Mark 6: 30-32* and *46; 7:24.* But it is clear, too, that His work was more important to Him than His rest—*Mark 6: 33-34* and *7:25ff.* Back of His entire way of life is another basic attitude that connects with our thinking about leisure time.

If we were planning a 3-year tour on earth for the Son of God, what changes in His program would we

160

have introduced? Would we have scheduled the tour in the pre-TV era? Surely Jesus Christ knew how many ill and demon-possessed were in the regions He never visited. Surely He knew how many more people there were in the world than in Palestine. Yet He lived one Man's life. He balanced rest and work in proper ratio, content to get done as much as one person could get done in a normal working day.

Now—the hard part. Let's list the things we do in our leisure time and figure out whether our Lord would have used time that way. *Philippians 4:8* is a good passage ✠; try *Colossians 3:17* and *4:5; 1 Timothy 6: 17-19; Ephesians 5:15-16* ✠; *1 Corinthians 9:19-23.* This chapter begins with St. Paul's comments on his free time! These are his conclusions. Note that the chapter ends with the Epistle for Septuagesima.

worshiping with the church

Life as Worship

We should be able to begin each leisure-time activity with a prayer to God to enjoy it with us, and end it with thanksgiving to God. But try it—can we put prayer at the top of the schedule of things we do in our spare time?

The Worship Life

An interesting contrast to the study of Sabbath Day passages might be made by considering how we look on our Sundays. Days of rest? "Our" time? "Free" time? We've stretched our Sabbaths into weekends. Where does our responsibility to "do our liturgy" fit in? How much *responsibility* do we feel to participate in the celebration of our Lord's Supper?

"Catching" the impetus from God certainly involves receiving the benefits of the Eucharist. It's a sobering thought that the Lord's love is to be *caught.* He gives His life. We are to receive it. He is present with us on the altar and with us as we receive the Sacrament. This is a heavenly food. He reaches us and enters our lives as we eat and drink the Holy Supper.

"Given for" and "for given" are the same words. What goes in between? You! "Given for—you—forgiven." Remember the Catechism's words about the Lord's Supper ". . . the true body and blood of our Lord Jesus Christ, under the bread and wine, for us Christians *to eat* and *to drink. . . .*" That is the way God instructs us to catch this Word.

But love also demands that "you" is to be written *before* "forgive" and "give for." *You* forgive. *You* give for. God's love means His Son's dying for us, and it means our living for Him. Whoever has forgiveness of sins has "life and salvation." That life is to be lived out by sharing that salvation. The man who is forgiven forgives. The man for whom Christ gave Himself gives himself.

my ministry

to my community

Lent is not so much a time to meditate on the death of Jesus Christ as it is a time to do something about the lives of men. . . . Agree or disagree?

Jesus Christ came not to be served but to serve and to give His life as a ransom for many. . . . Agree or disagree? Go and do likewise! . . . Agree or disagree?

word and work

I
The Proper Point

There is no doubt about the propers' push, but what's the proper point? How far do we have to go with the love business St. Paul urges on us in last Sunday's Epistle? Love yourself — your neighbor as yourself — but does all that mean going to the point of *Galatians 6:9-10?* ✠ Then there's simply no stopping point! And it's not just a matter of deciding who is your neighbor, but of proving yourself neighbor *(Luke 10:36)*. To whom — to the nation? the community? other races? the poor? orphans? sick people? old people? the world?

II
The Right Reaction

Agree or disagree? . . . This is the way a Christian should act:

TEACHER SPENDS SUMMERS
DOWN IN THE DUMPS

Yarmouth, Me., Sept. 12 (AP) — Augustus F. Jones looks like a garbage collector to at least 50 families on Littlejohn and Cousin islands.

To scores of students and the faculty at Dean Junior College in Franklin, Mass., Jones looks and acts like a sociology professor.

He is both. For nine months a year he teaches, and he went back to that life Wednesday. For the other three months the 64-year-old professor takes waste off the islands to a piggery and dump.

"I have been doing this summers for more years than I care to count," he said. "It's sort of a mission with me. Somebody's got to keep the island clean and if the rubbish isn't collected regularly it becomes a problem. Some solved it by burying it, but a lot of others would just start small dumps all over the place. Not neat at all, and not right."

— (St. Louis Post-Dispatch, Sept. 13, 1964)

Agree or disagree? . . . a Christian should run for mayor. Or senator. Or President.

Agree or disagree? . . . A Christian may not know much about the issues, but it is his duty to vote.

Agree or disagree? . . . *Romans 13* makes clear that the Christian's duty toward government is to obey authorities and pay taxes, and that's that.

There are areas closer to most of us than the government in which we are challenged to exercise our ministry. With passages like those below making God's opinion clear, we could work out our own "agree-disagree" statements. They could be in any or all of three relationships — our families, the "household of faith," or all our fellowmen.

What about poor people — that is, anyone who has less than we? It could be a sister whose allowance is all spent, or a member of our parish who is out of work, or hungry nations in the Orient. *(Ephesians 4:28 ✠; Proverbs 21:13* and *19:17; Matthew 19:21; James 2:1-6)*

Old people — What about them? Our parents and grandparents; old people in the inner city with no relatives, or the elderly in nursing homes; friendless old and invalids in our congregation? *(The Fourth Commandment; Leviticus 19:32; Isaiah 46:4)*

One more — about people whose skin or nationality or race is different from ours. Our reaction *should* be, "What difference does that make?" — but the sad truth is that it does seem to make a difference in the minds of some men in our world. *(Ephesians 2:11-16; Acts 2:5-12; 17:26-28)*

We could go on and on: talking about widows and orphans, about the sick and those whose minds did not grow strong and mature, about the emotionally ill, about the unemployed, about war and relations between nations, about two girls we know who aren't speaking to each other. In *2 Corinthians 5:14-17* is a good summing up. There is no one in the whole world for whom Jesus Christ has not died. Anyone we meet has already had his dying done by our Lord. That means we ought to look at every man as a forgiven person as far as God is concerned. The trouble is, some people don't know it has happened. They don't know about God's new life, that God wants to do a new creation on them! It would be terrible if they didn't find out because we didn't *show* them, or tell them.

worshiping with the church

Life as Worship

Every person who believes God *forgives*, must *give for* the rest of mankind whom God forgives. It's that simple. And that difficult. Worship God in the community today. Need a start? Pick up some litter and put it in the trash can — not just your own, somebody else's!

The Worship Life

"No sooner do we believe that God loves us than there is an impulse to believe that He does so, not because He is Love, but because we are intrinsically lovable" (Clive Staples Lewis, *The Four Loves*, N. Y.: Harcourt Brace & World, p. 180). God's grace must give us the ability to remember always how much we need to *catch* His love, so that we can accept it as something we need and not as something we deserve.

Perhaps it is even more difficult for us to remember that we need the love of our fellowman—the love that loves us even though we are not lovable. We want to be loved because we *are* something; we need grace to admit that we aren't very much—grace to accept the love fellow Christians give us because God is everything.

As we do our liturgy, thinking about all who do it with us, we practice catching the love of our brothers. In every celebration of our Lord's Supper we hear His words teaching us we are in this together: "Drink ye all. . . ." We can't be God's new creation by ourselves, *they're* here, too. We must love, but—sometimes it's even more difficult—we must let ourselves *be* loved.

God must change us so that we aren't always fighting to maintain our pride. He gives us peace—with Him and with ourselves. The *Pax* in the service, "The peace of the Lord be with you all," can help us love and be loved. The pastor offers us the Lord's love, and his own. We accept it with "Amen." Sometimes we offer ours to him with, "And with thy spirit." With our "Amen" we can turn to our brother on the right and on the left and let him know we mean, "And with you, too!" It's part of our task to give it. Can you take it?

punch ın

Some companies use time clocks to record how much time an employee puts in at work. The clock marks the time he begins and ends his work each day. Most time clocks are electric now. All an employee does is slip his time card into the clock's slot, and his hours are automatically registered. Time clocks had to be punched before electricity took over. *You* said what time it was. *You* punched the time when you began and punched the time when you stopped working.

In our ministry, that is, our lives of serving God by serving men, we must punch out our own schedule. We get some help.

God marked Sunday into our 7-day week. (But we still have to schedule the hours of Sunday.) Our parents help punch us out of bed on time in the morning. (But we have to schedule most of the day.) Teachers have the class hours all punched out. (But we have to decide whether we'll

have our minds in gear during the class hour or simply let them idle.) The hours where it's up to *us* to really come out punching are our homework hours, our leisure time hours — the time that's left when everybody else has claimed his part of our time.

"What I want to do is get some sleep!" Correct. Schedule it. It's important. But don't spend 16 hours half asleep instead of 8 hours really sound asleep. If we've agreed on the phases of our ministry we've been studying, we know there's plenty to do! The amount of time we have is the same. God sets that amount.

But how much we can get done depends partly on how we punch the time clock. The hardest part of the Christian job is getting started on the task at hand. No — perhaps the hardest part is scheduling our time so that we know when to get started on what.

A good passage from the Scriptures that urges us on is the first part of *Ecclesiastes 9:10* ✠. "The Preacher" is not very optimistic about our success. But the Spirit is our big help!

word and work

I
The Proper Point

There are forty days in Lent — not counting the Sundays. (Sundays are always celebrations of Easter.) Lent begins on Ash Wednesday. How many days of the 40 set aside for our preparation for celebrating Easter this year are already gone? Punch in — those days would make a useful check on how we schedule our time. Did we serve God with our time at home, in school, in leisure time, in our communities? The contrition accent of Ash Wednesday should say something to us. But the accent of Ash Wednesday's Gospel *(Matthew 6:16-21)* says something about our action, too. The time we have left is time in which to serve.

Begin with the apostle's urgent note in the Epistle for Invocavit. With our own time clock in mind we could make a quick list of the times in which we're tempted to let God's grace go to waste.

The Holy Gospel for the first Lenten Sunday makes a point of our Lord's conflict with Satan. Perhaps our biggest problem with our scheduling of time is the failure to recognize the devil. He surely didn't appear to Jesus in a red suit with a forked tail. It's no trick at all for him to take on the form of an excuse in our mind, and to make himself appear very logical.

With the promise of the Introit, the assurance of the Gradual, and our recognition of our time-clock problem, we should be able to make the Collect really collect our prayers.

II
The Right Reaction

A good reaction motto is *Ephesians 5:15-20* ✠. A good task for these days is the filling out of a typical time card for a weekday, and another

for a Sunday, which you can use during the Lenten season.

A checklist: Is there a time slot for direct conversation with God? One for serving God in home work? How about for serving the members of your family—or of just being *with* them as fellow Christians? Any spot for your community?

Now—punch in! That's the Lenten task: use the grace of God!

worshiping with the church

Life as Worship

Time *is* worship if we live it thoughtfully and if we have God in mind.

The Worship Life

God doesn't install a time clock at the entrance to the nave of His church buildings. But you put a mental one at the end of your pew, just for experiment this Sunday. Remember there are four principal tasks—to catch (to *imply* God's lessons for us from His Word); to give (to *reply* to the good God who gives to us); to share (to *supply* the wants of our brothers by sharing our faith); and to live (to *apply* what happens to us in our time of worship to what we can make happen in all our time of living).

The last one begins when you punch in for your life after the service. But the first three are tasks for the time we do our liturgy in church. If we set ourselves the task this Sunday, we can check our time cards after the service to see how well we do the work of worship.

Since Septuagesima we have stressed how we can *catch* God's power in the liturgy to live the Lenten life. Any improvement? Can we sing in the Nunc Dimittis "Mine eyes have *seen* Thy Salvation"? Keep looking!

39

keep the change

It's usually the big spender who says, "Keep the change." He may try to give the impression that money means nothing to him. Money *should* mean a lot to us. Money too is for worship. And God has much to say about our attitude toward money.

For one thing, God says to us, "Keep the change." But the change He means is the one spoken of in *Ephesians 4:22-24* ✠. That change does have something to do with money, though, as *verse 28* points out. The reason given for the thief to change is also a good reason for us to be careful with our money and to think about our attitude toward it. Ash Wednesday's *Matthew 6:19-21* makes it clear to us that our attitude toward money is not simply a matter of dollars and cents but a matter of the heart.

Put your heart into this lesson, and God will help you keep the change.

WORD AND WORK

I

The Proper Point

The Gospel for Invocavit gives us the chance to see that real living is not a process of getting but of giving. Remember that Jesus Christ took on humanity's nature in order that He might live life for us as it was designed to be lived. When His words make it clear that money is no object *(Matthew 8:20),* and that only the heavenly Father can be the Director of life *(Matthew 6:24),* we realize that real life is to be lived that way. St. Paul understood that and urged the Philippians to realize it, too. *(Philippians 2:3-8 ✠)*

Any other approach to life — like seeing how much He could get out of it, or wondering what was in it for Him — was totally foreign to God's plan. It would have ruined everything. The devil knew that and moved in on Jesus with temptations that practically wore dollar signs *(Hebrews 4: 15).* As we think through the temptations in Sunday's Gospel we can see how the devil was trying to get through our Lord's guard by tempting Him with things that money can buy. He practically told Him that "living" was a matter of having enough to eat, popularity, and possessions. "If you really are the Son of God," he tempted, "then make sure you get your share." But Jesus said that *having* was not *living — giving* was.

II

The Right Reaction

Imagine what Jesus Christ would say about the advertisements if He were turning the pages of one of our magazines. *(Luke 12:15.* The parable from verse *16* on to verse *21* should remind us never to forget the riches God has already given us in the manger of the barn He used!)

Wouldn't it be simpler — and more God-pleasing — if an owner of a factory employing a thousand men would simply sell the business and divide up the value of it with the workers? *(Matthew 19:21-22; Matthew 25:14-30; 1 Corinthians 13:3)*

Some people seem to think that trying to make a profit is unchristian, that trying to get ahead is wrong, and that the really Christian life today would mean that Christians would share and share alike. Is this right? *(1 Timothy 6:6-19; Acts 2: 44-45; 5:4; Jeremiah 22:13-17)*

The trouble with thinking about money is that finally I have to begin thinking about *my* money. (One may have only an allowance and what one gets by selling papers or by baby-sitting.) But what I have, I have to do something about. What? First of all, it's mine. . . . Then again it isn't. . . . It's mine to blow. . . . Then again it isn't — not if I'm worshiping the Giver. . . . What to do? What not to do? *(Malachi 1:6; 14; 3:8-10)*

worshiping with the church

Life as Worship

Lent is not so much a time in which to give *up* something as it is a time to *give* something. The biggest thing we have to give is ourselves. You could scarcely sell yourself as a slave and give the money to God. But you could consider yourself a slave and give yourself to God.

The Worship Life

We dare not think the task of giving is finished when we have offered our whole self to God. The hardest job is breaking off specific pieces of ourselves and giving them to God or to our fellowmen. That's true about pieces of money, pieces of time, pieces of love. Giving God pieces of love—adoration—is the heart of worship. When we give Him our loving adoration, we acknowledge that He deserves it. That's "the glory due His name." To give that to God is to be worshiping Him. It's tremendously important, because giving God our love is the first step in giving Him our living. If we are not ready to *say* our love for Him, will we be apt to live our love? But if we *say,* "God, I love and adore you," we are taking the first step in practicing what God's Word preaches.

Since "doing our liturgy" is a good way to think about the Sunday service, and that the service is at the central point of our lifelong liturgy, let's think through the opportunities we have to *give* during the service. That would be a good accent during these weeks of Lent. What we do as an offering to God in the hour of worship will be the first step in our work of worship throughout the entire week.

Take *the Preparation,* for instance, on page 15 in *The Lutheran Hymnal.* As soon as we think of it, we say, "That's a place in the service where we *catch!"* Right! The absolution brings us the forgiveness that God has given to all the world through Jesus Christ. The pastor pronounces that Absolution to *us.* That's the forgiveness that changed the world and that changes us.

That's no small change! But now we want to "keep the change," and the only way we really can is by *giving!* We're so apt to be living life as a *getting* process instead of seeing it, and living it, as a *giving* process. The real change begins when we begin to give. And the one to whom we begin our giving is *God!*

We give in the *Invocation*—it's our way of helping one another remember that God is God! He really is! But unless we think the Invocation with the pastor and unless we mean our "Amen" to those words, the reminder might go right past us. It is a reminder—but what's more to the point—it's an opportunity—to *adore.*

How about the *Confession of Sins?* Do we think of that as something we offer God? Or do we think of it as something we do to ourselves? We try to make ourselves feel bad "like a good Christian should"? No. We must of course think through the things we have done wrong, but we should by now have reached the conclusion that we *are* wrong. That's the very person we offer to God. A broken and contrite heart God will not despise. The reason He will accept us is that He *has* accepted us! We know that. We believe that. So in the very act of confessing, we adore! God is no Indian giver. When He gives, He says "Keep the change!" We've got it! Praise Him!

saints and sex

word and work

I

The Proper Point

"Remember, O Lord, Thy tender mercies and Thy loving-kindnesses; for they have been ever of old." These words of the Introit give Reminiscere Sunday its Latin name and give us our start in doing our liturgy. What good does it do to remind God of what kind of a God He is? Can we be sure that He will act as He always has in the past and be loving and merciful toward us? The psalmist thought so. We Christians do, too.

Can God operate on the same principle with us? "Remember, fellows and girls, what kind of persons you are, the children of God, redeemed saints." He remembers, and He expects us to respond. But He's too often disappointed. What's wrong? Our own worst problem is — ourselves. Sunday's Collect includes the confession each of us must make: "O God, who seest that of ourselves we have no strength. . . ."

Both Reminiscere and Oculi Sundays have Epistles aimed right at the saints who sin. These lessons had a special purpose in the early years of the Church. They were directed toward the men and women who were catechumens preparing to join the Church by Holy Baptism on Easter. They speak to us, too, who are using the Lenten Sundays to get the devil on target and fight against him. Even after our Baptism has made us saints in the sight of God we find there is still a sinner inside each one of us. We ought never underestimate the power of the enemy. The guide who knows where the quicksand is in the swamp carefully walks around it. We who realize the terrifying strength of our sinful flesh will be careful to hang on to the strength of God. We'll pray the Collect: ". . . keep us both outwardly and inwardly. . . ."

Sunday's Epistle includes Saint Paul's warning from God to "abstain from immorality." The warning is applied to those who are married and to those who think about getting married sometime. That includes most males and females in the world. But it includes more than the marriage relationship and more than words like "adultery" and "fornication."

It has something to say about holding hands and kissing on first dates. The Phillips translation of the Epistle includes the words, "Every one of you should learn to control his body." Our age has made sex seem so important and sexual sins sometimes seem so unimportant — and *sometimes* so damning. It's hard to see the sinner for the sin. But that's the person we want to see — the sinner in the saint. Once we realize that we too are "grievously vexed with a devil," we will be turning to our Lord and His grace for help.

II

The Right Reaction

St. James says that if a person could control his tongue he would be able to control every other part of his personality *(James 3:2)*. Wouldn't the simple thing be to cut it out? And wouldn't the simplest solution to the control of sex in our lives be to "cut it all out?" *(Matthew 5:27-30*  *)*

Even if such an operation were a "success," the patient would die. A person without sight is not quite the person God had in mind when He created. And a person without sex would not be the person God created. When God created men as "male and female," He put a wonder-

175

ful element into life. We call it "sexuality." That term includes all the differences that sex makes in our living. It's the way mothers feel about children, and the way boys look up to their fathers while growing up. Brothers and sisters, girl friends and boy friends—in almost every relationship in life the fact of our human sexuality adds a new dimension to our living. Sex is one of the Creator's *good* ideas for His people.

Jesus' strong words about "cutting it out" were meant to help men realize how terribly serious our sinning is. It's not just a matter of what we do, however. It's even more seriously a problem of what we *are* (*Matthew 15:19* ). The pharisai-

cal attitude, that thinks by washing one's hands (*Matthew 15:20*) or by not "going all the way" in sexual acts one will be able to stand on his record before God, is what Jesus is condemning.

Our problem is still that the bodies we saints live in are bodies out of control. The devil whom our Lord is fighting in the Lenten Gospels is fighting us, too (*James 3:6*). If our bodies were under control, we would use them in such a way that we give glory to God and do good to our neighbor. If we use sex simply as "a passion of lust" as the Epistle describes it, we are like people who do not know God. Real living is helping others—in terms of our sexuality, too. Our being the best kind of man can help another become a better kind of woman. Being the woman God helps you to be is one way you can help fellows be the men God's Spirit urges them to be. If sex is just a matter of self-gratification, it is sin. God has called us to holiness. This means "set-apartness" for service.

What's the answer to our "sinner-in-saint" problem? Sunday's Gospel describes how a mother kept begging and begging Jesus to help her daughter. "A devil has got into her!" she cried. Finally Jesus told her, "You certainly don't lack faith! It shall be as you wish." At that moment her daughter was cured. She was a Canaanite woman. Jesus was still working out God's Old Covenant plan by showing His grace to the Hebrew people. But He was moved by her faith in His grace. Now God's forgiving grace and His powerful Spirit have been poured out on His Church; God gives His Spirit to those who ask! (*1 Thessalonians 4:8*)

worshiping with the church

Life and Worship

God has certainly followed through on His good ideas of creation. He has redeemed us, body and soul. He has made *our bodies* the temple of His Holy Spirit. This means that sexual drives, from holding hands to being married, can be acts of worship. But not by themselves — by *ourselves*. We must put ourselves into every act of worship. And we must do the serving of God "in our bodies which are God's."

The Worship Life

Thanksgiving and supplication are major movements in our *giving* acting in the liturgy. Both are part of our worship action while the Introit is chanted. In the Kyrie and Gloria we are supplicating, but we are also giving. We ask what we do in the Collect because our thankful hearts know God will hear and help. As we hear the Epistle we give thanks that God has "called us to holiness." Where He calls, He supplies the help we need to answer!

41

GOD'S CALL IS TO PURITY

What is your first reaction when you see a person staggering down the street? "Drunk"? There's a person who "isn't in control of his body" to use the idea of last Sunday's Epistle. We think it's shameful, disgraceful. But we don't particularly worry about him. "He'll sleep it off. Tomorrow he'll be all right except for a hangover."

Sometimes our diagnosis can be all wrong and our prescription a tragic mistake. Some people have diabetes and carry a card imprinted with these words: "If I am uncon-

scious or my behavior is peculiar, I am not intoxicated—I am diabetic. Call a doctor or emergency hospital." *This* kind of staggering is much more serious. Letting a diabetic try to "sleep it off" will probably mean his death.

It is a matter of life or death that we be able to recognize when our conduct is *sin*. "Staggering" would have been a word to describe us when as little children we tried to see how many times we could spin around before we were so dizzy we would fall down. The child has fun; the drunk does wrong; the diabetic dies. All three stagger. We must be able to recognize sin when we do it. If we pass off sinful acts as something that "everybody does," if we try to "sleep off" sin, we're doomed to death.

The way of life is not reached, of course, when we correctly identify our sin as sin. For years doctors recognized diabetes, but there was nothing they could do about it. When insulin was discovered, it proved to be a miraculous means for controlling the disease. We can really begin to *live* by God's curing power, more wonderful than insulin. He enables us to bring our bodies under control. The sinfulness—like the crippled pancreas of the diabetic—is still there; but we *live* in spite of it. We live God's life given by the Spirit. This new life is not just a matter of taking in forgiveness every so often. We live when we avoid the sin, just as the diabetic really begins to live when he admits he needs a special diet and follows it. We really begin to live when we accept the new forgiven life God gives and by the Holy Spirit follow God's call to purity.

WORÒ anÒ WORK

I
The Proper Point

Are we ready to look back at last Sunday's Epistle and forward to next Sunday's and think about holiness and the Holy Spirit? *(1 Thessalonians 4:3 ✠; Ephesians 5:1-2 ✠)*

God's will is our sanctification, our holy living. He wants us to imitate Him, our Father, as beloved children. St. Paul gives us information about "how we ought to live and to please God." The code word is "love"—"Walk in love, as Christ loved us and gave Himself up for us, a fragrant offering and sacrifice to God."

These Epistles warn us to recognize *sin*. They concentrate on sins that are connected with sex. That is probably because the sexual drive is one of the strongest forces in our lives. Sex is one of God's good ideas for His people, but the disease of sin has made it terribly easy to turn it into bad thoughts and bad acts. Our troubles multiply because advertisers and writers and motion picture producers know how strongly sexuality influences us. They use sex to sell. Even when we don't buy, their advertising sticks in our minds like a singing commercial. We may really think it terrible, but we can't keep from humming it to ourselves.

Our job is to recognize the difference between God's good idea and sin's bad thought.

The ruler with which to measure our acts is suggested in *Ephesians 5:1-2.* What we do should be done "in love" — and that means "done for others and offered to God." Do we agree that St. Paul suggests that? Then we could use that measure with the things mentioned in these two Epistles and see how such acts fall short of the goal of "our sanctification." What about those in *1 Thessalonians 4:1-8?* "Immorality, take a wife, passion of lust, uncleanness." And in *Ephesians 5:1-9?* "Impurity, covetousness, filthiness, silly talk, levity." All the modern words too can be measured by the rule of "Does it help others? Does it honor God?"

II
The Right Reaction

God's cure is greater than our sin-damaged body. God forgives all sin. God's Spirit is ready to help all men repent, that is, to turn away from their sin and live. And that means "live right." All of us need to take in God's forgiveness day after day. But we want to follow the diet God gives, too. We want to follow God's call to purity. We want to live in manliness and womanliness that helps others be God's woman and God's man.

This is not an impossible goal. (*1 Thessalonians 4:8b; 1 Corinthians 6:11* and *19-20* ✠; *Ephesians 4:22-24* ✠). The Holy Spirit, who *is* holy, *makes* holy as well!

Life as Worship

One doesn't learn to control his body overnight. That's especially true when one's body seems to be changing week after week into something totally different from the body to which one had become accustomed. But the change is wonderful. We become men and women — almost like magic. That means we are becoming even more useful to God and to one another. Keeping your body pure and "treating it with respect" is an act of worship when you do it for God.

The Worship Life

Can we still give God our worship when we "stagger" and dishonor the body He gave us? Be courteous enough to accept Him at His word! He promises to forgive all those who will accept His love. His Spirit urges us to turn back to God and begin again. His Spirit helps us to "go and sin no more." Even when we "sin more" His grace "doth much more abound." Every day in every liturgy, give to God your honest confession. He will give full absolution. Thank Him for that each time you hear the holy Gospel. Adore and thank the Creator who made you with your kind of body, whenever you confess the Creed. Sunday after Sunday keep offering your body to His service as in the Offertory you ask for a clean heart and a right spirit.

42

GIVE SOMETHING
DIFFERENT THIS YEAR

"Is there a *difference?* The difference between day and night, that's all!"

Would people say that about our lives? Could they? Are our lives different from the lives of those who aren't Christians? Next Sunday's propers give us a great opportunity to think about *the different life.* Worship is something that we give to God. Our entire lives are to be worship. That means we are to give our lives to God. We ought to give something different—not only this day, but every day; not only some things, but everything we do!

word and work

I
The Proper Point

Sunday's Epistle at first strikes us as being *against* things—it warns us about things that are "not fitting among saints." Actually it is *for* almost as many things. We like to concentrate on a few negatives. Then, if we can keep from doing them, we feel "good." But the strong Christian life concentrates on the positives. That's a much harder way to live, because there's never any end to doing good. But that's the Christian way of living. For the Christian there is no Law. He lives by the Gospel. And that's the stress of *Ephesians 5:1-2* ✠ , the first verses of Sunday's Epistle.

The Gospel for next Sunday warns us not only to spring-clean our life but to refurnish it. "Nature abhors a vacuum" is an old saying. But Satan loves it. If our lives are "vacuum clean," all kinds of evil can rush in. If the time of our lives is filled with deeds that the good Spirit of God enables us to do, evil is crowded out.

Both Epistle and Gospel speak of the kingdom of God. The kingdom of God is not a matter of boundaries ("That's the edge of the Kingdom everybody on this side is in; on that side is out.") It's not a matter of having paid taxes ("Pay up and you're a citizen"), or of registering ("If your name is on the book, you can vote"). The Kingdom is the rule of God. When God is ruling your life, you're in the Kingdom. Through Christ God moved right into our lives. The Kingdom exists inside of us when the Spirit of God gives the orders and

directions for our living. We're subjects of the King when we begin to *want* to live the different life. That kind of people really pray Sunday's Collect.

II
The Right Reaction

Take the last verse of the Gospel. Mix well with *John 8:31-32* ✠ . Meditate with *John 8:34-36*. Pour into your mind to mold it.

We remember that the Word of God always has the thought of the work of God mixed into it. The words Jesus spoke were always working changes in people. They either moved people to call Jesus a partner with the devil, or they moved them to call Him Lord! Those who wouldn't hear His word, who wouldn't continue in His word, became more and more the slaves of sin. But those who were ready to hear and to continue became really *free!* They came to

the point that they fell on their knees and cried, "My Lord and My God!"

After that there was no longer any argument. They were God's. They were in the kingdom of His Christ. Their wills were in agreement with His will. They were free, because they could do whatever they wanted to do. What they wanted to do, even though they didn't always manage to do it, was what God wanted them to do. A famous father in the Church once said, "Love God — and do what you please."

Jesus Himself is the only really free Man who ever lived. He was the Word — He really continued in God's Word. He could meet publicans and prostitutes, lepers and national leaders, those who were wealthy and those who were poor, friends who were men and friends who were women — and never sin. Would Saint Paul have had to write next Sunday's Epistle to Jesus? Jesus knew the will of God and wanted what God wanted.

We are not quite free because we do not quite love God. We are not always ready to "let go and let God." The old Adam in us still *wants,* and sometimes we forget that we are *new men,* and that the real *we* wants God's will. That's why we need to read the Word of God two ways. Try it. Read Sunday's Epistle as you would read the riot act to the old Adam. Find the Sixth, the Seventh, the Eighth, and the Ninth and Tenth Commandments in it. Then read the Epistle to the new man. Read it as a reminder to love God and do as you please.

We have been made free because God forgives even when we forget. He has given us His Spirit so that we can give ourselves to Him. That's worship. He made us different so that we can give Him something different this year, this day!

184

Life as Worship

Often when we sin it is because we have forgotten what we really *want* to do. We let the old Adam in us cry out his lusts instead of letting the new man remind us what we really want. We will find that one thing helps us. If we *tell* God how we love Him — that is our worship life — we are at the same time telling ourselves what we really want. Kneeling to adore God is the best start for running the race for Him. It's like a sprinter's crouch before the starting gun. That's why we begin the day with adoration. Then we can live the day practicing the presence of God.

The Worship Life

When our Lord *gives* us His body and blood in the Holy Supper, our first action will be to accept His gift. But that means we *do* something. We *give* to God our willing obedience to what He told us to do. One of the reasons He wanted us to celebrate His Last Supper was that it would *bring to mind* all that He did for us, all that He said to us — His *Word*. He wanted us to "continue in His Word." One of the reasons some people are reluctant to commune is that they don't want the Lord so close to them, right inside their minds. But if we really want to offer to God *a different life,* there's nothing more helpful than to receive that real presence of our Lord through the Sacrament into our living. When we kneel at His altar, it's the sprinter's crouch again. The strength is from Him, whose body and blood we receive. But from our hearts our love is given to God. When we give our love to Him, we have made the first step in "doing what we please."

43

the transformed life

We are seldom aware of how many times in every day voices tell us what to eat, what to wear, what to do. The worst part of it is that we find ourselves listening. Instead of living our way, Christ's way, we find ourselves imitating everyone else. Instead of imitating Christ, we copy the world.

Listen to this conversation in Mexico between Don Cipriano Viedma and Kate Leslie in D. H. Lawrence's *The Plumed Serpent*.

"When you say you are free, you are *not* free. You are compelled all the time to be thinking U. S. A. thoughts — *compelled,* I must say. You have not as much choice as a slave. As the peons must eat tortillas, tortillas, tortillas, because there is nothing else, you must think these U. S. A. thoughts, about being a woman and being free. Every day you must eat those tortillas, tortillas. — Till you don't know how you would like something else."

"What else should I like?" she said, with a grimace at the darkness.

"Other thoughts, other feelings. — You are afraid . . ."

It could be a conversation between any one of us and God. Most of us know what else we *should* like — but how many of us are really *free* to think the other thoughts and to value the other feelings that make up *the different life?* How many of us are really escaping from the world's pressure that would make us live conformed lives and really managing to live *transformed* lives day by day?

Our day-to-day decisions make up the answer to those questions. Even more important — when those decisions are added up at the end of our lives, they *demonstrate* whether or not ours was a *transformed life (Romans 12:1-2 ✠; Matthew 25: 31-46).* The final judgment is made on that basis.

WORD AND WORK

I
The Proper Point

In last Sunday's Gospel there are helpful illustrations of the way religious issues are at stake in day-to-day decisions. In the midst of different kinds of people and different kinds of problems, *God took a place* in the person of Jesus Christ. Now that He has done that, every decision must take Him into account *(Luke 11:23 ✠)*. Since God has actually shown Himself in the middle of our life, we do not only marvel *(verse 14)*; it's ridiculous to try to shrug it aside *(verse 15)*; it's deadly to delay a decision. *(Verses 17-23)*

If everyone flunks an exam, the teacher must look at it again. Perhaps it wasn't clear. If no one had recognized God-in-Christ, if no one had discovered how His power could change the way men live, it could be argued that everyone should be excused. But there *is* no excuse today. *(Verses 19-20)*

The Christian life is not merely a matter of being *(verse 25)*; life must always be a matter of doing *(verse 28)*. "Having heard the Word of God, let *us* . . ." That's the way the Confessional Service phrases the suggestion that we all kneel and confess. We should say those words to ourselves whenever we have heard the Word of God. Then we begin to apply it to ourselves. That's where our Lord tells us we should look for the blessing. And keeping God's Word doesn't mean saving. Much more, it means spending! We pass it out to others as we live transformed lives.

II
The Right Reaction

The Word of God is a blessing only if we *keep* it. That is true about Jesus, the Word *(John 3:18-19 ✠; Luke 12:8-9)*. It is equally true about the Word reaching us through our minds. If we don't pay attention to the *reminders* about what's to be done and what's not to be done, we come under judgment. If we don't use the power of God (and the Word of God in our lives really is power) we judge ourselves. We as much as say we don't care; we don't care *for* God nor *about* God, we try to tell off the Holy Spirit. *(Romans 8: 9; 1 Corinthians 3:16 ✠; Romans 8:14 ✠; Luke 12:10-12)*

This is so serious that we are wise to put our lives under the magnifying glass of Lent. In our day-to-day decisions, are we led by the Spirit of God? Or do we do "what *everybody* does"? Or do we do "what *I* think is best"? Sometimes we don't even realize who's pushing us around.

This Lent we should think through how we arrive at our conclusions. What standards do we use to reach our decisions? What influences really move us? What pressures do we bow to and which ones do we reject? Every aspect of our day-to-day decisions has religious significance.

There's quite a tug-of-war going on in life. Conformity and popularity are on one side. Guess who is often pulling on that side!

The transformed life is usually at the other end of the line. There's no need to guess who's pulling for you over there!

Life as Worship

"Practicing the presence of God" really describes the life that lets God say His piece about the everyday decisions that need to be made. We don't control God's presence. He promised to be with us always, and He is. But He is not going to interrupt if we are doing all the talking. One of the ways we practice His presence is by being still to listen to Him. And when we hear Him, the blessing comes in obeying!

In both cases we must *give*—give Him our attention and give Him our obedience.

The Worship Life

The Lord gave us the Holy Communion as an aid to living the transformed life. We are to eat His body and drink His blood "in remembrance" of Jesus Christ. The greatest and most miraculous thing about the Lord's Supper is in what *Christ* gives us—His body and blood.

But He commands us to *do*—we are to eat and drink. That we *do* do is the second part of the miracle. God has transformed us into people who are different, who want to live the different life. It's a miracle when we commune. But it's a miracle that, in a sense, *we* perform; it doesn't get done unless we do it. It is because of the Spirit in us that we can do it, but because of the Spirit *we can* do it. When we do it, we do it because we love God. That makes our communing an act of worship. We do it for God, even while we do it for ourselves. The Eucharist is a Word of God, too. Blessed are they that hear this Word of God—and do it!

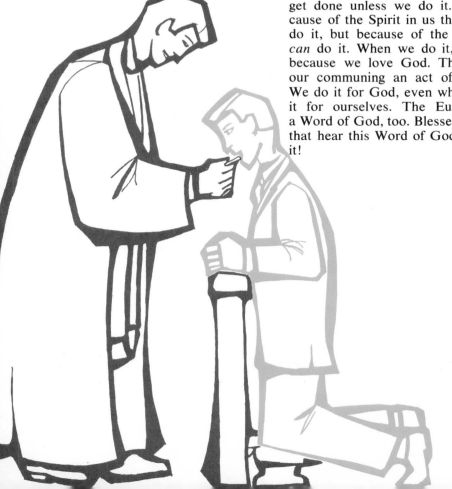

the Lifesaving God

Lent puts us under a continuous strain. We concentrate on living the transformed life, on being different. The more we succeed, the more we realize how much we fail. The Sunday called "Laetare" (Rejoice) is mid-Lent Sunday. Sometimes it is called "Refreshment Sunday" because its propers bring a note of joy to the sober stress of Lent. In England it was called "Mothering Sunday," perhaps from the reference to Jerusalem as "the mother of us all" in the Epistle. On that day children who had left home to set up house for themselves traveled back to visit with their parents. Mothers baked a "mothering cake" for the occasion.

These things give the day a special flavor. But our real need can't be met by a piece of cake or an extra portion of mother love. Our problem is that we realize more and more that we are not being what by God's grace we have become. The good that we would we far too frequently don't, and the evil that we would not, we find ourselves doing again and again. St. Paul summed up our problems in *Romans 7:21-25* ✠ and also pointed out the reasons we have for rejoicing. God is our life-Savior! His life-saving love continually reaches out for us in both the Law and the Gospel. Because of Him—*Laetare!*

word and work

I

The Proper Point

The victory which God gives us through Jesus Christ our Lord is the Gospel, the good news that by His great love He has forgiven us and accepts us as His sons. Because of that adoption we can rejoice. Then what's the trouble? Why are we ever troubled? Isn't it because we don't *deserve* to be loved by God? Of course that's true. The Law of God makes that terrifyingly obvious. The Collect for the day gives us the

chance to be perfectly honest before God: "we, for our evil deeds do worthily deserve to be punished." Yet, why should that make us discontented?

The Collect continues with words that all Christians are ready to pray: "Grant . . . that by the comfort of Thy grace we may mercifully be relieved." All Christians who know of God's undeserved kindness surely believe that their God answers that

prayer with complete relief: with forgiveness of sins and with the assurance that we are still His children.

Then "Why are you cast down, O my soul, and why are you disquieted within me?" *(Psalm 42:5* ✠ *)* Isn't it because *we want to deserve* to be loved by God? It is utterly humiliating to be loved by God on His terms. He tells us frankly that even our righteous deeds are "like a polluted garment" *(Isaiah 64:6).* We want to be loved — but we want to be loved for our own sake. We take another's love as a compliment. It means that in some way at least we are lovable. "But God shows His love for us in that while we were yet sinners Christ died for us." *(Romans 5:8* ✠ *)*

To accept that kind of love requires us first of all to confess that we are "poor, miserable sinners." To admit we need that kind of love is to accept the fact that we are creatures who are completely dependent upon God. Man has been trying to get away from that relationship ever since Adam and Eve first sinned.

That pride of ours is the basic sin. Our own opinion of ourselves is our own biggest problem.

Now watch — see what we begin to do with the Law. In order to avoid admitting what it reveals us to be, lost and condemned sinners, we begin to act as if we could keep it. "Oh, not perfectly. But I try. Surely God doesn't expect more than that." It just doesn't work that way.

We can't change this terrible truth about ourselves made clear by God's law. It is not a mistake to try to do God's will. Our mistake is that we think we can *earn* God's love. But we don't make God fall in love with us. The fact is that in spite of our fall, God loves us.

This mistake is what the Epistle warns us about. We need to know the Old Testament story *(Genesis 16* and *21)* in order to understand St. Paul's point. He uses it as an illustration that Christians should not give up the privilege of being sons of God just to be able to boast that they are first-rate slaves.

We should learn another lesson from the Epistle. Every time we worry that we are not "good" enough to be sons of God we are really doubting the power of God's grace and the extent of His love. We are minimizing the Gospel and mistaking the purpose of the Law.

II
The Right Reaction

St. John tells us how we ought to use the Law and the Gospel *(1 John 1:8-9 ✠)*. When a lifeguard swims out to rescue a drowning man, he sometimes has to hit him in the jaw and knock him unconscious before he can be rescued. That is what our life-saving God is doing for us with His law. He is trying to make us realize how desperate our condition is, in order that we will turn to Him and accept the forgiving love that He has given us through Jesus Christ. What a mistake it would be if a swimmer concluded from that kind of an experience that by hitting himself on the jaw he could swim to the shore. We should learn instead that we can survive even in the deep water of a sinful world, confident that the lifesaving God is continually rescuing us, is always holding us up. *(Deuteronomy 33:27a ✠)*

worshiping with the church

Life as Worship

In the early Church the candidates for Easter Baptism were permitted to remain in the service for the reading and explanation of the Holy Gospel on this Sunday. *Psalm 122* was an especially appropriate Psalm for them to sing. It is for us too, because we know the Gospel and live in it!

The Worship Life

The candidates for Baptism used the Creed on this Sunday for the first time, too. One of the things they were now able to confess was, "I believe in the forgiveness of sins."

We see again that *believing* always includes *doing*. What we catch we give!

That is what every communicant does as he approaches the altar to receive the body and the blood of our Lord. He "shows forth the Lord's death." He testifies that he believes it is most certainly true that by Christ's death he and all men have been given the forgiveness of sins.

But he does not show it only to others. He makes it clear also to himself. That is another reason that participation in Holy Communion is so important. By it a Christian confesses that he is a sinner. By it he preaches to himself that "God is faithful and just and will forgive our sins and cleanse us from all unrighteousness." As a result communing is filled with our worship. When we know that He has given us "forgiveness of sins, life, and salvation" we are filled with thanksgiving. We worship!

living in the forgiveness of sins

How do we think of our lives, especially during Lent as we prepare to celebrate Easter worthily? Is our life to be lived primarily as a struggle not to commit sins? Or are our lives to be lived in the power of the *forgiveness of sins?* Of course we know that God forgives us; but we can't let *that* be the foundation of our life, can we? Or can we?

Won't it be a little like knowing what your own I. Q. score is—once you know you're just an average brain, you'll quit trying to get A's? Or does that bring out exactly the point: God *does not believe in giving grades?* That's not the way He runs His school. He can spot anyone who tries to get "brownie points." Whenever anyone is just working for grades, God will accommodate him—with an F.

"That's all very well—in theory. Everyone ought to study to learn, to make something of himself. But you know as well as I do that grades count." If we think that about studying, what do we think about living, about *living in the forgiveness of sins?*

WORD AND WORK

I

The Proper Point

Perhaps it is unreasonable to expect people to live for something else than grades. But that doesn't mean God wouldn't expect exactly that. *Matthew 11:25-30* is important reading at this point. Use it for background—but then let's look at the Gospel for *Laetare*.

It seems to be a simple story of how the Lord fed 5,000 people in the wilderness. It shows His compassion for people who are hungry. He had said about food and clothing in general, "Your heavenly Father knows that you need. . . ." His point was partly that we should stop worrying. But was that the main point *(Matthew 6:31-33* ✵ *)*? The fact that God looks out for us should make us free to be on the lookout for God. He volunteers for the kitchen work so that we will get involved in the Kingdom work.

The Lord did not come to earth to hand out free food nor to heal the sick. He had a greater purpose *(Matthew 9:2-8)*. Since all the distortions of life—hunger, sickness, death—are the result of sin, He performed miracles that solved problems of hunger and illness. This shows His power to solve all of man's problems. And He did—by the forgiveness of sins!

Can we see the connection? With our sins forgiven, we are freed from the constant burden of trying to *deserve* God's favor. We can live in the forgiveness of sins. It's a very special kind of environment, like being in outer space where gravity's pull has disappeared and the drag of one's weight is gone.

Jesus was using the miracle of the feeding to teach the people lessons about living in the kingdom of God and seeking God's righteousness. (That's about the same thing as *living in the forgiveness of sins.)* Take *John 6:4-5;* add to it *verses 27* and *31-34.* The sum will be the lesson Jesus was trying to teach. But subtract *verses 14-15, 28-29, 35-36,* and *41-42,* because they are the items of unbelief that the people put into the equation.

Now we can put ourselves into the computation. Are we part of the problem or part of the answer? Take *verses 35-40, 43-51,* and *66-69,* add them up, and see if they total your number.

II

The Right Reaction

Look again at *Matthew 11:25-30.* God decided to make His point so clear that children could understand it. He would make it visual and keep it simple. And He did! From manger to cross, including the feeding of the 5,000, it's very clear that God loves us, that He accepts us even though we are sinners. He forgives us!

Jesus Himself revealed that to us about the Father. Thank God we are among those to whom He has chosen to reveal it. (Many people can only say, "I wish I could believe the way you do.") Now Jesus says to us, "Come unto Me—instead of laboring and being weighed down with ideas about deserving God's love. I will

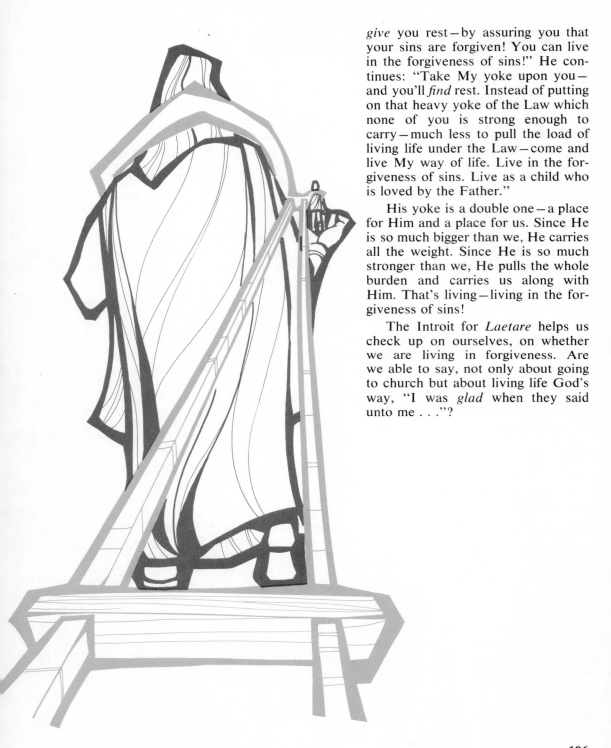

give you rest—by assuring you that
your sins are forgiven! You can live
in the forgiveness of sins!" He continues: "Take My yoke upon you—
and you'll *find* rest. Instead of putting
on that heavy yoke of the Law which
none of you is strong enough to
carry—much less to pull the load of
living life under the Law—come and
live My way of life. Live in the forgiveness of sins. Live as a child who
is loved by the Father."

His yoke is a double one—a place
for Him and a place for us. Since He
is so much bigger than we, He carries
all the weight. Since He is so much
stronger than we, He pulls the whole
burden and carries us along with
Him. That's living—living in the forgiveness of sins!

The Introit for *Laetare* helps us
check up on ourselves, on whether
we are living in forgiveness. Are
we able to say, not only about going
to church but about living life God's
way, "I was *glad* when they said
unto me . . ."?

worshiping with the church

Life as Worship

It isn't much of a compliment to God if we check off things we have done and tell Him, "There, God, I did that for You. Chalk it up on my record." After all, hasn't He made it clear to all His children that He has done all that's necessary? The only life that can really be worship is the life lived in the forgiveness of sins. That life actually adores and thanks God for what He has done. That life confesses it was necessary. That life can ask for the right things — Kingdom things.

The Worship Life

As we read the words of *John 6,* we can understand why the Church included this Gospel in Lent as we approach the remembrance of Christ's last Passover. In His Supper Jesus gives us His body to eat and His blood to drink. "Make it visual and keep it simple" — our Lord did just that. It's miraculous, but any child can believe it. We children of God do.

And therefore we *do this in remembrance of Him.* All that Jesus did for mankind by offering His body and shedding His blood we call to our minds as we commune. We remember *that He is forgiving us now, always.* We can live in the forgiveness of sins! And we do!

forGivinG one another

People who live in the forgiveness of sins must live in forgiveness with one another. It is not only a matter of having similar interests: "I am interested in Jesus Christ; you are interested in Jesus Christ; therefore we have something in common and should be interested in one another." It is more than a "love-Me-love-My-brother" kind of proposition by Jesus Christ: "I love everyone in the whole world; if *I* love those other people, there must be something good about them; and so you should love them, too."

The real point is that living in the forgiveness of sins is living the new life, the life in Christ. It is living in our salvation which has already had its beginning here in time. We are members of the one body (the Church) of which Jesus Christ is the Head. If we truly are—then loving other members of the body is natural to us.

But it does not stop there. That kind of love is God's kind—the kind that puts itself out for every other person. That love put God's Son out of heaven in order to bring the world forgiveness. That love moves us to continuous forgiveness of all those for whom Christ died. We accept those whom God accepts. We do not merely *know* the will of God and what He did for mankind; we have been *changed* by His will and His action. The forgiven forgive!

WORD AND WORK

I

The Proper Point

The Epistle for Judica dramatically pictures Jesus as our High Priest and at the same time our perfect sacrifice. His blood cleanses us from dead works. But the purpose of our forgiveness is not that we should be neutral. With living deeds we should serve the living God. Forgiving other people is something we *do*. It is more than an attitude. It always demands action. If we forgive, we will "give for." By forgiving we do the will of the forgiving God.

The Gospel indicates that the offer of forgiveness is not always a welcome gift. A person must do much more than decide whether or not he wants to accept God's forgiveness; it is first of all a problem of accepting God's opinion of him. When God says, "I forgive you," He also says, "You are a condemned sinner." Unless a man is down on his knees before the holy God and admits this, the offer of forgiveness is insulting to his pride. That's the way some of the "children of Abraham" reacted to Jesus' gospel. What must finally happen to people who throw stones at God and won't let Him forgive them?

II

The Right Reaction

Matthew 18 is required reading for forgiven people who wish to live forgiving lives. In it our Lord tells us what *we* must be like if we would be the forgiven *(verse 3* ✠*)*. He tells us how He feels about the little ones

and the lost ones *(verses 5 and 12-14 [14* ✠*])*. He speaks very vividly of how *we* should feel about them since *He* feels that way about them. We must be very careful not to tempt them to sin *(verses 6-11)*. And we must be even more eager to share the forgiveness of God with them. *(Verses 15-20* ✠*)*

The attitude that must move us is the desire to gain the brother. It is true that when we call a brother to repentance he will hear a judgment against his sin. But we must make sure it is God's judging voice he hears, not ours. In our voice he must hear only the sound of a confessed sinner calling another sinner to confess . . . and be forgiven. *(Matthew 7:1-5)*

There is a limit on forgiveness, but it is God's, not ours *(Matthew 18:21-22)*. That limit is reached with people when stubborn hearts rebel at the accusation of the Law and refuse the forgiveness offered by the Gospel. At this point Christians can do only what their Lord did—withdraw from them *(Matthew 23:37; 7:6; 18:18)*. But even then forgiven people pray for those who need forgiveness. *(Matthew 18:19-20; 7:7-12)*

When we know what it is like to live in the forgiveness of sin, we know what a good thing it is we have to share. When we do not pass along the good thing God has done for us, we show that we have not really entered the forgiven life *(Matthew 18:23-35)*. It is only the Christian, who lives in repentance and forgiveness, who is able to pray the Fifth

Petition of the Lord's Prayer. He knows his own continuous need for forgiveness, and that forgiveness overflows to help the need of his neighbor.

All of this is the task of every Christian, and every Christian needs help to do it. Our Lord sent out the apostles to preach the Gospel and by the Gospel pronounce forgiveness and administer the sacraments of Holy Baptism and the Lord's Supper. St. Paul commanded Titus to ordain elders, or bishops, in every city where there were Christian people *(Titus 1:5, 7).* And that is what Paul did *(Acts 14:23).* Their task is to minister to Christians so that they can better minister to others *(1 Timothy 3:5; Acts 20:28).* Pastor and people are to live in the forgiveness of sins, forgiving one another and sharing God's forgiveness with all the world.

worshiping with the church

Life as Worship

"Forgiveness of sins" is our greatest need if we are to live lives of worship. When we hear that term now, we don't think only of having sins forgiven, do we? We think of living lives in the brand-New-Testament atmosphere of forgiveness! Such lives are continually praising and thanking God—not only in their living but in their forgiving!

The Worship Life

We need all the help we can get! Our Lord knew it. That is a reason for His taking bread and wine and with them giving us His body and His blood, the very body and blood which He offered as a sacrifice for our forgiveness. By His death He secured for us the right *to live in the forgive-*

ness of our sins. By our partaking of His body and His blood, which were given for the forgiveness of our sins, we enter further into the atmosphere of *the forgiven life.*

We do have individual sins that must be forgiven. The pastor our congregation has called to minister to us does exactly that in the Absolution. We may confess our sins to God and to the pastor. When he forgives us it is God's forgiveness that he gives to us. Then we continue in the liturgy to receive the Holy Sacrament, *for the forgiveness of our sins.* That forgiveness means the life in Christ that is ours, the salvation in which we are already living! We can never get enough of that!

There is more than *confession* in our communing. There is also *adoration* and *thanksgiving* because we receive forgiveness of sins, life, and salvation through our Lord's body and blood. We call the celebration the Eucharist, the Thanksgiving. As we kneel beside our brothers at the altar we show our concern for them too, and *supplication* is a part of our worship. Even those who are not yet communicants can think on these parts of the service that belong to the Lord's Supper.

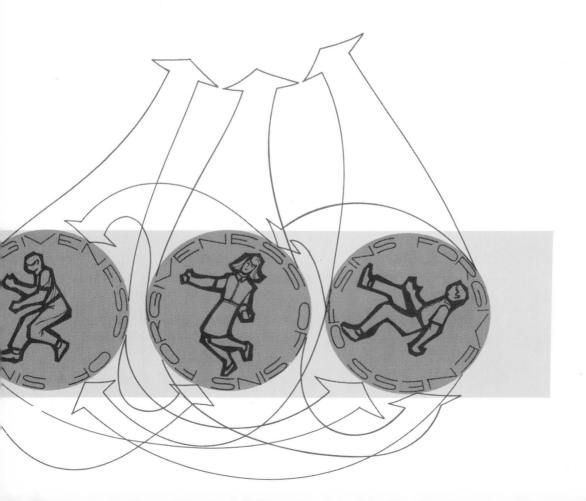

one for all and all together

In Passion Week and Holy Week we want to "remember" our Lord Jesus, who is both our High Priest and the perfect sacrifice for our sins. The Lord's Supper was given to us to do in remembrance of Him. When we eat our Lord's body and drink His blood we vividly remember all He did for us. One for all!

But this is more than recollection. Jesus Christ is present! This "doing in remembrance" means making present *today* what He did *then,* so that we are receiving all that He secured for us by His death and resurrection. It was an amazing thing that God proceeded to give us forgiveness of sins and life and salvation by taking on human nature in the flesh-and-blood-life of His Son. God saved us, adopted us, and gave us new life through the body and blood of Jesus, the Son of God. It is just as amazing that He continues to give us these blessings through the body and

blood of Jesus Christ in, with, and under the bread and the wine in the Lord's Supper. "Given for you." One for all!

"Take, eat. Take, drink." "Whosoever believeth in Him shall not perish but have everlasting life." "He is truly worthy and well prepared who has faith in these words, 'Given and shed for you for the remission of sins.'" Don't forget that for Christians "you" is plural.

"One for all and all for one" — that's the way the saying usually goes. It's true for us, too. We all are *for* the One, Christ Jesus. But it should be clear to us that when our Lord instituted His Supper He wanted us to become more and more "all together." It was a meal for us to eat together. He said, "Divide it among yourselves." *(Luke 22:17)*

"All of you," He said. He gave His life that all men might be reunited with God and might be brothers with one another again. He gave this sacrament, too, to bring about that double communion — with God, and man to man. What He accomplished in the first giving, He also bestows in the sacramental and repeated giving of His body and His blood.

"This is" what the Sacrament offers. "This do" is the direction for our response if we understand "one for all and all together." Remember — "forgiveness of sins, life, and salvation" is a way of life, a way of life together. It describes our way of life with the forgiving God and with the others in the Church who have salvation through His Son.

word and work

I

The Proper Point

What God *did* is what God *does* for us in His Word. The Word is Jesus Christ, the Scriptures, the sacraments. When we remember all this, and are thinking about the Lord's Supper, words from last Sunday's lessons take on added significance *(John 8:47; Hebrews 9:13, 14* ✠*)*. He gave Himself for all. He gives Himself for all.

Look ahead to the lessons for Palm Sunday. We are to have the "mind of Christ" *(1 Corinthians 2:16; 1:10; Philippians 1:27; 2:1-4)*. What our Lord had on His mind *(Matthew 20:26-28* ✠*)* He demonstrated by His entry into Jerusalem. He entered as a king, but He was meek — humble, glad, confident that God was with Him, wanting to do what God wanted Him to do. That is described in the Epistle. It is *this mind* that is to be in us. Those words describe *life as worship*. It is a tremendously big assignment; but it is the kind of life that ends in exaltation!

II

The Right Reaction

The *"this do"* which is expected of us is difficult. We can understand it, but how can we undertake it?

On Thursday of Holy Week, Jesus Christ gave His new commandment, that we should love one another. This is the *mandatum* which gives Maundy Thursday its name *(John 15:12 ✖)*. This is "the mind of Christ" which we are to "have among ourselves." But it is also something *which we have in Christ Jesus (Philippians 2:5).* Loving our neighbor is something we *can* do as well as *should* do since we are His disciples. We can put out the extra amount of friendship that repairs the breach between ourselves and our Christian brothers.

Only one thing can patch up a broken friendship: a real friend who will give an extra amount of friendship to fill up the distance that separates one person from his friend. One of the two who have "broken up" must be ready to forgive—and that always involves his whole self which he must "give for" his friend.

We realize that our friendship with God had been broken when man first fell into sin. But we ourselves have broken off with God time after time when we have deliberately left Him and gone our own way. Now remember what God-in-Christ did to patch up our friendship *(John 15:13;*

10:11 ✖). He gave His body and He shed His blood for His friends. Whoever accepts what He gives accepts the friendship of God once again.

Jesus made all this clear on the night before He gave His life for His friends on the cross. It was on this night that He instituted His Supper. "This is it," He said. "This is My body which is for you. . . . This cup is the new covenant in My blood" *(1 Corinthians 11:24-25).* God makes us His friends. All He did for us is made ours when we believe His *"This is. . . ."*

We are the people who *have* the mind of Christ *(Philippians 2:5).* We can love the other brothers who have been made His in the new covenant of His blood. Since the "this is" has been accomplished, all that remains is the *"This do!" (John 15:14-17)*

But we "have a mind of our own," too. Our Lord knew that. That is one of the reasons He added to the words of institution, "Do this in remembrance of Me. . . . Do this, as often as you drink it, in remembrance of Me" *(1 Corinthians 11:24-25).* When we *do this* we participate in what our Lord has done for us. *(1 Corinthians 10:16 ✖)*

When we *do this* we participate in one another's lives, too. This is "the communion of saints." There is one loaf; we who are many are one body, for we all partake of the same loaf *(1 Corinthians 10:17 ✖).* To get started in loving the brothers by putting ourselves out for others, Christ gives us this clue—*"This do* in remembrance of Me."

"This is" becomes ours as we obey His instruction, *"This do."*

worshiping with the church

God's Word doesn't only speak, it works! It does what it says. The message of Passion Week and Holy Week will build the brotherhood which the deeds of our Lord in those days created. The celebration of the Lord's Supper unites us to one another. Is there any brother who does not want to be drawn into the body?

How could anyone announce his intention *not* to commune? One for all — and all together!

We show concern for our brother when, kneeling at the altar, we intercede for him. Our presence at the altar is a witness to our belief that Christ died for us all.

join the family celebration

When a boy decides to marry a girl he needs to be reminded that he is also marrying her family. They probably won't move in with the new couple, but in-laws are relatively important. All of us have been shaped by our families. Their influence goes on in our lives no matter where we move. The wonderful thing that can happen is for a couple to have two full families, each of which is filled with people they love and who love them.

When we celebrate our Lord's Supper we are rejoicing in the blessings inherited from two sources, from an Old Testament family and a New Testament one. We need to understand the Passover lamb in the Old Testament background. At the same time we join all the generations of New Testament Christians who have gathered around the altar to receive the body and blood of Jesus Christ, "the Lamb of God who takes away the sin of the world."

We ask the same question that Jewish children asked *(Exodus 12:26)*. Before we can understand we must study the answers they received and then go on to learn the answers we get in our day. We wouldn't want it any different, really. God had His people before we became persons. God taught His people to worship before we had hands to fold.

Our task is to understand what is going on in the family of God into which we've been born by Holy Baptism and to fit into it. That's what we've been doing in all these lessons. What we are doing in Holy Week is to see how everything comes to a climax in the death and resurrection of Jesus Christ, and how our Lord shares it all with us in the celebration of the Eucharist!

word and work

I

The Proper Point

As a boy, Jesus probably asked the Exodus question about the Passover, too. He learned fast. By the age of 12 He knew the answers to more than that question. But then He had to live out the connections between the Old Testament and the New Testament.

Some of the important words are in the Easter Epistle, the Maundy Thursday Epistle, and the Good Friday Epistle. The important things our *Lord* did are in the Good Friday and Easter Gospels. The things that *we* should do are taught us in the Maundy Thursday Gospel

II
The Right Reaction

and the Easter Epistle. It all connects up with the celebration of the Lord's Supper. We keep that feast because Christ our Paschal Lamb has been sacrificed for us.

We need to realize that the 12-year-old Jesus deliberately lived out the connection between the Old Covenant and the New. When it was all brought together, He gave us His body and His blood of the New Covenant to eat and to drink "in remembrance." If we don't understand when we're children, He understands. He asked questions as a boy, too. But if there are any who don't *try* to understand, who don't join in the celebration He arranged, He must wonder if they really want to be in the family.

Exodus 24:3-8 and *1 Corinthians 11:23-26* help us connect the two covenants. Jesus deliberately showed the connection when He sacrificed Himself to shed His blood. As Israel was made God's people by the blood of the covenant, so we are made His people by the blood of Christ. *Isaiah 42:1-7* speaks of the Servant of the Lord. *Verse 6* said that the Servant was the covenant in person. Jesus lived out the Servant role as He died and made *Isaiah 52:13* to *53:12* become real for His disciples. By the shedding of His blood He would "bear the sin of many." That blood He gives in the cup of the Supper. *Jeremiah 31:31-34* spoke of Israel's hope for a better life under a new covenant. Jesus made sure that they would see a new covenant coming through His blood, given "for the forgiveness of sins."

Every Christian in the New Covenant inherits the family traditions of the Old Covenant. "Do this in remembrance of Me."

In *1 Corinthians 5:7* we see the deliberate connection our Lord made between the Passover *(Exodus 12: 27)* and His Passion. He went steadfastly to Jerusalem at the time of the Passover. He instituted the Supper at the Passover meal. He fulfilled everything necessary to change us from a slave people to the people of God by His giving of His life on the cross. When the Old Covenant people celebrated the Passover they "became" the people God had brought through the Exodus. When we New Covenant people keep the feast made possible by the death of our Paschal Lamb, we show that we are the people of God.

Moses sprinkled the blood on the people to establish the covenant. Jesus, the Prophet greater than Moses whom God promised, finally came and gave His blood of the New Covenant. Now His people wait for an even greater day *(Matthew 26:29; 1 Corinthians 11:26 ✠)!* He *is* present always—and present at the altar *(Matthew 28:20 ✠).* He is coming again *(Revelation 22:20 ✠)!* Each time we celebrate in remembrance, we rejoice in hope!

worshiping with the church

The Lord's Supper is God's Word made visible to us in the bread and wine. It is Jesus Christ giving us the benefits of His Passion in the body and blood. Forgiveness of sins, life, and salvation! It is one of the ways He is "with us always"—right now. It is God's way of renewing His covenant with us—of making us and keeping us His people. There is more. The food we eat is not merely a lamb that ceremonially connected the Old Covenant people with God; we eat and drink the body and the blood of our Lord. This is a food of eternal life!

Why does the Church celebrate the Eucharist *often?* The Church

found that in the celebration of the Lord's Supper they could best express their worship! When God made present for them again all they "Remembered," they could best adore and thank, repent and pray; they could best accept His absolution and be made strong in faith; they could best witness to one another and express their oneness in Christ. So, Lord's Day after Lord's Day they celebrated "in remembrance." And so do we!

The Eucharist is both a sacra-ment and a service. As a sacrament, God gives Himself to us. But we offer ourselves. This is service. Yet it is God at work.

While we do our liturgy, it is Christ dwelling within us who does it. In our service in the Sunday liturgy, we join ourselves to Christ's offering for all men. We rejoice to know that the Father has already accepted this service. No wonder the Holy Communion is such a joyful service!

209

VOCATION

49

δoing what comes unnaturally

The job our God did for us on Easter should change the way we go at any job we ever have on earth.

It doesn't seem to work that way much of the time. Just to illustrate: compare life to an Easter egg hunt. Are there parallels between the way children gather eggs and the way people go at their jobs? The point of the hunt comes out in shouts: "I've got more than you have!" "I win! I win! I found the most!" "Here's a pretty one. I'm only gathering red ones." "I saw it first. It's mine."

OCCUPATION

WORD AND WORK

I

The Proper Point

"Do I like them—you mean *to eat?*"

If a hungry tramp or an adult who skipped breakfast got caught in an Easter egg hunt, he'd have a different motive. But would his approach be a better way to go at the matter of a lifework? He'd be "doing what comes naturally." Is that enough? A person who really believes in the Resurrection should be doing "what comes unnaturally."

God used His Word to work on us during the Feast of the Resurrection. Did He get the job done? Some children at an Easter egg hunt never think about why they gather eggs. Some parents explain that an egg is a symbol of new life. The Easter egg should remind us that in the enclosed sepulchre the dead body of Jesus Christ came back to life. But their children may fill their baskets and go home again without thinking of the Resurrection. Has *our* celebration of Easter made us more sure that Jesus is actually alive and that we shall live too?

The Easter Gospel is *the Word,* not only a symbol of the word. Rising from the dead is about the most unnatural thing in the world. But not only did our Lord do it, He made it quite clear that resurrection would be for all men *(John 14:19b ✠; John 5:25-29).* He has taught us that we can expect with confident faith that we shall live forever with Him! When a person believes that, he dies differently.

When a person believes that, should he not *live* differently? The Epistle told us so. But it said it realistically. Just as the congregation in Corinth had to excommunicate the proud sinner, so we must purge ourselves of the natural in order to live unnaturally. To believe that right now we have risen to newness of life, seems even more unnatural than our Lord's resurrection. But the Spirit of God is doing, has done, and will do exactly that resurrection miracle to us *(Romans 6:48 ✠; Romans 8:10-11 ✠).* Remember, the Spirit works *in us.* He moves *us* to do. We must "set our minds" to live the risen life. *(Romans 8:1-8)*

Nowhere is that more important than when we try to make up our minds about what we want to do "when we grow up."

II

The Right Reaction

Our "vocation" as Christians is our "calling" by God. Just as Abram's vocation changed the whole course of his life, so our lives should be changed. God changed us from being natural to being unnatural *(Philippians 3:17-21),* and keeps on changing us. Our big job in life is to answer His calling. *(Ephesians 4:1-6)*

Our occupation is usually something that appears to be very natural to men. It's our way of earning our living. It's the things we do with our minds and our muscles to reach a goal. Since our goals as Christians are not the same as those of the natural man, what we do and how we do it should be different as well. But the natural man that is still part of each one of us makes it difficult for us to do what comes unnaturally. We must work at it. Our work is cut out for us both in choosing our goal in life and in the way we set about reaching this goal.

Are there any jobs in the world that a Christian could not take on as a lifework? How about being a slave trader? A Christian couldn't, if he did what comes natural to a slave trader. But what if he went at his work "unnaturally?" What if he bought slaves in order to set them free?

Somebody says, "He wouldn't live long that way," or "He wouldn't get rich that way." Or, "How would he get three meals a day if he went at it that way?" Well, he might not *get* rich, but might he not *be* rich *(Luke 12:16-21)?* That would be a good switch, wouldn't it—not to be interested only in how many eggs he could get into his basket? We ought to have as many Christian slave traders in the world as we possibly can. This is a bit extreme, perhaps, but every job that can be lived unnaturally can be a Christian job. Only when we work at our jobs in an unnatural way are we following our Christian *vocation* in our *occupation.*

worshiping with the church

Life as Worship

Now we're right back to the beginning of this catechism. Our whole life must be worship. When we do things unnaturally we are living our liturgy. If we are alive, we are doing things. Whatever we are doing *now* is our occupation. Our vocation must affect the way we undertake our occupation. Is your calling affecting your living right now? In the Sundays after Easter let's see how doing our liturgy helps us to *live*.

The Worship Life

Remember the way we talked about the diver who climbs up the steps to the high board, then dives, and then swims back to the ladder to dive again? The *whole* process is part of being a high diver.

But if we are to live a life as worship, we must be faithful in our worship life. Every Sunday as we *do our liturgy,* we are getting the necessary height to be able to dive into our work and *live our liturgy*. We have reached the high point of our Christian faith in the celebration of Easter. We'd better pay attention to the way we stroke and the way we kick every day of our lives or else our high dive will just mean that we are going under. God is always faithfully standing by with His life preserver of the Word, but He's hoping that we are learning to *swim!*

the work of ministry

50

How we do what we do reflects our sense of vocation. But what we do in *itself* is often part of our call. God calls some of His people to special tasks. He tells them quite specifically, "This is what I want you to do." A man is a bit foolish to try to tell God what he ought to be called to do *(Mark 10:35-40)*. But God can shape even our mistakes to help us learn the real meaning of ministry *(vv. 41—45)*. When God calls us, even though we are young, we should have the right answer. That answer is "Yes." *(Jeremiah 1:6-8; Isaiah 6:8-9)*

Translators of the Bible sometimes have troubles with punctuation. The old manuscripts don't always make clear where the commas go. In *Ephesians 4,* should there be a comma after "saints" in *verse 12?* A comma means a pause. Should the saints be equipped "for the work of ministry, for building up the body of Christ," or should the saints be equipped and then allowed to pause while the apostles, prophets, evangelists, pastors and teachers do the ministering?

Actually the issue doesn't hang on that passage. Every Christian is called by God to minister. But we should carefully study the grace that has been given to us to enable us to do what God wants us to do. Some of us will discover that God has called us to be "evangelists, pastors, or teachers" *(Ephesians 4:7 and 11)*. Our "Yes" to God's call will mean for us lifework in some phase of the Church's activity.

word and work

I

The Proper Point

Life is simple for a newborn baby. All it needs to do is to eat and sleep. That's what we think. It's true that a baby doesn't have to make decisions about a job, but psychologists say he must learn more in the first years of his life than in any other comparable period in his life. He's working. The way he wants his milk shows how hard! The Introit which gives next Sunday its name (the Latin words for "As newborn babes") tells us as "risen-with-Christ" Christians to make sure we get enough of the one food that enables us to do our ministry.

The Epistle spells out exactly what a man needs in order to "live." No one is born alive in that sense. God must give a man a second birth. What it is that means "life" for a man is described very clearly in the last verse of the Gospel, too.

All this has something very definite to say about the special ministries to which God calls some of His children. *Romans 10:14-17 (17*  *)* and *1 Corinthians 1:18-25* help us see how important in God's plan is the ministry of the Word. The Gospel for Quasimodogeniti shows how important Jesus regarded it that Thomas should say "Yes!" to His

215

call. He promised a special blessing to those who believe without seeing.

Those who preach the Word help bring that blessing to God's people. Those who are freed from other work to be able to do this work with the Word as a vocation are greatly blessed and are great blessings.

II
The Right Reaction

It is always difficult for a person to be sure to which task God is calling him. Yet we can expect that God wants us to do those things for which His gifts make us best suited. Check up on yourself. 1. Ask God for help. 2. Study yourself. 3. Use aptitude tests. 4. Discuss yourself and your problem with counselors, parents, pastor. 5. Read about different job opportunities. 6. Talk to people who are doing the kind of work that interests you. 7. Try to get part-time work in the kind of job that interests you.

What if God wants to call you into the special ministry of the Church?

Would you expect Him to make the call as clear as if you heard Him talk, or saw Him in a vision? Or would it be sensible to apply the same checklist to this possibility?

If God does want you as a pastor, a teacher, deaconess, or any other church-related task, when does He expect you to get ready? If a man is going to be a doctor, he can't wait until he's ready to get to work and then just *be* one. It takes years of training to be a doctor. That's true about the special ministries, too. It's not only a matter of deciding on schools and courses of study. There are things involved that are even more important. *(Titus 1:5-9; 1 Timothy 3:2-12)*

The things that should be done to prepare for the special ministries are the same things that every Christian needs to do to be ready for his ministry. That says something to each one of us, doesn't it?

If a man has a chance to do a job for God, a chance really to be a big help to his fellowman, should he take it? *(1 Timothy 3:1; 2:20-22)*

worshiping with the church

Life as Worship

Practice makes perfect. Ministering makes ministers. In doing the things God wants us to do, we are being prepared to be the people God wants us to be. If we live our lives as worship in what we are doing now, we will be ready to make our occupation a real vocation.

The Worship Life

The Sunday after Easter is sometimes called "Low Sunday." For us it ought to be as high a day as Easter, for every Sunday celebrates Easter. Remember, the things that make a Sunday great are the things that God does. When He raised Jesus Christ from the dead, that was a great day! When He gives us the same Spirit that raised Jesus from the dead "to quicken our mortal bodies," that's a great day. When the same Word that created the worlds and became man comes into our lives, that's a great day. All that's necessary for any Sunday to be high day is for us to climb up the ladder of opportunity and *do our liturgy!* For in the divine service God does to us great things.

When we deliberately dive we make a definite beginning in living. When we worship God with our offerings, for instance, we are very practical. We collect money to help others. The first step in living for others is at the very center of our worship.

the family of god worships

When is a person ready to strike out on his own? Parents have a rough time deciding that teen-agers are able to manage their own affairs. Between "Act your age" and "Wait until you're grown up" the teens find a terribly irritating tension. In the midst of all the forces trying to break the family bond and the other forces that knot the apron strings, home life sometimes seems like the inside of a boiler at high pressure.

Note 1. The Christian family is actually the Church under a certain roof. We could make a neat little list of the things which we expect should happen in the Church which should therefore also happen in the family. Let's make that list!

2. Even after He had been with His disciples for 3 years, Jesus concentrated 40 days more of visible appearances on making sure that they would remember. That wasn't all, of course. There was the Supper which He had told them to do "oft, in remembrance." And He added another thing, "Lo, I am with you always," before He ascended. We could add some comments to our list as to what's important for a family Church if it is to remember and be the Church. Let's!

word and work

I

The Proper Point

How many lists have included "family worship?" If we have it listed, let's look at it critically. Just what purpose do we see it serving? What kind of form do we have in mind as we propose it? Have we thought it through, or do we list it because we're always told we *ought to?*

Last Sunday's Gospel suggests that it is important for us to be in Christ's company if we are to be His disciples. But seeing is not needed for believing. The blessing is in believing. Anyway, that choice is not ours to make. Since the Ascension our Lord has withdrawn His visible presence. Now the Spirit is our Counselor, to bring to our minds what our Lord did and said, to fortify us with His companionship (that's comfort!), and to guide us into all truth.

But where does Bible reading come in, for instance? We stress that as an important part of family devotions. How much were the Jews accustomed to read the scrolls? Did Jesus write anything? How many years went by before the Spirit guided an apostle to write a book of the New Testament? Before there were Bible books, or when people didn't have them in their homes, what kind of a pattern existed for family devotions?

That should stir up something. Now mix in the accent of *verses 30* and *31* of *John 20*, last Sunday's Gospel. Add to it the *11th verse* of *1 John 5*, the Epistle. It would help to attach *verse 13* to that addition. If we have a good thing, certainly our pattern need not be based on a time when they didn't have it. We use electric lights to help us see, even if early Christians didn't have them.

The opening words of the In-troit seem to remind us of the im-

portance of intake in our devotions. Also *1 Peter 1:23-25* (✠) tells us something about how God worked on us to give us new life. Then *1 Peter 2:2* (✠) urges us to desire "spiritual milk." Try *John 8:31-32* (✠). What does this say about using the Scriptures in family devotions? *Psalm 81:8* is the source of the Introit's second line. How does it chime in? But now check out *Psalm 81:1*, the last line. What does it suggest to us as family, as Church under one roof, as people thinking about family devotions?

II
The Right Reaction

This would be a good time to look back at the opening chapters of this catechism. Lesson 8 especially helps us to see that "worshiping makes worshipers." The family that wants to *be* the Church together will stress worshiping together. They will remember the relationship of the "catch, give, share, and live" forces in worship. Sunday will be the day to do their liturgy, both those who commune and those who look forward to communing.

Every week's time will be time that fits into the scheme of the church year. Each week will live out the liturgy and the labor of the Sunday before and express the accent of the season. Each member of the family will remember the "Well begun is half done" theory that urges us to "think God" the first thing in the morning. The practice of His presence is part of every Christian's life. But each member will see times of family worship as times to "share."

The Epistle reminds us that the testimony of God to Jesus as His Son and our Savior is within us *(1 John 5:9-10)*. We can bring it out. We can discuss it, apply it, ponder it. And we can deepen and correct and grow in our knowledge through the Scriptures God has inspired for our use *(2 Timothy 3:14-17* ✠*)*. Then every period of family worship will obey *Psalm 81:1-5*. Each time we gather together we will rejoice because of God's great promises to us in Jesus Christ. *(Matthew 18:19-20* ✠*)*

worshiping with the church

Life as Worship

We need not wait for a Sunday or a church service in order to worship with the Church. The Church is the people of God, and the people of God worship. Our goal is only partially stated if we say that we want to have family worship. What we really want the Spirit of God to do is to help us be the Church together in our house.

This is the time to talk through ways we can arrange the worship which helps us be the Church in our house.

The Worship Life

Life for God in the family at home and among men in the world begins with lively worship with the family of God in the liturgy at church. Take the General Prayer, for instance. Sometimes it is called "the prayer for all sorts and conditions of men." Actually no prayer can include that much. But the words of a corporate prayer are only tracks and cars on which we load the specific freight of our petitions and move them to God. The cues for praying about *our* family needs and those of people in other parts of the world are certainly there.

Could we possibly be asking God to do something about them without intending to follow through ourselves?

221

52

a matter of death and life

The resurrection of Jesus Christ affects everything we are and do. Some people in His day on earth thought of His death as just another criminal's crucifixion. They paid no attention to the rumors of His coming to life again. But that matter of His death and life is a matter of life and death for every man in the world.

We believe that by His death all the guilt of our sins has been forgiven and that by His resurrection God has assured us that we can live before Him as forgiven children.

We think of His death and life as guaranteeing us the good life. Ought we not also think about how it guarantees us a good death?

Taken in their chronological order, this is the way the different "lifes" and deaths fit together: His life, then His death, then His life again; our life, then our death, and then our life with Him eternally. It would be short-sighted for us to be concerned only about our first life part. There's a matter of *death* and *life* still to be reckoned with.

word and work

I

The Proper Point

Misericordias Domini means the goodness of the Lord, the steadfast love of the Lord. That's the Vulgate, the King James Version, and the Revised Standard Version. However you translate it, the earth is full of it *(Psalm 33:5b* ✠*)!* The Introit tells us to do something about it!

This is a good example of how the Introits often urge us simply to *worship,* without setting any kind of theme for the day. "Praise befits the upright"—that's reason enough *(Psalm 33:1* ✠ *)*. Sometimes the

voices of the other propers set a theme for the day.

The Epistle and the Gospel for next Sunday show several accents. The "Good Shepherd" idea merely serves as an illustration. *John 10: 10b* and *15b* bring together the most important thoughts, and they can all be summed up in the words "life" and "death." Whenever we think about the very heart of the "steadfast love of God" we think about what He did for us through our Lord's death and life.

222

Since we are such practical people, we usually ask, "What shall we do about it?" The Epistle is really the reason which the apostle gives for what we should do about it. Then *1 Peter 2:11-20* gives specific directions. That would be one of the themes Christians could contemplate on Misericordias Domini Sunday. It would be a stress on the first *life* part of the chronological scheme of our existence: life, death, life.

The Collect suggests that we should have another dimension in our thinking as we worship. What our Lord did for us to make this life a time for rejoicing, He also did for the future life. He took the sting out of death to make us partakers of *eternal* life. Every Christian thinks about his own death and resurrection whenever the Easter Gospel is preached.

The Gradual brings it all to our minds again. It reminds us that we too, like the Emmaus disciples, will

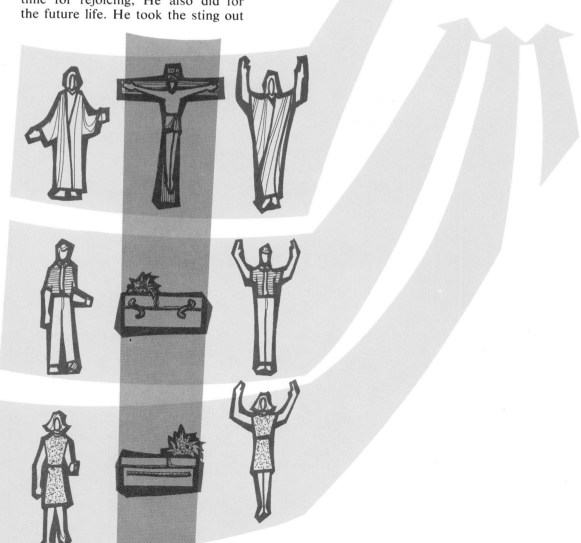

come to the end of our journey, to eventide. The Jesus Christ who made Himself known to them in the breaking of bread is present with us, too, in the Sacrament. He knows us. He will give us eternal life! In these weeks after Easter the matter of our death and *life,* eternal life, ought to be at the top of our thinking list.

II
The Right Reaction

How about planning your own funeral, right now?

Would that be fun?

Should it be? Not for fun in the funny sense, but fun in the "rejoice in the Lord, O ye righteous" sense. That "befits" us!

There are a few basics that must be decided on first of all. Dying, that's one. Before we can plan our funeral, we must plan on our dying. If God would let you know that your dying day was set for next week Tuesday, what would your reaction be? *(2 Timothy 4:6-8 and 18; Romans 8:31-39 [38-39 ✠])*

How about tears? Where does sorrow come into a Christian's death? *(1 Thessalonians 4:13-18; John 11:33-37 [25-26 ✠])*

What arrangements would you make for the funeral? In church? Funeral home? How about flowers? Would you like an expensive coffin? What about giving your body for medical research, or your eyes for the blind? Cemetery lot? Cremation?

Is a funeral service a time for a sermon? Write your own. *1 Corinthians 15* is a chapter that has so much to say about our joy in the day of dying that a whole class could select different texts and each one could sketch out his own sermon.

Of course arranging for the funeral is only the beginning. How about planning for after death when the matter of *life* comes up again? Of course that is really something God will take care of. We'll think it through in the next lesson. But it would be interesting if each member of the class would put down what he thinks life after death will be like.

woRshipinG with the chuRch

Life as Worship

"Rejoicing in the Lord" should be our way of life. If we are confident that our Lord has saved us and has great things in store for us, nothing should frighten us. The thought of our own death should make us happy, and the thought of the death of loved ones should make us happy for them.

It doesn't always work out that way. Satan always tries to frighten us, and death is a terrible thing that sin and Satan brought into the world to spoil God's creation. We can expect the thought to be difficult to live with. There is a way to find strength and peace of mind—in the worship life.

The Worship Life

Someone has said that the best way to prepare for the death of our loved ones is to give them to God every day. After we adore God when we awake, we might commit our loved ones to Him. We thank Him for giving them to us to live with so far. We ask His blessing for them. But we say, "They are Yours, God. We're glad they are Yours. Your will be done with them and in their lives and in their deaths." That's practice for the time when He takes them to Himself. It's practice for the time when He takes *us* to Himself, too. Each celebration of our Lord's Supper marks this hope until He comes.

The time to learn to live with death is while you are still alive. Like now.

"i make all things new"

Have you ever tried to draw something that looks "like nothing on earth?" Even if your drawing has no resemblance to any creature man has seen, in order to explain it you must say, "This is its head, its mouth, its eyes." We can't imagine anything totally unlike anything we've ever known.

That's our problem when we try to think what life will be like after death, too. God knows our problem. He helps us by describing the conditions of our eternal life in human terms. But we must be on guard so that we don't think, "That's exactly the way it's going to be," instead of thinking, "Oh, it will be *like* that."

Take what the Scripture tells us about the fate of our earth, for instance. *2 Peter 3:10* ✠ tells us about its destruction. *2 Peter 3:13* ✠ points us to a new earth. "Heaven and earth" are what God created in the beginning *(Genesis 1:1)*. They will "pass away." *(Luke 21:33; Hebrews 1:10-12)*

But in *Romans 8:18-25* St. Paul speaks about all of creation awaiting deliverance from the bondage of sin. This word picture says the world as we know it now will indeed pass away. But it will then be a new world. The pictures drawn for us in *Isaiah 65:17; 66:22; 2 Peter 3:13;* and *Revelation 21:1-4* help to darken the lines of Paul's picture. But the language makes clear that it is still only a picture. God has not decided to make the future any clearer than that.

Phillips translates *Romans 8:19:* "The whole creation is on tiptoe to see the wonderful sight of the sons of God coming into their own." That's the way we should feel. — To be with our God for ever and ever! One of the ways we help ourselves live as God's people on earth is to think about what life will be like in heaven. Get up on tiptoe. Look!

WORD and WORK

I

The Proper Point

A good way to begin is to pray the Collect for last Sunday. Note what we say about the wonderful things God has done: "Who by the humiliation of Thy Son didst raise up the fallen world . . . those whom Thou hast delivered from the danger of everlasting death." Now see how we ask Him to help us look and run to what He has in store for them that love Him.

II
The Right Reaction

We don't look clearly at the eternity after death unless we realize the possibility of eternal damnation. *Matthew 25:46* and *John 3:36* ✠ make it plain that hell is as certain as heaven. Man will not disintegrate. He will live forever. God will not force a person to live with Him forever. It is necessary that there be a place for those who want to be without God. That place is hell. And *2 Thessalonians 1:9-10* tells about the "exclusion from the presence of the Lord." We know that would be a terrible way to live.

But we know many people who live that way now and don't seem to mind it. People choose to live without God, and after the Judgment Day, God grants them their wish. If after all He has done through Jesus Christ and the work of the Spirit, they still prefer to live without God, what can God do? He makes room for them in the place He provided for the angels who sinned.

But now think about being "partakers of heavenly joys"! If we've taken care of our funerals, we're ready to prepare for heaven. Before we begin, take a moment to remember what a blessing it is that "through Jesus Christ" we can think so calmly about what awaits us. The "should not perish" of *John 3:16* is as great a blessing as the "have eternal life." What manner of love the Father has given us!

There are two ways eternity can begin for a man. In *1 Corinthians 15:35-50* we read about those who are dead and buried by Judgment Day, and *1 Corinthians 15:51-53* tells about those who are still alive on that day. But in either case, read *verses 54-57* ✠. While *you're* waiting for one or the other, read *verse 58*.

The Bible uses the word heaven as if to describe a place. But do the words speak of a place like the earth, or are they trying to help us understand something we've never experienced *(Matthew 5:12; 6:20; 1 Peter 1:4; Mark 16:19)*? We use the language of *Revelation 21:10-27* to speak about heaven, but we know that no human words can really describe what that life will be like.

1 John 3:2-3 and *Philippians 1:23* ✠ suggest additional helpful words to use as we try to describe how wonderful it will be. It is good to read *2 Corinthians 5:1-10* while we're waiting for the time when we are made "partakers of eternal joys!"

Worshiping with the Church

Life as Worship

"So whether we are at home or away, we make it our aim to please Him." *(2 Corinthians 5:9* ✠ *)*

The Worship Life

In every Communion liturgy we say "with angels and archangels and with all the company of heaven." When we are in heaven we will join our praises with the angels and all the faithful whom God has raised up to eternal life. We look forward joyfully to that time.

This is a great anticipation in our

every participation in the Holy Communion. Our Lord ended the first Supper with words that promised He would join us in the meal "When the Kingdom comes." What a celebration that will be! "Even so, come, Lord Jesus!" While we wait, while we rejoice in His certain coming, we celebrate His present presence. He promised to be with us and His real presence even now gives us life and salvation!

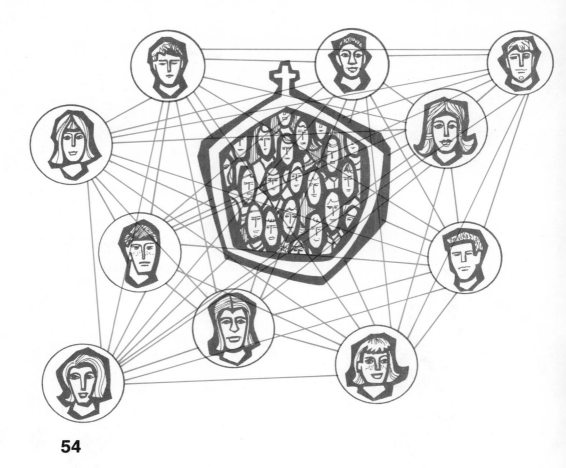

54

looking after one another

You can't be human alone. It's not too important to know that this is a title of a book. It is important to know it is true about your living. Crowded cities, crowded schools, crowded homes make us think we could be more human if we could just be alone for a while. We are sometimes tempted to make "Help stamp out people" our motto.

But when we go away from home for the first time, or when we move to a new city, or go to a new school, then we realize we're enlisted in humanity. We're in the human race, and it's no race if you're running alone. Robinson Crusoe had nothing on us when he tried to figure out his feelings on seeing a human footprint in the sand.

If we are to live worshipful lives, we must be aware of our involvement with one another as human beings, and of our special needs and opportunities to help one another in the Church.

WORD AND WORK

I

We're made for each other and we're stuck with each other. It's easy to think of both of these expressions as partly jokes. But passages in the creation account show us how true they are *(Genesis 2:18-24; Genesis 3:16-19).*

II

We need each other and we help each other. God tells us that the first part of that *is* true, and the second part *should* be. We know the first part is true. Each one of us must answer to God for whatever is untrue in the second part. In *Genesis 4:9* God's question and Cain's question are not looking for information. What God is trying to teach us, no sarcasm can make unimportant.

Brothers should help one another. *Hebrews 11:4* tells us that Abel believed in God, but *Genesis 4* does not give any indication that he tried to help his brother. It might have made a wonderful story. *Genesis 37* shows how the first generation of the Children of Israel got along together. Brothers should help one another. The only time these brothers really cooperated was when they decided to "get" Joseph.

All mankind needs to understand the world's brotherhood. But the Christians who are God's new humanity should surely live as brothers. *(Galatians 6:10* ✠*; Romans 15:1-6 [1-2* ✠*])*

Jesus Christ is always the perfect example of how we ought to love. *(John 13:1-17; John 19:25-27)*

Every society needs some rules — but Jesus gave His Church only one rule: *John 13:34-35* ✠. The apostle Paul made the rule very clear in *Galatians 5:13-15 (13b-14* ✠*).*

In *John 3:14-18* and *4:7-21* are some of the clearest directions for what we are to do and the most powerful reminders of what God has done for us in Jesus Christ our Lord.

In *Matthew 18* the Lord spells out a number of things we should realize about the way we ought to help one another. At other times He told His disciples to minister with a cup of cold water or with any other service to the "least of my brothers." But here He tells us to service one another with the forgiveness of sins. He said, "Admit you need forgiveness of sins yourself. . . . Don't cause others to sin — cut off your hand before you let it lead others to sin. . . . Be as concerned for every little sinner as God is. . . . If anyone sins against you, it's your responsibility to see that he gets forgiveness from God. . . . Make sure he always has your forgiveness, too. . . . Put no limits on your forgiveness of your brother or you limit your own forgiveness by your God."

worshiping with the church

The divine liturgy is a continuous sharing of the forgiveness of sins. We are faithful in doing our liturgy as much for the brother's sake as for God's sake or our own sake. When we eat the body and drink the blood of our Lord in the Sacrament, we "show forth His death." We show to one another that we are sure He did die for sins and that He surely does give us all forgiveness. If a member of the Church does not eat the body or drink the blood he doesn't "show forth" anything. He even suggests that the forgiveness of sins isn't the greatest thing in the world. But it is!

Perhaps we need help in remembering that during the liturgy "we're in this together." Because some of the parts of the service are phrased in the singular, we forget that Church always means *us*. The very fact that *we* came *together*, that the liturgy is *corporate*, should remind us of the Church. We don't come together just to make it easier for a sermon to be preached to everyone at once. We come together to *be* together and to remind ourselves that we *are* together.

In the very beginning of the liturgy, in the Invocation, we should be conscious of how many we are in the body of Christ. *I* was baptized, and *I* may make the sign of the cross to remind me of it at the Invocation, but I am never alone. Even if I "enter into my closet" and shut the door, I am not alone. We are all baptized into the glorious company of the apostles and prophets and the whole company of the saints, living and dead. Look around at the Invocation on Sunday — think of the Church.

Each one of us must catch the reminders. Take the Confession of Sins, for instance. It is called the Preparation, because it is that. The service traditionally began with the Introit. Everyone said his confession privately and received private absolution. When there is a public confession, we begin with the statement *"Our* help is in the name of the Lord" before we start to say "I." Each one of us sinned, each one of us needs forgiveness for himself, but we are still "we."

When we confess that we are "poor, miserable sinners" and that we (each one of us) is "a poor sinful being," we also remind *ourselves* that we are sinners. As a member of the human race I am a sinful being. It's all there in the words — we must be working at it to have it in our minds.

When the pastor pronounces the Absolution, he does it in the name of God, but also as "a called and ordained servant of the Word." The Church called him and ordained him to the ministry of the Gospel of forgiveness. We're in that together, too. We are absolving one another, as the pastor absolves us in the name of the Father and of the Son and of the Holy Ghost.

names of the church

Sometimes we can tell more about a person by his nickname than we can by his real name. "Red" tells us something more about what a certain boy looks like than does "Frederick." "Hotshot" might be a compliment or it might be a description of an attitude.

When we try to understand all the marvelous things there are to know about the Church, we need to depend on the words which the Bible uses. The big advantage with those names is that God gave them, and we can depend on their accuracy. The Church certainly *is* what and how God says it is. It is *His* Church. He should know.

Neither given names nor nick-names will actually tell us what a boy will be like when he grows up. "Only time will tell," people say about boys. But it is not time but eternity that will reveal the truth about the Church. Since only God understands and dwells in eternity, only God can tell us the truths about His Church. We ought not think about the Church only as we see her in time but as God knows her to be in eternity. We ought not to think of the Church only as we see her "By schisms rent asunder, by heresies distressed." She is already what only God can see she will be, and believers should know God's vision is accurate, and believing, rejoice.

word and work

I

The Church is the family of God.

In Biblical language the Church is "the gathered group that comes to the meeting." It is the people of God that is called apart from other peoples by God. They meet together to *be* God's family around God's table and to hear the Father's words. Then they obey the Father, each one saying, "I go, Sir!" then actually *going* to serve Him by serving the world.

It is the company of those that belong to God through Jesus Christ.

When we talk about a family, we sometimes use the expression, "Blood is thicker than water." Since *God* created the Church through the *blood* of Jesus Christ and through the Spirit's work in the water of Baptism, there is a "thick" relationship between the people and God Himself, and between Christian and Christian.

We can learn much by thinking of the Church's names, the picture lan-

guage God uses to describe what people in time cannot yet see. *The people of God: Ephesians 2:11-22; Romans 9, especially v. 25; 1 Peter 2:9-10. The building of God: 1 Corinthians 3:9-17; Romans 9:33; Ephesians 2:11-22; Matthew 16: 13-20. The Vine and the branches: John 15. The Shepherd and the flock: John 10; Matthew 18:12-14; Luke 15:3-7; 1 Peter 5:1-4. The body of Christ: 1 Corinthians 12; Romans 12; Ephesians 1:15-23; 5:21-33.*

When in the Creed we confess that we believe in "the holy Christian Church, the communion of saints," we are saying that we are sure it exists and that it is a fellowship so wonderful it must be *believed.* But the Church is at the same time so real, it is so obviously a company of people all over the world, that it must be *experienced* to be believed. And it can be, by the grace of the Spirit of God! God's people also share in the holy things by which God establishes communion.

II

But there are weaknesses in the Church.

It is the Church, who knows what she should be, that is able to recognize her own terrible weaknesses *(1 Corinthians 1:10-13; 5:1-5; 11: 17-22; Revelation 3:14-22; Jude 3-4; 10-13).* The *weaknesses are not* merely "other people"; they are *in us.*

III

The Church is under attack by the world.

Sometimes "the world" is represented by anti-Christian forces *(1 Peter 4:12-17; Acts 12:1-4);* and sometimes these forces are very active among Christians: *1 John 4:1;* Galatians 1:6-9. Some of the fiercest attacks by the world are expressed in the voices that simply say, "Don't go overboard. Take it easy. You don't have to get fanatic about the faith."

IV

The Church is one and it will never perish!

We need to remember that the Church is what God made her to be. She is what God knows her to be *(Ephesians 4:4-6).* The Lord Himself is the Head, and He prays for her *(John 17:20-23).* The Church will never perish! *(Acts 12:24; Matthew 24:35 ✠; Matthew 16:13-19 [15-16 ✠])*

WORSHIPING WITH THE CHURCH

The liturgy is a celebration! Our Lord is risen from the dead. He really is with us alway. When He gives us His body and His blood, we celebrate that He won the victory. We sing "Blessed is He that cometh in the name of the Lord!" We give thanks that He entered into Jerusalem to suffer, and we give thanks that He enters into our lives in His sacrament.

It is the whole Church that celebrates. Our congregation is the church we can see, but we rejoice "with angels and archangels and with all the company of heaven." We rejoice with the believers in Christ all over the world. That is happening. But if we don't remember it, we may miss it.

There are many of the parts of the liturgy that cry out to us to remember the Church of the ages as we celebrate. The Introit, with which we really begin, is a voice from the Church of the Old Testament. It connects us with Abraham and Moses and David. The Kyrie (a Greek word) reminds us of those centuries when many in the Church spoke Greek. The "Lord have mercy" is the kind of cheer that people gave for

236

conquering kings who came home to have a triumphal procession. That's the way we greet our King, and that way we remember all our fellow subjects. The Gloria in Excelsis makes us one with the shepherds in the Christmas fields, and unites us with the Church through all the long centuries since that day. When we gather to celebrate the liturgy, we can each make sure that we think of who we are and praise the God who made us the Church!

Our biggest task, however, is to see that the Smiths and the Schneiders, the Macmillans and the Oraveks —all of our local family of God—are saints in the communion through the forgiveness of God. Their weaknesses are the very reason *we* are in the Church—to provide help. When they fall because of the attacks of the world, *we* are God's helping hand to lift them up. Surely if we see them as our brothers and sisters we will be ready to help. That is why the Church gathers around the Lord's Table on the Lord's Day to make sure that we look around and *see* the family of God, and then by His grace *be* the family of God!

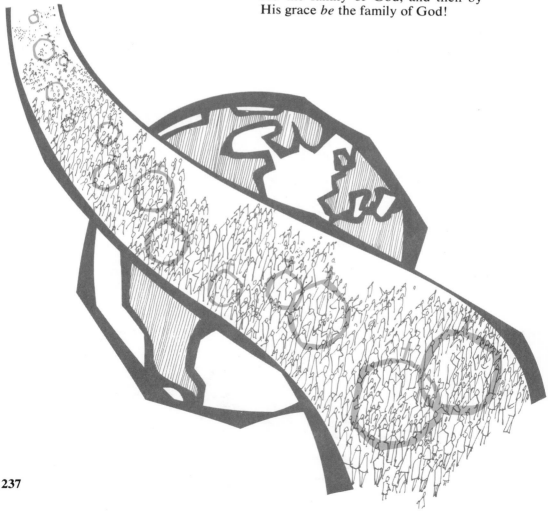

the church
and the churches

We can understand the comparison of the Church to the Vine and its branches—every member of the Church is connected to Christ. Every Christian lives by the strength of the Spirit of Christ.

But what are we to say about the obvious fact that so many of the branches of the Church are spread around the earth having almost nothing to do with one another? Can we be united with Christ and not be united with one another? Or is the union with the Vine and one another just a matter of definition and not of fact that one can see?

It's a very practical matter. Your family is traveling on vacation. At 11 o'clock Sunday morning you drive into a small town with six churches, and all the bells are ringing. Which one will you go to? Why? The church people with whom you decide to worship are celebrating the Lord's Supper. He is your Lord, too. Will you commune with them?

WORD and WORK

I

For one thing, we need to be clear on whether Communion is something we do, or something that is done to us. When we describe the Sacrament as "the Holy Communion" we think of three communions. The body and blood of our Lord are united with the bread and wine. Each Christian who communes is united with Jesus Christ and therefore with the Father and the Spirit. And every Christian who communes is united with every other Christian in the body of Christ. What we *do* is very small compared with what God does in making those communions. Yet without our "doing" there would be no Communion.

Is it the same with the unity in the Church? Is it already there and yet not quite? One could almost set up two columns, one headed "Something Given" and the other "Something Gained," as he checks out Bible passages about the Church. *(1 John 1:3 and 6-7; Romans 12:4-5 and 16; 15:5-6; John 17:11, 20-23; Ephesians 4:1-7 [4-7 ✠] and 11-16)*

II

With the bells of six church buildings ringing, then, can we simply pick one and go in and work on "maintaining the unity of the Spirit in the bond of peace?" For one thing, the Scripture talks about the Church as being a local congregation *(Acts 20:17)*, but at the same time it says that something much bigger than a congregation is present *(Acts 20:28)*. Evidently the Church is not the addition of the sum of the churches, nor are the churches little pieces of the Church. The Church is to be found in the places called churches. The Church is *catholic* [universal, general], and we do not really know her unless we know her in that way.

Yet our Lord made clear another standard for measuring the Church *(Matthew 28:18-20* and *Matthew 5: 17-19)*. And in His own words He warned about false teaching *(Mark 13:21-23* and *Matthew 7:15 ✠)*. His apostles were just as specific. *(2 Peter 2:1-2; Galatians 1:6-9)*

Evidently it is not quite as simple as going into any building that has a steeple and ringing bells.

III

God has given us a unity in Christ but we must work at it. The Church is to be found in every Christian congregation, but we must measure the congregation by its teaching. Our fellowship also is described as something that we should express and that we shouldn't express.

Anyone who can confess "Jesus is Lord" has been converted by the Holy Spirit *(1 Corinthians 12:3)*. And *1 Corinthians 13* shows us how to live with one another—in love. But *1 Corinthians 5* is very sharp about what should be done with deliberate sinners in the congregation. *Galatians 1:9* shows one side and *6:1-2* the other. *Romans 15:1-3* and *16:17-20* make the same comparison. *1 Thessalonians 2:13* shows the source of strength, and *2 Thessalonians 1:8* and *2:9-12* shows the cause of unbelief.

Perhaps *2 Thessalonians 3:14* is the summary of all that we should do about fellowship and denominations. We should recognize and thank God for the unity He creates. We should recognize the disunity which our sin and our failure to follow God's Word creates. We should show our unity so that the world will believe that Jesus came from God. We should mark disunity and withdraw from those who persist in error, in order that God may make us all one in Jesus Christ.

worshiping with the church

The liturgy is the *evidence* of our worldwide fellowship in the Church. It is also a way to *express* that fellowship. But each of us must deliberately "share" as we do our liturgy. Everybody who orders a turkey dinner in a restaurant eats a bit of the same bird, but that doesn't mean they're celebrating Thanksgiving together. Each one of us must *think* of his brother and *speak* to his brother and *pray* with his brother if he is really to share.

"Let *us* pray" before each collect reminds us to remember the whole Church, holy and catholic, that prays and has prayed these words for centuries. It doesn't mean, "Let's each one pray by himself." When we confess the Creed, we should think of the baptized brotherhood and how vital is our unity. The lessons were chosen by the Church, "built upon the foundation of the apostles and prophets." Today the sermon is given by one man, but it is still the message that all of us who called him as pastor are saying to one another. We should listen to it that way, sharing in it. The Lord's Supper is a sharing with one another, too. We "show forth His death till He comes" —to the brotherhood.

Remember, our Lord told us He is *the Vine.* He is not the stem only, but the whole thing. We, as branches, are a part of Him. To be "in Christ" is to be part of Him. In Him we are united. The unity He has given is where we begin. The disunity we have created is where we have work to do. We cannot ignore our divisions by closing our eyes and pretending they are not there. We cannot close our minds and hearts and prayers to them. We seek to heal these divisions.

57

my place in the church

A member of a confirmation instruction class was given a final assignment: to write an essay on "My Place in the Church." It was longer than this, but this is about what it included:

"When I join the church at my confirmation, I will take on certain obligations. I will be expected to go to church each Sunday, to attend Bible class, to have family devotions, to give for the support of the church, and read my Bible. But I will have many advantages too, chief of which will be the promise of a place in heaven."

We have been studying about our place in the Church long enough to be able to correct that essay and to write a better one. It would be interesting to have your essay's first draft written before you go on studying this lesson. Without looking ahead, describe your place in the Church . . . then do the

WORD AND WORK

I

I am a member of the body of Christ.

How it all happened will surely include some of the things St. Paul wrote about to Titus, chapter *3:3-11* and *14 (4-7* ✠ *)*. In *Ephesians 4: 20-24* there is a description of the difference it should make. *Romans 8:9-14* shows that life has a totally new dimension. *Ephesians 5:15-20* adds some extra notes about what we should do for one another.

Acts 2:42 ✠ and *43-47* describe a church life that sounds quite different from the essay. *Acts 4:19-20* describes an attitude that should be ours in the Church today, too. *Almost everything in the essay the confirmation class member wrote should be said a bit differently,* and if we realize what it means to be a member of the body of Christ, our essay will say it all differently.

243

II

I am a member of the body of Christ in this place.

Only God, who knows all things, including what is in the heart of all men, can see the whole Church. He makes this His business, too. None of His children will be plucked out of His hand. The problem of who really belongs to the Church and who doesn't is none of our business. For us the Church is very visible—it is all those people who call Jesus Lord and who take their place in the community that regularly assembles to do its liturgy. We can heed the warnings St. Paul gives and do the right things he urges. *(1 Corinthians 11:17-33; 12:27-31; 14:12)*

The constitution of our congregation will show us some of the opportunities we have to live for our fellow members in this place. The societies of the parish are groups who gather together to help their members *be* the Church toward one another.

III

I am a member of the body of Christ in my denomination.

I am not more important than the rest of the Christians in my congregation. My congregation is not more important than my denomination, my Synod. My Synod is not more important than the universal, the catholic Church. But we can *be* the Church as we should more effectively by using the advantages of our Synod.

The Articles of Incorporation in the synodical *Handbook* as well as the Objects listed in the Constitution provide a good summary of the things we join together to do.

It is important to help one another remain true to the truths of God *(2 John 8-11)*. The Lutheran Confessions help us by summarizing and arranging the teachings of Scripture.

This would be a good time to study all the different ways our Synod goes about training workers for schools and congregations and to study the many mission fields in which we are working.

IV

I am a member of the body of Christ.

After all has been said, we ought to remember this truth again. Our task is also to work for the unity of the Church for which Jesus Christ prayed *(John 17:20-26)*. But I *am* this member since my Baptism and *before* my confirmation.

worshiping with the church

The early Church found that one of the best ways to remember they were one body was to have all things "in common," to have everything belong to everybody. In the service, the Offertory can remind us that we belong to one another. The first thing we are doing is to offer ourselves to God; but we are offering ourselves to one another and to the world as well. Our gifts in the alms basin are representatives of *ourselves*. Our muscles and effort are part of the money they earned.

In some churches the bread and wine for the Holy Communion are also brought to the altar in the offertory procession. That reminds us that when we celebrate the Lord's Supper we are offering ourselves to the Lord. That is a very small thing compared to what He is giving to us — His body and His blood, Him-

self! But still, when we resolve "henceforth to amend our sinful lives," we are offering ourselves as living sacrifices to our God. God has told us that one of the ways we give ourselves to Him is by giving ourselves in service to one another.

We really do this in our prayers in the church service, too. We pray "for all sorts and conditions of men." As we pray, we lift up their needs to God — and God uses us to give them His answers.

All of this demands action from us, worship action. We must *put* our money in the offering plate; we must put our mind to the praying; we must be thinking of others as well as ourselves as we go to Holy Communion. And we must take our place in the working church after the Benediction is spoken!

his order of worship

Our response to God begins with our action *directly to God*. Week after week we gather together to worship. We offer adoration to God and receive the gifts of His Word from Him in liturgies and rituals and ceremonies. The things we do are similar to the things Christians have been doing in worship for centuries. Some of them are things that the people of God were doing in the Old Testament days.

We worship liturgically. Some of us do, that is. Every year thousands of young people stop coming to church to worship. Other thousands keep coming, but they aren't very happy about it. One of the things you can hear them complain about is the form of our worship. "We can't understand what's going on. Why do we keep using the same old order of service?"

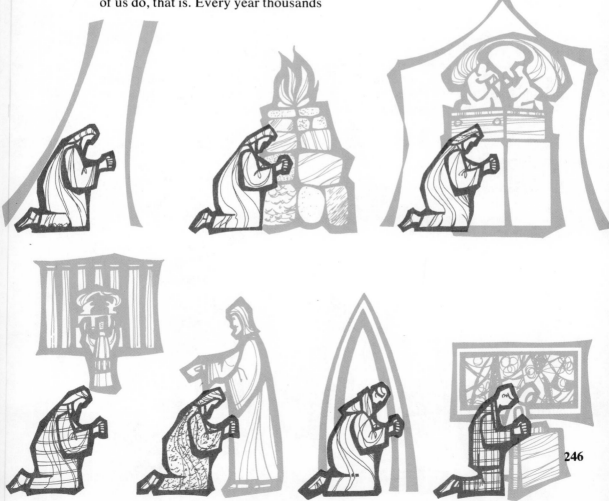

246

"They've got a point there." Who said that? It sounded as if it came from somebody in your class. Even after all the talk we've had about the way we worship, some are still asking, "Whose idea is all this liturgical stuff, anyway?"

It's natural. When a 16-year-old first gets his driver's license, his response is automatic. He gets into his father's car and drives. He isn't very fussy about what kind of car it is—he wants to drive! But it's a different thing when he is able to buy his own car. Then he begins to shop around. Things like cylinders, horsepower, torque, and color begin to concern him a lot more! Then he's not ready to buy a certain kind of car just because his dad owns one.

When we first begin our worshiping life, we worship the God of our fathers in the way our fathers did. But after we come to the age when we decide for ourselves what we are going to do, we look around a bit more. Sometimes we begin to wonder whether the way we've been worshiping all these years is the best way to worship.

Look at the record. We discover that God Himself has been at work in the developing of our present forms of worship. That says something to us about keeping on with them—quite a bit!

WORD AND WORK

I

The Creator made it clear that He should be worshiped by His creatures. What do we make of it when He lets His people know that He is a jealous God? It's strange to hear God admit He's jealous. Usually we think of jealousy as something wrong. Then what about God's jealousy? *(Exodus 20:4-6; Genesis 3:22-24)*

These passages tell us about God's attitude. The Bible has many examples of the attitude of the people who knew God intimately. They worshiped, and they used altars and actions to help them worship. These things were natural reactions of every man who was aware of God and wanted to worship Him. *(Genesis 4: 2-4; 4:26; Genesis 8:20)*

II

The Chooser gradually unfolded His order of worship to His chosen. The gracious God revealed Himself to His people in different ways. Always His people responded in forms—some of the forms God Himself prescribed. Over fifteen hundred years there was a wide range of things that God did and things that men did. When God changed His way of acting toward men, they changed some of their ways of acting toward God. But certain forms were handed down from generation to generation. People of every age found them helpful for worship.

Follow some of the changes and the climaxes in the worship relation between God and men:

Genesis 12:1-3 and 7-8
Exodus 25:1-10; 33:7-11
2 Samuel 7:1-16
1 Chronicles 23:25-32
Exodus 20:1-11 and 21-24
Exodus 40:33-38
1 Kings 5:1-5; 9:1-3
2 Chronicles 8:12-16

The destruction of the temple and the exile of the people broke up the centralized worship in Jerusalem. But most people had not been able to get to Jerusalem often anyway. And when they did, they watched more than they performed. The important thing was that the law of God was being obeyed. That important thing they could also do at home. So the synagogues developed. Around the Word of God men gathered to hear and to worship. Many of the earlier customs were kept. Some were changed. But the worship went on.

Then came Christ!

III

The God and Father of our Lord Jesus Christ is worshiped in the Spirit. What can we make of this passage *(John 4:21-24 [24* ✖ *])?* Does it urge New Testament Christians to value an inward and mental worship more highly than worship that is focused at a certain place—more than worship which is expressed in ceremonies and sacraments?

Worship "in spirit and in truth" is that kind of worship which is made possible by the coming of Jesus Christ who is Himself the Truth. It is that worship offered by the people in whom the Spirit of God dwells. God has chosen to use Scripture and sacrament to come to man. Man does well to accept God's form of worship and to respond in form as Spirit-filled children of God.

worshiping with the church

Life as Worship

If we will work through the Order of the Holy Communion together, we can find a number of places where the Old Testament forms of worship are still being used in the Church today. When we use them on Sunday we will be able to remember that we are worshiping in the company of the saints of all the generations of God's people.

Whenever we use a verse from the Introit as a waking-up thought of God, we are joining the Old Testament worshipers. But we are also in touch with all the people of the New Testament who kept on using these forms until we took over as the living members of the Church. Remembering all the saints who are joined with us in worship of the holy God makes our daily worship much richer.

The Worship Life

Doing our liturgy helps us to understand how we are to bring all creation into the service of God. We know we are God's creatures with bodies, who live by eating and who communicate by symbols. In Communion we place some of the bread God shares with us and some of the wine He gives us on the altar to use as God directs us. They remind us how all creation is God's when we receive Christ's body and blood in His holy meal.

59

we take ourselves seriously

Health books persuade us that a sound mind needs a sound body to function at its best. Agree to that?

Let's try this as an example: We're members of a building committee. We're planning a new church. One committee man suggests, "Let's not have a chancel. Give the pastor a place to preach from and a place to stand and pray, but that's enough. We could save $50,000 by not building on those 18 feet, by not buying a stone altar, the carved reredos, the paraments, the stained glass, the crucifix, and the candlesticks—not to mention the candles we keep burning up year after year."

What about that? On which side of that fence would we be?

Now . . . we're in the new church, and we're Sunday school teachers. We teach kindergartners how to pray in church. "Fold your hands and shut your eyes. . . ." (There goes $50,000 out the window!)

And what's more, isn't it a contradiction? "Fold your hands"— why? But then "shut your eyes"— why, again?

When a created being wants to worship the Creator God, he needs all the help he can get. We should recognize need when we have it and recognize help where we can get it.

worᴅ anᴅ work

I

Let's take ourselves seriously.

A bit of quiet meditation could help us all. "Just who do you think you are?" (Not God . . . *Genesis 3:5.* But God-like . . . *Psalm 8:3-8).* "You'll never be an angel." (True— but not because angels are so few. Rather because a man's a man . . .

Genesis 1:26-27 and *2:7-8; Psalm 8:3-8).* "When we know the worst, we can try to make the best of it." (It's bad enough . . . *Genesis 3: 16-19; 32:9-12; Romans 7:24.* But we are God's good idea, and even death and decay in the grave do not change His mind about our bodies being worth saving . . . *Genesis 1:31; Romans 7:25; 1 Corinthians 15:22; 35-56 [53-56 ✠]).*

II

God certainly takes our humanity seriously.

There's no argument in Scripture about the importance of God. The Scriptures assume it. But there's so much question about the importance of humanity in our guilty minds that God didn't stop to argue about it. He *assumed* it! He assumed our humanity . . . *John 1:14.* That was just the climax of all that God did in taking our humanity seriously. Passages like these indicate how clearly God recognizes our human limitations *(Genesis 3:8; Exodus 3:2-6; 1 Samuel 3:1-18; Jeremiah 1; Luke 1:26-35; Acts 2: 1-4; 37-39; 1 Corinthians 11:23-26).* Divine ideas are said in human words. Deity is made visible to humanity's eyes.

Divine thoughts result in sound waves and vibrate human ear drums. Divine concepts are illustrated in earthly images. Passages like these show us that God expects human worship to be expressed in human ways and with human words. Humans will take human positions for prayer and use human movements, human art, symbols and music. *(Psalm 95:6;*

Acts 21:5; Mark 11:25; Luke 18: 11, 13; Joshua 5:14; Mark 14:35)

We can think of other words that show God's use of human things: sacrifice, sackcloth and ashes, incense, fasting, tabernacle, temple, the ark, the vestments, ceremonies, washings, and ceremonial meals. God *directed* Israel to use these things. He takes humanness seriously. God isn't merely being sorry for us. He's in favor of our bodies. The idea of a combination body-soul creature was His idea, and His actions in His plan of salvation tell us He's still convinced His creative idea was very good.

III

Throw your self into worship.

It's certainly not the expected thing that God would enter the world through the natural process of being born, yet our Lord took on a human body in birth. Who are we to argue about our bodies? Mary said, "Let it be to me according to Your word."

We too should accommodate ourselves to God's approach—we who actually can't do anything else but! We ought not try to worship with only our minds, or only our voices. We should throw our whole selves into it! And we should take creation with us! *(Romans 8:19-23)*

wORSHIPING WITH THE CHURCH

Sunday

Check out the different movements that go on in the worship service. The reason for the liturgy and the ceremonies and the Sacrament is humanity. Not every parish does everything the same way. In the Philippines they hunker [crouch];

in England they kneel; in Canada and the United States perhaps, they stand. We can make what we do have significance. Then when we do it, the action has a power to help us worship.

Everyday

Dr. Martin Luther's rubric before the Morning and Evening Prayers is "to bless thyself with the sign of the holy cross." If we have not seriously tried that or if we have not seriously tried kneeling; let's! If we are already doing these things, let's make sure that we continually fill the symbolic action with meaning. None of these actions will automatically make our daily living more holy. But if we make the proper connections in our own minds, we help ourselves grow in holiness.

These lips have sung the praises of God—shall they now speak slander? This body has knelt in adoration of the holy God—shall it now act as if it were its own master? The Lord has given to me His body and His blood—shall I now act as if I were not His temple? These feet have walked before God's altar and in the company of the saints—shall they now deliberately walk into sin?

We are living with our whole selves in the liturgy and with our whole selves in the world. We practice involving our selves in the liturgy. We follow through in everything we do throughout the week.

60

the voices of symbols

When the other kind (spelled c-y-m-b-a-l-s) *bongs,* you can feel the vibrations in your bones as well as in your ears.

There isn't really any reason why we should limit our hearing of the Word of God to our ears. (Of course technically only what our mind understands by interpreting the vibrations that the eardrum transfers to the brain is called hearing.) Actually, we never do. If you really are interested in a sermon, you usually want to be able to see the preacher. He says things with gestures and with the expressions of his face just as he does with his words. We say things to one another in the pew, too, with eyebrows, smiles, frowns, and touches.

Every one of these things is a symbol, a sign by which one knows or infers a thing. Sometimes a symbol tells us something at a glance that it would take many words to explain. Sometimes it makes visible something that is actually invisible.

When the things that symbols say are Christian things, they are really words of God. Just as He uses letters of print, each of which is a symbol, to speak His meaning and convey His power, so He can use other symbols to get His points across.

Whenever an international meet-ing is held, many different languages will be spoken. That's a fact of our life ever since Babel. In order to make the meeting successful, translating devices must be used. Every participant is given earphones. By turning the proper switch he can listen to speeches as they are translated into a language he can understand. It's not very difficult to move the switch. But everything depends on whether the delegate *moves* it. If he is concerned, he'll tune in on the right symbol, the one that will give him the meaning.

The Church is universal. It has existed through many centuries. It has spoken Hebrew and Aramaic, Greek and Latin. It speaks many languages in many places today and has many symbols that are only meaningful to the Christians of a certain land. But some of the truths of the Word the Church has been saying for centuries and will keep on saying to Christians of every age and every land. For that reason some of its symbols are truly universal. Wherever the Church lives, these symbols are used.

Now, here's the point: it's up to the new delegate to the Church's meetings to move the switch which will enable him to understand the symbols the church uses. When he does, God's Word can work on him through all his senses.

WORD AND WORK

See

1 John 1:1-4 makes an interesting starting point. What God made visible to sight in the Incarnation, He also made visible to sight through inspiration. Whether men saw Jesus Christ or saw John's letter they were enabled by the Spirit to know God.

How many voices of symbols are ready to speak to you in your church building? You don't even have to be there to understand their word — you can think the symbols into your mind. A list would include things on the outside and on the inside of the church. Have you taken any of the symbols into your home, and into your room to speak to you there?

Don't forget — Christian symbols

may also speak the Word, but just as we must "catch" the Word, we must "turn on" the symbol!

Hear

Psalm 92:1-4 and *Psalm 98: 4-9* ✠ are Bible passages that remind us of the place of sound in His words to us and our words to Him. Every sound is something of a symbol—but which sounds have become special symbols of God's presence for us? If we take sound seriously, perhaps we could deliberately use those sounds to make us know God is near.

Touch

It's very natural to want to "feel certain." Some Bible verses illustrate that yearning *(Matthew 9:21; 14:36; Mark 3:10; Luke 18:15).* Are there some things used in your church that you like to touch? Or things that you can almost feel just by looking at them? (Their feel is conveyed by sight.) In the early Church the liturgy included the "kiss of peace." We don't kiss quite so casually today, but we do shake hands. The Church of South India, for instance, has included this in its service. Would this be a help for us in our services?

Taste

Psalm 34:8 and *1 Peter 2:3* ✠ are passages that remind us how much we appreciate what our sense of taste can tell us. Peter is so excited about God's goodness that he uses this sense too when speaking about it. We may also think about tasting the bread and wine in the Holy Communion. Can we find ways in which we might use this sense in our worship at home as we try to stress the meaning of the seasons of the church year?

Smell

See *Psalm 141:2* ✠ for a symbol that appeals to our mind through our sense of smell. The Bible often uses this symbol as though God shared in our sense of smell, and describes our Lord's offering of Himself as an incense offering. *(Ephesians 5:2* ✠ *)*

One could hardly imagine a person with switches all over his body—one marked Sight, another Sound, and others Taste, Touch, and Smell. But every one of us has the ability to switch on or off the senses through which the Word of God tries to reach through to us. Just as we can train ourselves to sharpen the senses, so we can increase what we take in through these other channels of the Word.

worshiping with the church

Sunday

Take a moment during the church service to recognize how your senses are working for you to catch the Word. While we're at it, we should realize that we are sending out signals to others, too. Or sometimes we are refusing to broadcast! At the Pax in the liturgy we might shake hands with

fellow Christians to the right and left of us in the pew.

Everyday

The easiest symbols to use are those which we see. It's like learning a new language. Make a point of increasing your symbol "vocabulary" this week. But make every new word of "symbol-talk" speak the Word. Anyone can *understand* it. Only a Christian can really *use* it. We can!

We can make our everyday handshake speak the Word this week by adding the words of the Pax: "The peace of the Lord be with you."

61

psalms, hymns,

spiritual songs

This is a "Muzak" world. One would think that no argument at all would be necessary to sell hymns to worshipers. But maybe that is just the trouble. We are so accustomed to having music of one kind or another poured over us while we are in a state of only semiconsciousness, that we are not ready to take up hymnody as part of our work of worship. But that is exactly what hymns should do for us—be tools for the work of worship.

This work of worship, of course, is something that we *want* to do. Since music helps us do what we want to do, we *want* to use hymns. Since worship must be something which *we do* (if we don't do it, it doesn't exist as far as we're concerned!) we put ourselves into the hymns. The Bible talks about angels playing their harps. The Church should see each one of us singing our hymns!

WORD AND WORK

All people are singers; some are better singers than others. We all believe that music expresses some of our feelings better than words alone can do. Not many of us can make up our own songs, so we welcome the songs that others make for us. We use their songs to express our joy or our sorrow, or we hum them just because they give us pleasure.

The Bible is filled with references to music and songs. There is the Book of Psalms, the collection of the hymns which God's people sang in their worship. We read about Jubal who was the "father of all those who play the lyre and pipe" *(Genesis 4:21)*. An example of a song not contained in the Book of Psalms is found in *Exodus 15:21.* Jesus and His disciples followed the Jewish custom of singing *(Matthew 26:30).* St. Paul urged the Christians of his day to use the psalms and hymns in worship *(Ephesians 5:19* ✠*; Colossians 3:16* ✠*).* The Canticles *(L. H.,* pp. 120–122) provide other examples.

It's not difficult to match up the different ACTS of worship with our use of hymns. The context of the Colossians passage, chapter *3:12-17,* is an example of this. *Psalm 149* not only urges singing but tells us something about God's attitude toward His singing people. *Psalm 106* is a good example of the way the Word can be taught at the same time it is being sung. Many of the Psalms were marching songs for the pilgrims going up to Jerusalem, and they give us a pattern for marching out to our work in the Lord's name. *(Psalms 120–134)*

In *The Lutheran Hymnal*, pages 837 and 838, entire sections of hymns are suggested for adoration, confession, and supplication. The hymns of sanctification urge the Christian to live his life as worship.

If we page through the Order of the Holy Communion in our hymnal we will find that about 50% of the service seems to be set to music. The sermon is not usually sung, but the lessons are often chanted in addition to the other parts of the liturgy which are usually chanted. When the hymns used in the service are added to all this, we can see that the Lutheran Church puts great stress on music in worship.

A good way to investigate how much the music of the service helps in our worship is to imagine what happens when the organ breaks down. (Some churches don't have organs at all — some use pianos; the Church got along without organs for a long time!)

Pick a hymn. Instead of singing it, read it aloud together! Does it carry its message as well? Take "All Hail the Power of Jesus' Name" (No. 339) for instance. With some hymns, part of the trouble is that they are not very good poetry; but singing puts the real spirit into hymns.

There's another side to the story. If you didn't sing the words of hymns, how would you go about telling one another the truths the hymn verses convey? One of the things we want to do in worship is to share the Word with one another; we want to admonish and edify one another. That's not very easy to do. It's impossible for everyone to do it at once in a large group — except through joint speech like hymns. When the hymns are sung to a rousing melody we are doing even more for one another than we could ever do by just saying the words.

Sometimes people (boys whose voices are changing, men who think that music is rather feminine, some girls, too) sort of stand back and let others do the singing in church. Actually no one can do your singing for you any more than he could do your praying for you. Since we are all touched by music, and since we are all to reach others in worship with our witness, we all ought to take our part in the hymn singing. Since God likes to hear us worship in song, let's sing!

woRshipinG with the chuRch

Sunday

A good way to remind yourself of how much hymns help is to notice how they do the job of preaching the Word, how they give you words with which to praise God, and how they put words into your mouth to speak

1 Flung to the heed-less winds Or on the wa-ters cast,
2 The Fa-ther hath re-ceived Their lat-est liv-ing breath,

The mar-tyrs' ash-es, watched, Shall gath-ered be at last.
And vain is Sa-tan's boast Of vic-t'ry in their death.

And from that scat-tered dust, A-round us and a-broad,
Still, still, tho' dead, they speak, And, trum-pet-tongued, pro-claim

Shall spring a plen-teous seed Of wit-ness-es for God.
To man-y a wak-'ning land The one a-vail-ing Name. A-men.

to your worshiping neighbors. Try it Sunday.

Every Day

At the end of Dr. Martin Luther's suggestion for Morning Prayer is the direction that we go to our work singing a hymn. Pick a hymn of the week and see how helpful it is to use that hymn every day during the week.

Martin Luther played the lute from the time of his student days. While on the way to the Diet at Worms he entertained the guests at an inn in Frankfurt by singing and playing the lute. He even composed a ballad in 1523 about two young men who were martyred at Brussels. In *The Lutheran Hymnal* it has been translated as "Flung to the Heedless Winds." But you may be interested in looking up the background to the writing of this hymn.

This ballad started Luther off on a career as a hymn writer. He wrote over 35 hymns that became very popular. Many of these hymns are sung in all Christian denominations even today. But Martin Luther would probably rejoice at the efforts by ballad singers to put the Gospel message in the language of our day, and at the efforts of musicians to sing the songs of the Church in the music of today. But most of all he would underline "unto the Lord" in the words, "Oh, sing *unto the Lord* a new song!"

62

that ı may
Be hıs own

This is the end of the book. If its message were all to end here, everything up to this point would have been a failure. But if each one of us in whom God's Spirit lives makes it his resolution to keep on writing new chapters week by week, the whole study will be a success. "And live under Him in His kingdom." That was the idea with which we began. The King is not about to abdicate, just because the last lesson has come around. He wants us to live from Lord's Day to Lord's Day, trying to make every day—from Monday through Saturday—His days, too.

This lesson is yours to write; it can be a kind of pilot project for the Sundays ahead. The God who made us and saved us and lives in us looks for our response.

It was His idea that a day be set aside in His honor as a token of the giving of our entire life. By His grace we have inherited a great tradition in the Church. We can use the propers of each Sunday to be ready to catch His Word's power. We can set ourselves to give to Him the glory due His name. We can be "the people of the meeting" who gather to do the liturgy and thereby can build one another up in Christ. Together we can resolve to live the Christ-life in the world, and together we can take the first step week by week in the liturgy. All this we know.

Now if we plan our worship for the coming Sunday, we will be get-

ting set for the way we should approach each service. If we meet together to discuss what our thoughts will be in Sunday's service, we will *be the Church* to one another.

word and work

I
The Proper Point

As you read through the propers for next Sunday, try to phrase the theme of the day. How does this theme stress something we should believe? What should we *do* about this belief?

Once you have seen the central thrust of the propers, note the big thought you will try to *catch* as each of the propers is used in the service. Or plan what kind of *giving* to God you will want to do when the proper is used. There will be reminders to *share* with fellow Christians, but the very fact that you are together with them doing your liturgy will be the best kind of sharing. If the theme of the day includes what we ought to *do* about our faith, there will be voices in the propers urging us to live out our faith in our life. Listen for them.

This is what we have been doing together. Do it now by yourself. Then share your ideas with the rest of the class. That should be practice for an every-Sunday sharing — with a class or with our families or with friends.

II
The Right Reaction

After you have done that work with the propers, test out your own reaction.

What if you have the opportunity to go on an outing on Sunday or to play golf or to sleep? How *do* you feel about *doing your liturgy?* You've climbed up the ladder to the top of the high diving board. You've dived many times before. During the week, God willing, you'll be swimming the right direction to get back to the shore — is it important to you to make the dive, to *do your liturgy, this Sunday?*

After all, now you know what the Word will say to you. You're set to make your response. Will you feel that you are missing anything if you are not "in the meeting" to share with the Church? If you *must* miss it, will you *really miss* it?

If the answers are the ones the Church hopes will be your reaction, they will all fit into the pattern of the explanation of the Second Article in Luther's Small Catechism: I am His own to live under Him in His kingdom and serve Him in everlasting righteousness, innocence, and blessedness, even as He is risen from the dead, lives and reigns to all eternity!

woRshipiNG with the chuRch

This can be the best service you've ever attended and the best liturgy you've ever done!

Some of you will discover that your congregation does not plan to celebrate the Lord's Supper in next Sunday's service. This might be the time to meet with the pastor and the church officers to ask that the opportunity to commune together be provided for your class in Sunday's service. It is important for you to put down on paper the reasons you want to commune together. If your congregation will be celebrating the Eucharist, it would still be a good idea to gather together your thoughts as to why the opportunity to commune is important for you.

Would it be a help for every member of the class if the entire group would sit together this Sunday? Are there some members of the group who should be visited so that they will remember to "do this in remembrance of Him" and to take their place in the "one body"? If they are to be able to do their liturgy, it would be helpful to be prepared for what they should *catch, give,* and *share* in the

divine service. A visit to the brothers should be more than an invitation. It should include a sharing of the Word.

There may be some in the group who are not yet confirmed and who will need to do a special rethinking of the blessing of being *in* the liturgy, even if they will not be communing. The communicants need to make these unconfirmed people a part of the Church just as much as those who commune.

And now—to worship. Remember: "This is"—in the liturgy all that our God has done for us to make us His people will be made present for us once again. "That I may be His own. . . ."

And remember: "This do"—all that our God expects of us in our living can be undertaken as we celebrate. "And live under Him in His kingdom, and serve Him."

And remember: "in remembrance of Him." All our failures in the past and the times we will fail again in the future, all these have been forgiven by the God who loved us and who loves us so much that He gave His only Son and continually gives His Spirit. We can serve Him "in everlasting righteousness, innocence, and blessedness!"

the small
catechism

The Ten Commandments

THE FIRST COMMANDMENT

Thou shalt have no other gods before Me.

What does this mean?
We should fear, love, and trust in God above all things.

THE SECOND COMMANDMENT

**Thou shalt not take the name of the Lord thy God
  in vain.**

What does this mean?
We should fear and love God that we may
not curse, swear, use witchcraft, lie, or deceive by His name,
but call upon it in every trouble,
pray, praise, and give thanks.

THE THIRD COMMANDMENT

Remember the Sabbath day to keep it holy. *(Thou shalt
  sanctify the holy day.)*

What does this mean?
We should fear and love God that we may
not despise preaching and His Word,
but hold it sacred and gladly hear and learn it.

THE FOURTH COMMANDMENT

**Thou shalt honor thy father and thy mother
that it may be well with thee
and thou mayest live long on the earth.**

What does this mean?
We should fear and love God that we may
not despise our parents and masters nor provoke them to
    anger,
but give them honor, serve and obey them,
and hold them in love and esteem.

THE FIFTH COMMANDMENT

Thou shalt not kill.

What does this mean?
We should fear and love God that we may
not hurt nor harm our neighbor in his body,
but help and befriend him in every bodily need.

THE SIXTH COMMANDMENT

Thou shalt not commit adultery.

What does this mean?
We should fear and love God that we may
lead a chaste and decent life in word and deed
and each love and honor his spouse.

THE SEVENTH COMMANDMENT

Thou shalt not steal.

What does this mean?
We should fear and love God that we may
not take our neighbor's money or goods
nor get them by false ware or dealing,
but help him to improve and protect his property and
business.

THE EIGHTH COMMANDMENT

Thou shalt not bear false witness against thy neighbor.

What does this mean?
We should fear and love God that we may
not deceitfully belie, betray, slander, nor defame our
neighbor,
but defend him, speak well of him, and put the best
construction on everything.

THE NINTH COMMANDMENT

Thou shalt not covet thy neighbor's house.

What does this mean?

We should fear and love God that we may
not craftily seek to get our neighbor's inheritance or house
nor obtain it by a show of right,
but help and be of service to him in keeping it.

THE TENTH COMMANDMENT

**Thou shalt not covet thy neighbor's wife
nor his manservant nor his maidservant
nor his cattle
nor anything that is thy neighbor's.**

What does this mean?

We should fear and love God that we may not
estrange, force, or entice away from our neighbor
his wife, servants, or cattle,
but urge them to stay and do their duty.

THE CLOSE OF THE COMMANDMENTS

What does God say of all these commandments?

He says thus: I, the Lord thy God, am a jealous God,
visiting the iniquity of the fathers upon the children
unto the third and fourth generation of them that hate Me,
and showing mercy unto thousands of them that love Me
and keep My commandments.

What does this mean?

God threatens to punish all that transgress these
    commandments.
Therefore we should fear His wrath and not act contrary
    to them.
But He promises grace and every blessing to all that keep
    these commandments.
Therefore we should also love and trust in Him
and willingly do according to His commandments.

271

THE FIRST ARTICLE

Creation

**I believe in God the Father Almighty,
Maker of heaven and earth.**

What does this mean?

I believe that God has made me and all creatures;
that He has given me my body and soul, eyes, ears, and
    all my members,
my reason and all my senses, and still preserves them;
also clothing and shoes, meat and drink, house and home,
wife and children, fields, cattle, and all my goods;
that He richly and daily provides me with all that I need
to support this body and life;
that He defends me against all danger
and guards and protects me from all evil;
and all this purely out of fatherly, divine goodness and
    mercy,
without any merit or worthiness in me;
for all which it is my duty to thank and praise, to serve
    and obey Him.
This is most certainly true.

THE SECOND ARTICLE

Redemption

**And in Jesus Christ, His only Son, our Lord,
who was conceived by the Holy Ghost,
born of the Virgin Mary,
Suffered under Pontius Pilate,
was crucified, dead, and buried;
He descended into hell;
the third day He rose again from the dead;
He ascended into heaven
and sitteth on the right hand of God the Father
    Almighty;
from thence He shall come to judge the quick and
    the dead.**

What does this mean?

I believe that Jesus Christ,
true God, begotten of the Father from eternity, and also
true man, born of the Virgin Mary,
is my Lord,
who has redeemed me, a lost and condemned creature,
purchased and won me from all sins, from death, and from
     the power of the devil;
not with gold or silver but with His holy, precious blood
and with His innocent suffering and death,
that I may be His own and live under Him in His kingdom
     and serve Him in everlasting righteousness, innocence,
     and blessedness,
even as He is risen from the dead, lives and reigns to all
     eternity.
This is most certainly true.

THE THIRD ARTICLE

Sanctification

I believe in the Holy Ghost;
the holy Christian church, the communion of saints;
the forgiveness of sins;
the resurrection of the body;
and the life everlasting. Amen.

What does this mean?

I believe that I cannot by my own reason or strength
believe in Jesus Christ, my Lord, or come to Him;
but the Holy Ghost has called me by the Gospel,
enlightened me with His gifts,
sanctified and kept me in the true faith;
even as He calls, gathers, enlightens, and sanctifies
the whole Christian church on earth, and keeps it
with Jesus Christ in the one true faith;
in which Christian church He daily and richly forgives all
     sins to me and all believers,
and will at the Last Day raise up me and all the dead,
and give unto me and all believers in Christ eternal life.
This is most certainly true.

Our Father who art in heaven.
Hallowed be Thy name.
Thy kingdom come.
Thy will be done on earth as it is in heaven.
Give us this day our daily bread.
And forgive us our trespasses,
**   as we forgive those who trespass against us.**
And lead us not into temptation,
but deliver us from evil.
For thine is the kingdom
and the power and the glory forever and ever.
                                        Amen.

THE INTRODUCTION

Our Father who art in heaven.

What does this mean?
God would by these words tenderly invite us to believe
that He is our true Father and that we are His true children,
so that we may with all boldness and confidence ask Him
as dear children ask their dear father.

THE FIRST PETITION

Hallowed be Thy name.

What does this mean?
God's name is indeed holy in itself;
but we pray in this petition
that it may be holy among us also.

How is this done?
When the Word of God is taught in its truth and purity
and we as the children of God
also lead a holy life according to it.
This grant us, dear Father in heaven.
But he that teaches and lives otherwise than God's Word
    teaches,
profanes the name of God among us.
From this preserve us, heavenly Father.

274

THE SECOND PETITION

Thy kingdom come.

What does this mean?

The kingdom of God comes indeed without our prayer,
  of itself;
but we pray in this petition
that it may come unto us also.

How is this done?

When our heavenly Father gives us His Holy Spirit,
so that by His grace we believe His holy Word and
lead a godly life here in time and hereafter in eternity.

THE THIRD PETITION

Thy will be done on earth as it is in heaven.

What does this mean?

The good and gracious will of God is done indeed without
    our prayer;
but we pray in this petition
that it may be done among us also.

How is this done?

When God breaks and hinders every evil counsel and will,
which would not let us hallow God's name
nor let His kingdom come,
such as the will of the devil, the world, and our flesh;
but strengthens and preserves us steadfast
in His Word and faith unto our end.
This is His gracious and good will.

THE FOURTH PETITION

Give us this day our daily bread.

What does this mean?

God gives daily bread indeed without our prayer,
also to all the wicked;
but we pray in this petition
that He would lead us to know it and to receive
our daily bread with thanksgiving.

What is meant by daily bread?

Everything that belongs to the support and wants of the body,

275

such as food, drink, clothing, shoes,
house, home, field, cattle, money, goods,
a pious spouse, pious children, pious servants,
pious and faithful rulers, good government,
good weather, peace, health, discipline, honor,
good friends, faithful neighbors, and the like.

THE FIFTH PETITION

And forgive us our trespasses, as we forgive those who trespass against us.

What does this mean?
We pray in this petition
that our Father in heaven would not look upon our sins
nor on their account deny our prayer,
for we are worthy of none of the things for which we pray,
neither have we deserved them;
but that He would grant them all to us by grace,
for we daily sin much and indeed deserve nothing
but punishment.
So will we also heartily forgive and readily do good to
those who sin against us.

THE SIXTH PETITION

And lead us not into temptation.

What does this mean?
God indeed tempts no one;
but we pray in this petition that God would guard
and keep us,
so that the devil, the world, and our flesh may not deceive us
nor seduce us into misbelief, despair, and other great shame
and vice;
and though we be assailed by them,
that still we may finally overcome and obtain the victory.

THE SEVENTH PETITION

But deliver us from evil.

What does this mean?
We pray in this petition, as the sum of all,
that our Father in heaven would deliver us from every evil

of body and soul, property and honor,
and finally, when our last hour has come, grant us
    a blessed end
and graciously take us from this vale of tears to Himself
    in heaven.

THE CONCLUSION

For Thine is the kingdom and the power and the glory forever and ever. Amen.

What is meant by the word "Amen"?

That I should be certain that these petitions
are acceptable to our Father in heaven and are heard
    by Him;
for He Himself has commanded us so to pray
and has promised to hear us.
Amen, Amen, that is, Yea, yea, it shall be so.

The Sacrament of Holy Baptism

I. THE NATURE OF HOLY BAPTISM

What is Baptism?

Baptism is not simple water only, but it is the water
comprehended in God's command and
connected with God's word.

Which is that word of God?

Christ our Lord says in the last chapter of Matthew:
Go ye and teach all nations, baptizing them in the name
of the Father and of the Son and of the Holy Ghost.

II. THE BLESSINGS OF BAPTISM

What does Baptism give or profit?

It works forgiveness of sins,
delivers from death and the devil, and
gives eternal salvation to all who believe this,
as the words and promises of God declare.

Which are such words and promises of God?

Christ our Lord says in the last chapter of Mark:
He that believeth and is baptized shall be saved;
but he that believeth not shall be damned.

III. THE POWER OF BAPTISM

How can water do such great things?

It is not the water indeed that does them, but the
word of God which is in and with the water, and
faith, which trusts such word of God in the water.
For without the word of God the water is simple water
     and no Baptism.
But with the word of God it is a Baptism, that is,
a gracious water of life and a washing of regeneration
in the Holy Ghost, as St. Paul says, Titus, chapter 3:
According to His mercy He saved us by the washing
     of regeneration
and renewing of the Holy Ghost,
which He shed on us abundantly through Jesus Christ,
     our Savior,
that being justified by His grace,
we should be made heirs according to the hope of eternal
     life.
This is a faithful saying.

IV. THE SIGNIFICANCE OF BAPTIZING WITH WATER

What does such baptizing with water signify?

It signifies that the old Adam in us should
by daily contrition and repentance
be drowned and die with all sins and evil lusts
and, again, a new man daily come forth and arise,
who shall live before God in righteousness and purity
     forever.

Where is this written?

St. Paul writes, Romans, chapter 6:
We are buried with Christ by Baptism into death,
that
like as He was raised up from the dead by the glory
     of the Father,
even so we also should walk in newness of life.

Confession

What is Confession?

Confession embraces two parts.
One is that we confess our sins; the other, that we receive
absolution or forgiveness from the pastor as from God
Himself and in no wise doubt but firmly believe that by it our sins
are forgiven before God in heaven.

What sins should we confess?

Before God we should plead guilty of all sins, even of those
which we do not know, as we do in the Lord's Prayer; but before
the pastor we should confess those sins only which we know and
feel in our hearts.

Which are these?

Here consider your station according to the Ten Commandments,
whether you are a father, mother, son, daughter, master, mistress,
servant; whether you have been disobedient, unfaithful, slothful;
whether you have grieved any person by word or deed; whether you
have stolen, neglected, or wasted aught or done other injury.

The Sacrament of the Altar

What is the Sacrament of the Altar?

It is the true body and blood of our Lord Jesus Christ
under the bread and wine,
for us Christians to eat and to drink,
instituted by Christ Himself.

Where is this written?

The holy evangelists Matthew, Mark, Luke, and St. Paul
    (the apostle) write thus:
Our Lord Jesus Christ, the same night in which He was
    betrayed, took bread; and when He had given thanks,
    He brake it and gave it to His disciples, saying,
Take, eat; this is My body, which is given for you.
This do in remembrance of Me.
After the same manner also He took the cup when He had
    supped, and

when He had given thanks, He gave it to them, saying,
Drink ye all of it;
this cup is the new testament in My blood, which is shed
      for you for the remission of sins.
This do, as oft as ye drink it, in remembrance of Me.

What is the benefit of such eating and drinking?
That is shown us by these words:
"Given and shed for you for the remission of sins";
namely, that in the sacrament
forgiveness of sins, life, and salvation are given us through
      these words.
For where there is forgiveness of sins, there is also life
      and salvation.

How can bodily eating and drinking do such great things?
It is not the eating and drinking indeed that does them
but the words here written:
"Given and shed for you for the remission of sins";
which words, besides the bodily eating and drinking,
are the chief thing in the sacrament;
and he that believes these words has what they say
      and express,
namely, the forgiveness of sins.

Who, then, receives such sacrament worthily?
Fasting and bodily preparation are indeed a fine outward
      training; but
he is truly worthy and well prepared who has faith in
      these words:
"Given and shed for you for the remission of sins."
But he that does not believe these words, or doubts,
is unworthy and unprepared;
for the words "for you" require all hearts to believe.

The Office of the Keys

What is the Office of the Keys?
It is the peculiar church power
which Christ has given to His church on earth
to forgive the sins of penitent sinners but
to retain the sins of the impenitent
as long as they do not repent.

Where is this written?
Thus writes the holy evangelist John, chapter 20:
The Lord Jesus breathed on His disciples and saith
    unto them,
Receive ye the Holy Ghost.
Whosoever sins ye remit, they are remitted unto them; and
whosoever sins ye retain, they are retained.

What do you believe according to these words?
I believe that
when the called ministers of Christ deal with us
by His divine command,
especially when they exclude manifest and impenitent
    sinners
from the Christian congregation
and, again,
when they absolve those who repent of their sins
and are willing to amend,
this is as valid and certain, in heaven also,
as if Christ, our dear Lord, dealt with us Himself.

Prayers

MORNING PRAYER

*In the morning when you get up, make the sign of the holy
cross and say:*

In the name of ✠ the Father and of the Son and of the Holy
    Ghost. Amen.

Then, kneeling or standing, repeat the Creed and the Lord's
Prayer. If you choose you may also say this little prayer:

I thank Thee, my heavenly Father,
through Jesus Christ, Thy dear Son,
that Thou hast kept me this night from all harm and danger;
and I pray Thee that Thou wouldst keep me this day also
from sin and every evil,
that all my doings and life may please Thee.
For into Thy hands I commend myself,
my body and soul, and all things,
Let Thy holy angel be with me
that the wicked Foe may have no power over me. Amen.

After singing a hymn (possibly a hymn on the Ten Commandments)
or whatever your devotion may suggest, you should go to your work
joyfully.

EVENING PRAYER

In the evening when you go to bed, make the sign of the holy
cross and say:

In the name of ✠ the Father and of the Son and of the Holy
 Ghost. Amen.

Then, kneeling or standing, repeat the Creed and the Lord's
Prayer. If you choose you may also say this little prayer:

I thank Thee, my heavenly Father,
through Jesus Christ, Thy dear Son,
that Thou hast graciously kept me this day;
and I pray Thee that Thou wouldst forgive me all my sins
 where I have done wrong
and graciously keep me this night.
For into Thy hands I commend myself,
my body and soul, and all things.
Let Thy holy angel be with me
that the wicked Foe may have no power over me. Amen.

Then go to sleep at once and in good cheer.

BLESSING BEFORE EATING

When children and the whole household gather at the table, they
should reverently fold their hands and say:

The eyes of all look to Thee, O Lord,
and Thou givest them their food in due season.
Thou openest Thy hand; Thou satisfiest the desire of every
    living thing.

Then the Lord's Prayer should be said and afterwards this
prayer:
Lord God, heavenly Father, bless us
and these Thy gifts which we receive from Thy bountiful goodness,
through Jesus Christ our Lord. Amen.

THANKSGIVING AFTER EATING

Likewise after eating they should fold their hands
reverently and say:
O give thanks to the Lord, for He is good,
for His steadfast love endures forever.
He gives to the beasts their food and to the young ravens
    which cry.
His delight is not in the strength of the horse, nor His
    pleasure in the legs of a man;
but the Lord takes pleasure in those who fear Him, in those
    who hope in His steadfast love.

Then the Lord's Prayer should be said and afterwards this prayer:
We give Thee thanks, Lord God, our Father, for all Thy benefits,
through Jesus Christ our Lord, who lives and reigns forever. Amen.

The Nicene Creed

I believe in one God, the Father Almighty,
Maker of heaven and earth
and of all things visible and invisible.
And in one Lord Jesus Christ,
the only-begotten Son of God, begotten of His Father
    before all worlds,
God of God, Light of Light, Very God of Very God,
begotten, not made,

283

being of one substance with the Father,
by whom all things were made;
who for us men and for our salvation
came down from heaven
and was incarnate by the Holy Ghost of the Virgin Mary
and was made man;
and was crucified also for us under Pontius Pilate.
He suffered and was buried; and the third day He rose again
according to the Scriptures;
and ascended into heaven
and sitteth on the right hand of the Father;
and He shall come again with glory to judge both the
quick and the dead;
whose kingdom shall have no end.

And I believe in the Holy Ghost, the Lord and Giver of life,
who proceedeth from the Father and the Son,
who with the Father and the Son together is worshiped
and glorified,
who spake by the prophets.
And I believe one holy Christian and apostolic church.
I acknowledge one Baptism for the remission of sins,
and I look for the resurrection of the dead,
and the life of the world to come. Amen.

✠   ✠   ✠

The Practice of Confession and Absolution

The baptized child of God lives in repentance and faith as he responds to the Word of God in his life. Daily the Word of God shows him the mercy of God over against his sinful and needy condition. As he lays the misery of his sin and weakness before God, in faith the child of God trusts that God will forgive him for the sake of Jesus Christ.

When a Christian confesses his sin to God, he may do this before a fellow Christian (especially if he has sinned against him), and certainly before his pastor. The most important part of such personal confession is the absolution that is spoken to him. This is the Word of God that speaks forgiveness in the mouth of the fellow Christian. The confession is prompted by the promise of forgiveness.

If we say we have no sin, we deceive ourselves, and the truth is not in us. If we confess our sins, He is faithful and just and will forgive our sins and cleanse us from all unrighteousness. If we say we have not sinned, we make Him a liar, and His Word is not in us. 1 John 1:8-10.

God forgives those who confess and believe. He does this through the Word of the Gospel spoken to the sinner.

For growth in grace and knowledge and for the assurance of forgiveness, the child of God uses the special ministry of the pastor, who has been called to care for his soul with the Word of God. In private confession the pastor can offer the instruction and consolation of God's Word to the individual penitent sinner. Private confession should not be *demanded* of anyone. But it is offered to all believers as a means to help them remove the burden of a particular sin and to bring them back into their battle against sin with the sure Word of God.

It should be noted that when a person confesses before his pastor, he is actually not confessing his sin to the pastor but to God. The pastor hears this confession and when he speaks the absolution, it is God who forgives.

Here is a way in which an individual Christian may confess his sin before his pastor.

Individual: I confess before you, and to almighty God, that I am a sinful person, that I have sinned against God in my thoughts, words, and deeds. I make no excuse for my grievous sin. I stand under the judgment of God. There is no help for me except that God would look upon me in grace for Jesus' sake and cover me with His righteousness. My heart is troubled with my sin. Especially am I burdened with the weakness and sin of _____.
I pray God for Christ's sake to forgive me and by His Holy Spirit to give me a new heart.

Pastor: Do you believe that God by grace for Jesus' sake forgives you all your sins?

Individual: Yes, I believe this.

Pastor: Do you believe that through me, a called servant of God, you receive forgiveness of all your sins?

Individual: Yes, I believe this. (Here the person may ask the pastor special questions or tell of special problems for instruction in the Word of God.)

Pastor: Almighty God, our heavenly Father, is merciful and gracious and ready to forgive you all your sins for the sake of His Son Jesus Christ, who suffered and died for you. In His name and by His command I declare that you, being penitent, are absolved and free from all your sins.

For your comfort, your peace, and your encouragement, take the assurance I give you in the name of the Lord Jesus. Believe without doubt that your sins are forgiven in the name of the Father ✠ and of the Son ✠ and of the Holy Spirit ✠ Amen. The peace of the Lord be with you. Amen.

thanksGIVING

RED

reformation

RED